Democracy, Social Values, and Public Policy

Democracy, Social Values, and Public Policy

Edited by
Milton M. Carrow,
Robert Paul Churchill, and Joseph J. Cordes

Westport, Connecticut
London

Library of Congress Cataloging-in-Publication Data

Democracy, social values, and public policy / edited by Milton M.
  Carrow, Robert Paul Churchill, and Joseph J. Cordes.
      p.   cm.
    Includes bibliographical references and index.
    ISBN 0-275-95985-6 (alk. paper)
    1. Social values. 2. Political planning. 3. Democracy.
  I. Carrow, Milton M. (Milton Michael), 1912- . II. Churchill,
  Robert Paul. III. Cordes, Joseph J.
  HM73.D435 1998
  303.3'72—DC21   97-34748

British Library Cataloguing in Publication Data is available.

Library of Congress Catalog Card Number: 97-34748
  ISBN: 0-275-95985-6

First published in 1998

Praeger Publishers, 88 Post Road West, Westport, CT 06881
An imprint of Greenwood Publishing Group, Inc.

Printed in the United States of America

The paper used in this book complies with the
Permanent Paper Standard issued by the National
Information Standards Organization (Z39.48–1984).

10 9 8 7 6 5 4 3 2 1

For our wives, Barbara, Eileen, and Ann

Contents

Introduction

Milton M. Carrow, Robert Paul Churchill, and Joseph J. Cordes

Values have been at the forefront of modern political discourse. What they are and what they imply for democratic public policy are far from clear. Because contradictory values are held by individuals and different constituencies in American society, because there is confusion over values, virtues, and preferences, and because there is confusion over how well policies represent values, public discourse has created more heat than light. Definition and clarification are as essential as close attention to the policy process and logical rigor in argument.

This book deals with a significant aspect of value debates, namely, the social values underlying public policies in a democracy. In the United States we have learned that our democratic ideals are not based solely on the structural and institutional elements of a democracy, such as the Constitution and the Bill of Rights. This understanding is underscored as we observe the struggles in Eastern Europe, Africa, Asia, and Latin America to attain democratic societies. Simply adopting a constitution and providing for elections does not assure a democratic result. Likewise, democratic processes do not assure that public policy will be of high quality. Thus we have to look for firmer underpinnings and to explore more carefully the connection between values and policy outcomes.

Such underpinnings and connections undoubtedly include the common values of a society—the forces that hold it together. Among these are the social values of the community as a whole, although these may not be the preferences of particular individuals. As one of the authors in this book has aptly pointed out, social values are derived through a complex deliberative, cultural, legal, and political process.

Critical aspects of the strength of American democracy lie in its social values, on the way they influence public choice, and how they are reflected in public policies. What social values are, how they change and are perceived, how political institutions respond to them, how they are involved in the making of public policy are among the subjects of discussion in the various chapters of this book. Through the perspectives of anthropology, economics, gerontology and medical ethics, history, philosophy, religion, women's studies, policy science, as well as the view of practitioners, they are examined in depth and detailed in current areas of public interest.

This collection had its origins in a conference of the same title, held at The George Washington University in the fall of 1995 and sponsored by the Graduate Program in Public Policy of the Columbia School of Arts and Sciences and the vice president of Academic Affairs. From its inception, as organizers of the conference, we believed it was important that the perspectives of our respective disciplines—economics and policy analysis (Joseph J. Cordes), law (Milton M. Carrow), and philosophy (Robert Paul Churchill)—be reflected not only in the selection of topics and invitations to presenters but also in our roles in facilitating discussion and commenting on papers. Each of our disciplines places interestingly different emphases on the intersection of democracy, social values, and public policy.

We believe it is useful to summarize the perspective each of our disciplines brings to debates over the role of social values in a democratic policy process. In Sections I and II of this introduction, we present brief accounts of public policy and social values as viewed first by an economist and policy analyst and then by a philosopher. In Chapter 1, Milton Carrow offers a more extensive institutional approach to the subject of this book, one that emphasizes factors that are both conducive and inimical to the success of democracy.

SOCIAL VALUES IN ACADEMIC POLICY ANALYSIS

The opening chapter of a leading text on policy analysis describes policy analysis as "client-oriented advice relevant to public decisions *and informed by social values* . . . that is as much an art and a craft as a science. Just as the successful portraitist must be able to apply the skills of the craft of painting within an aesthetic perspective, the successful policy analyst must be able to apply basic skills within a reasonably consistent and realistic perspective on the role of government in society" (emphasis added).[1]

The authors of the text go on to observe that in order to effectively integrate the art and craft of policy analysis, it is important that a policy analyst be skilled in five areas:[2]

1. Policy analysts must be able to put perceived social problems in context. When is it in the public interest for the government to intervene in private affairs?

2. Policy analysts need technical skills to enable them to predict and to evaluate the consequences of alternative policies.

3. Analysts must be able to communicate the results of their analysis effectively to the public and to political decision makers.

4. Analysts must understand the political and organizational context in which policies are adopted, including the world views of potential clients and opponents.

5. Analysts need to have a professional ethic to guide their interaction with clients.

An understanding and appreciation of social values is an important, and in some cases, critical part of developing many of these skills. At the most fundamental level, social values are at the heart of defining the public interest, which sets the context for any public policy debate. It is difficult to see how one can understand the world view of potential clients and opponents without knowledge of their social values, and the conclusions of policy analysis are often most effectively communicated in the public arena if the results of policy research can be linked to deeply held social values.

Yet, despite the central role that social values play in the political discourse about public policies, formal training in policy analysis often tends to emphasize the more readily measurable aspects of public policy—(e.g., how to empirically measure the economic and social effects on children living in poverty of replacing the federal entitlement to AFDC with block grants). This emphasis on the quantifiable dimensions of policy is grounded in rational choice models of the policy process, which have their roots in disciplines such as economics and the decision sciences. Although the rational choice approach to policy analysis clearly has (and should have) an important place at the table in the ongoing discourse about policy in modern democracies, it often gives social values less attention than they deserve, largely because they are not amenable to quantification. There is, in other words, an implicit tendency to equate "rational" with "quantifiable."

This is unfortunate because, within the framework of the rational choice approach, there are numerous places where social values come into play. This is most clearly evident in the use of technical policy analysis to provide guidance to decision makers about whether particular policies are in the public interest. To offer such advice presupposes that there are some criteria for defining what the public interest is, and it has become commonplace in the rational approach to policy analysis to focus on two different dimensions of the public interest: (1) economic efficiency, or "getting the greatest aggregate good from available resources" and (2) distributional equity, or "fairness in the way . . . [the aggregate good] . . . is distributed."[3] Focusing on these can be quite useful analytically, but a good technical analyst needs to be mindful of several other issues.

Economic Efficiency as a Social Value

Cost-benefit analysis provides a generally agreed upon framework among economists and policy analysts for how in principle to measure whether a particular public policy is economically efficient. But one must recognize that the goal of achieving economic efficiency is itself a social value. In other words, although there are widely accepted technical procedures for calculating the benefits and costs of public policies, the decision to judge a policy on the basis of its economic benefits and costs is not value neutral. On one hand, there is a strong case to be made for making sure that the social value of economic efficiency be given considerable weight in many policy discussions. On the other hand, economic efficiency is one of several different social values, which also have legitimate claims in the policy debate. Thus, if economists wish to be advocates for efficiency in the policy process, they need to be sensitive to the range of social values that shape policy debates, if only to be able to make the best possible rhetorical case for giving efficiency the weight that economists believe it is due (see Chapter 6 by Klamer).

Social Values and Equity

The rational choice approach to public policy recognizes the importance of fairness as a social value for judging policy outcomes. This, however, raises numerous questions. How much weight should be given to the social value of fairness as opposed to the social value of economic efficiency? Are the weights the same in all cases, or do they change with the nature of the policy that is under consideration? Are there different social conceptions of what is fair? Is fairness only about the distribution of income and wealth, or also the distribution of power? Are concepts such as gender equity corollaries of broader social notions of fairness, such as equality of opportunity and/or equality of result, or are they distinct conceptions of fairness that exist apart from these concepts in some definable way?

Social Values Other Than Efficiency and Equity

There are also numerous areas of public policy where social values other than those of efficiency and equity play a central role. It matters, for example, whether the underlying social value behind affirmative action admissions programs to law or medical schools is to provide equality of opportunity or to promote diversity of background and cultures in those learned professions.

Similarly, one could ask whether it is economically efficient or fair to implement public policies that either facilitate or restrict research in areas such as genetics or cloning. But posing the question in this way might miss the point because the fundamental ethical issues that are raised by such policies turn on social values such as protection of human life and dignity that supersede what might be seen as secondary concerns about the economic benefits and costs of such policies, and who would gain and who would lose from their implementation.

Value Conflicts in Technical Policy Analysis

Policy analysis also needs to grapple with the possibility that social values can and will come into conflict with each other in the policy arena. In some cases, this conflict may be reducible to the trade-off between efficiency and equity that can at least be described in quantitative or measurable terms. But, the very idea that different social values can be traded off against each other or made somehow commensurable is itself a controversial proposition (see Chapters 7, by Sagoff, and 8, by MacClean). Whether or not the technical policy analyst agrees with the proposition that (at least some) values are not commensurable, it is important to understand the basis for this concern.

The Need for Reasoned Discourse About Social Values

Thus, to be effective, even technical policy analysis must pay serious attention to the nexus between social values and policy. But the rational choice paradigm that provides the overarching framing for technical policy analysis provides little guidance for exploring this nexus in a way that gives social values their due.

One possible reason is the typical analyst may be wary of giving too much credence to values without having some way of deciding which values deserve consideration in deciding a particular policy issue. Here, the analyst is well advised to look to other disciplines for guidance about how to construct a reasoned discourse about social values and their relation to public policy. Philosophy is a logical first place to look for such guidance because, as a discipline, it not only has a tradition of intellectually responding to critical ethical and moral issues as subjects for a community of dialogue, but also has sought to increase the intellectual quality and integrity of arguments for action as well as for the theoretical support or justification offered for plans of action.

A PHILOSOPHICAL PERSPECTIVE FOR REASONING ABOUT VALUES

Philosophical perspectives, whether offered by professional philosophers or by others, have tended to fasten onto three salient features of policy arguments. First, there is an abiding concern with persistent, often unquestioned and embedded background assumptions—ranging, for example, from the notion that policy choices ought be made democratically to the model of rationality presupposed by economists. Second, the moral dimensions of policy arguments are inescapable insofar as the policy process involves claims that some options are guided by principles, policies result from intentional actions that require justification, policy outcomes often have serious implications both for agents and all persons affected by a policy, and of course, because of the presumption that the objective of public policy is to promote the general welfare. Third, the philosophical perspective is concerned with epistemological and logical issues such as the logical validity of arguments, the clarification and analysis of key concepts, and the consistency of explanations.

Philosophical efforts to question persistent and embedded assumptions, and philosophical concerns with the moral dimensions of policy arguments are reasonably well represented by several chapters in this collection. Consequently, this section focuses instead on illustrating philosophical concern over conceptual clarification and analysis.

There is so much vague, loose, and ambiguous discourse centering around values that one who tries to find logic in discourse laden with value terminology should be reminded of the story of the Irishman who responded to a request for directions from a lost tourist by responding, "Well, if that's where you will be wanting to go, sir, then I wouldn't start from here." Thus, if one seeks analytical clarity about the meaning of "values," where should one start?

Perhaps one helpful way to begin is to distinguish between the things we value or describe as valuable—people, objects, ideas, actions, situations, and so forth—and values themselves. In ordinary discourse we usually do not make this distinction; for example, we usually do not distinguish honesty as a value, from deeds or actions that we find valuable and that flow from honesty, such as telling the truth or giving unbiased information. Yet, some warrant for this distinction can be drawn from etymology, as the English "value" comes from the Latin root *valeo*, "meant to be strong" (and hence the relation to "valor"), and more specifically, through a secondary meaning, to wit, "to be strong (enough) for some purpose." What associations might we make with both "strength" and "purpose"? We can think right away of "standard," "rule," and "test"; indeed of *criterion* which meant in Greek, "a means of judging." Possibly the direction of our thinking is already clear; to be explicit though, the reader might think of values as the criteria by which we judge things (persons and their traits, objects, ideas, actions, and situations) to be good, right, worthwhile, desirable; or on the other hand, bad, wrong, worthless, undesirable; or, of course, somewhere in between these extremes. By contrast, with values per se, the things we impute, or assign, value to, and hence regard as valuable, all have some particular substance or content: they meet our needs, fulfill us, satisfy ambitions, and so forth.

If this distinction is helpful, then it recommends a number of other points worthy of consideration. First, thinking about values as criteria helps us see that any adequate definition of the concept of value must be strictly formal. It alone could not specify the criteria persons might select; hence our standards for choice might run the gamut from rationally defensible moral principles to conventionally valued goods and then to wholly subjective desires, inclinations, and tastes. Likewise, a definition would say nothing about what particular things, or kinds of things are selected as valuable.

Indeed, disputes about what is of value, or valuable, cannot be settled by definition. To see this, we need only employ the simple analytic device made famous in the early twentieth century by G. E. Moore known as the open question test. The question, What has value? must always remain open because it always makes sense to ask of anything X defined as having value (e.g., as satisfying preferences), "Does X really have value?" Thus the relevance of this "test" is that it shows that claims about what is held to have value can never be necessarily true (as essentialists such as Plato might have thought) and are always empirical issues. Hence to discover what has value is just to discover certain facts about ourselves, other people, and the communities in which we live.

It might be noted that the open question test also applies to values understood as criteria. For example, someone who continues to press for answers when one of us has explained why he has chosen to complete a crossword puzzle during fifteen minutes of free time, and after being told that he finds that activity more satisfying than any other he can do in fifteen minutes of leisure, seems to be misunderstanding something important about the situation, preferences, or both. On the other hand, additional questions can be interpreted as asking what it is about one's ranking of preferences or the puzzle that makes it a chosen leisure activity. So, in general, if we want to reach a logical "stop," then we must rely either on the quality of the arguments we can make for our criteria for choice, or on agreements that we have reached a terminus beyond which it is fruitless to proceed, or both, since practically speaking, satisfactory arguments are often necessary and sufficient for such agreements. There would, however, seem to be many cases in which one can agree that sufficient reasons exist for accepting a value, or criterion, as really right, good, correct, or appropriate.

Recognizing the factual grounding of valuable things does not require that values—our criteria for selection—be subjective, or even that, despite changes, values necessarily presuppose relativism. This analysis exposes the obviously cognitive, as well as affective, dimension of values. Some things may be valuable for someone for no identifiable, effable reason, but certainly very many values look like commitments, principles, beliefs, points of view, reasons, and so forth for which defenses can be made. Some values, perhaps many, may be objective in the sense that they can be supported by reasons that virtually any impartial observer could accept, that is, values acquire objectivity to the extent that they cannot be overturned or discredited by arbitrary or capricious conditions (shifting desires, bursts of anger, whims, etc.) and resist pressure from particular political, ideological, religious, or economic interests. In addition, since as least some values may have much to do with the psychology of humans or features of sentient beings that are generally universal and remain more or less constant, some values may be fairly permanent or unchanging across cultures.

Second, the distinction between values as criteria and valuable things can help us distinguish among the bewildering array of things that are valued. It also helps us see the sense in speaking of the priority of some valuable things over others, that is, of some kind of hierarchy of values, if we attend to the kinds of reasons individuals and groups do and would give for their selections of the things to which they assign value.

Admittedly, investigating valuables in terms of reasons people offer for choices may lead to an unfortunate hodge-podge of overlapping categories. After all, many people are not very reflective about such matters and may have the same reasons for selecting different things and different reasons for selecting the same things. Further, difficulty in marking off categories of valuables may point to the presence of intrapersonal value conflicts as well as interpersonal conflicts.

Nevertheless, we believe that careful inspection of a sufficiently large sample would disclose at least five broad overlapping, but substantially different, categories. (1) Most primary are what one demands from life if one is to be free from need and able to regard life as at least minimally satisfactory. These demands call for criteria, or values, that relate to meeting basic needs such as freedom from pain and insecurity and to fundamental ends or aims that must be met if life is to be endurable. (2) Second, there are demands individuals may make upon one another, if they are to regard shared life as law-abiding, decent, and fair or morally adequate. Criteria, or values, related to these demands pertain to rights, duties, obligations, responsibilities, and moral principles.

Sharing roughly the same middle ground with valuables of type (2) are (3) what one seeks in order to achieve a fair measure of the "good life" as conventionally understood, which requires criteria reflecting higher ends or goals (such as education or a career) as well as various opportunities for satisfaction or pleasure in living. Next, consider (4) demands one makes, usually on one's own resources of effort and ability, but also on others, that enable one to call a life worthwhile or even excellent, in the sense that it represents genuine flourishing through the development of talents and abilities and the presence of opportunities for the exercise of skill and virtue. These demands require criteria, or values, that relate especially to beliefs about the meaning of life, to ideals, aspirations, and to commitments.

Finally, (5) there are demands people linked together socially make on one another to lessen the chances that some may aim at ends whose attainment would detrimentally affect the lives and prospects of others, and to increase the chances that some people will aim at ends that have the effect of raising the overall quality of life. In addition to rights and moral principles, the criteria, or values, most relevant to these demands concern what are urged and disputed as publicly sanctioned incentives and commitments and politically chosen ends or objectives.

Where among these categories are social values to be found? One might think most readily of the criteria for categories (3) and (5) because of their necessarily social dimensions, but of what significance are the goods in these categories if a society lacks effective criteria for securing for its members the goods in category (1)? It obviously does not take long to see that what one defines as crucial social values cannot be separated from a host of other, often controversial, views and beliefs about the meaning of life and the role of government. Fortunately, several of the authors in this book identify and attempt to defend what they regard as especially important social values.

Finally, thinking of values as criteria for selection tends to undercut the reductionistic or preemptory efforts of those who believe the diversity of values can be reduced or transformed into just one kind. We have in mind not only the economist who seeks to "cash in" all values as preference satisfactions, or the sociobiologist who argues that all values must serve adaptive fitness, but also philosophers with blinkers who would convert this unsettled and slippery linguistic terrain into a dry and stony ethics by arguing that values must be analyzed as value judgments and ultimately justified by ethical theory. Because some of the chapters in this book argue powerfully and eloquently against various reductionistic schemes, anyone who wants to pursue a reductionistic program must be able to show, not only that we can speak and think of our values as if they were all of the same kind, for example, as preferences, but also that there are no really significant differences between the kinds of reasons people offer for claiming things as valuable. And the latter task looks quite formidable indeed.

In conclusion, readers may remember the Irishman of lore and conclude that we started from the wrong point and ended up nowhere. In any case, being sufficiently impressed by the sheer complexity of our conceptions of and discourse about values, we hope that, even if our observations fail to suggest fruitful directions for thought or to raise interesting questions, they may at least help us keep this complexity in mind.

In the opening chapter, Milton M. Carrow, whose background is in administrative law and public policy, provides a framework for the ensuing discussions. He points out how fragile democracies are and identifies some of the erosive trends in the United States today. He emphasizes the necessity of looking beyond structure and institutions to reclaim democratic ideals, ideas, and practices. Carrow alludes to the work of others who point to "social capital" as the indicator of the success or failure of democracies, and he argues that, to understand the foundation of successful democracy, we must also focus on the underlying social values.

As Timothy Brennan notes in Chapter 4, "just because something is valued by someone does not make it valuable to support or provide it." The next two chapters are concerned both with the origins and nature of social values and with how distinctions might be made among values.

A key feature of British philosopher Jennifer Trusted's argument in Chapter 2 is her distinction between fundamental moral principles, which, she holds, are universal and absolute, and social values, which are relative to particular societies, cultures, and subcultures. One may agree or disagree with Trusted's view of morality as universal and absolute, or with her view of the content of its basic principles which, she argues, do not include consequentialist (utilitarian) standards. But her distinction between morality, on the one hand, and social values, on the other, should add needed clarity to debates over public policy. While societies may differently interpret the two basic moral principles identified by Trusted, and implement them as social values (as they may do with religious values), social values are typically much more inclusive and, unlike the two moral absolutes, subject to change. Indeed, Trusted holds that, although social values support changes in policy and law, they are derivative and subservient to the basic moral principles. Hence, morality provides criteria for assessing social values and dependent moral conventions.

Trusted concedes that the critical assessment of social values is often difficult and controversial, as she illustrates with respect to changing social values about the family, but such critical scrutiny is no less important than the assessment of social values in relation to present realities and past history. Moreover, appreciating the distinction between moral absolutes and social values will help us to remember that the latter are never sacrosanct, as well as to avoid reflexive, knee-jerk, responses to judgments that appear to conflict with predominant or preferred moral conventions and social values.

In Chapter 3, James L. Peacock, a cultural anthropologist, defines values very broadly as general conceptions of the desirable, including what Trusted would regard as the distinctive domain of moral absolutes. Despite this potential disagreement, Peacock focuses squarely on what Trusted would accept as social values, that is, on values that most specifically affect policy and that vary among societies, cultures, and subcultures. Two questions are central to Peacock's concerns: (1) Do social values change as a result of changes in economic, social, and environmental conditions? and (2) Can adopted policies induce changes in social values?

In contrast to reductionistic, causal-functional analyses of values associated with Durkheim, Marx, and Freud, Peacock finds the logico-meaningful analysis associated with Max Weber and certain neo-Weberians to offer the most sustained and comprehensive account of the wellsprings of values. Within this framework of meaning, values are integral parts of conceptual paradigms humans deploy in their quest to find life meaningful. Moreover, in response to the first key question, Peacock delineates a complicated dialectical process between change and stability. While social values are extensively constructed or transformed in response to influences elsewhere in society, Peacock finds that certain core values, such as those related to the Protestant work ethic in the United States, have a remarkable resiliency, so that "the old structures the seemingly new."

For Peacock the second key question can be answered more quickly. It might be possible to develop policies that seek to transform values. But the dialectic between stability and change among social values makes it difficult to predict what kinds of interventions are likely to produce desired outcomes. While considering some possible venues or intervention points, Peacock warns that outcomes are uncertain and potentially chaotic and dangerous. And yet, failing to intervene wisely is to risk that changes already in motion might undermine a heritage of democracy and liberty worth preserving.

Of course, many critics already argue that policies as designed and implemented by big government are disconnected from the values citizens actually hold. This is a claim that Timothy Brennan, a policy scientist and economist, confronts head on in Chapter 4. Is the lack of social consensus in public policy a result of the failure of policy institutions to reflect underlying social values held by the body politic or a result of these institutions faithfully reflecting the absence of social values in the body politic? Brennan disputes the widespread view that primary attention should be given to institutional reform, asserting instead, as Walt Kelly's Pogo said, that "[w]e have met the enemy, and they is us."

The issue is, of course, empirical, and Brennan argues not only that there is little evidence that people really are willing to make nontrivial sacrifices to promote the general good, but also that the evidence offers little support for the view that policy outcomes diverge from the consensus position on values. Such divergences that do occur are results, Brennan claims, of occasional market failures, and, ironically, voting paradoxes and vagaries associated with collective action.

Noting that "effective concern with public values is an exceptionally scarce resource," Brennan points out that it would be much easier to fix flawed institutions than to inculcate a strong sense of civic duty in citizens, to encourage them to voice their values, and to ensure that the system responds to them. Regarding this last issue, Brennan considers whether a "revolution" in concern with values, which likely cannot occur without public intrusion into private life, can be justifiably opposed by liberalism and its insistence on value-neutrality regarding visions of the good life. After carefully weighing arguments on both sides, Brennan rejects extreme versions of the principle of neutrality. His chapter closes with consideration of some broad recommendations for using political authority to increase civic responsibility in ways that are minimally intrusive, and with a warning that social stability may require a balance between "our individualistic neglect of each other" and some "hope of achieving agreement on specific theories of what a good society should be."

In addressing the relationship of the humanities disciplines to social values and public policy, Chapter 5 focuses on the role of religion in a modern democracy from the standpoint of the Roman Catholic religious tradition. J. Bryan Hehir, a distinguished theologian, analyzes the issues through three stages. First, he locates religious communities in the framework of nonestablishment and free-exercise clauses of the First Amendment. Second, he examines how a given religious tradition engages the public policy debate both as a voluntary association and with a religious voice. And third, he uses four important issues (safety nets, human rights, military intervention, and bioethics) that exemplify the interaction of religion, values, and policy formation in a democracy.

In differing ways, Chapters 6, 7, and 8 take a critical look at the role of economic efficiency as a social value for evaluating public policy. In Chapter 6, Arjo Klamer, an economist who occupies the chair of Art and Culture at Erasmus University in the Netherlands, uses the political debate about the North American Free Trade Agreement (NAFTA) as a case study of the relative importance of economic efficiency as a social value in policy discourse. The case is a good one because there is virtual technical consensus among economists that policies that promote free trade are economically efficient (e.g., help produce the greatest aggregate good from available resources). As a result, professional economists were able to speak with nearly one voice in favor of NAFTA. The question is whether such support was decisive or incidental to other issues. Klamer argues that arguments on behalf of NAFTA based on economic efficiency were certainly present in the debate, but that in the final analysis, other concerns, such as who would win and who would lose from NAFTA, and the perceived character of the principal protagonists in the NAFTA debate, were more decisive than economists' estimates of the projected gains in economic efficiency.

Chapter 7 by Mark Sagoff, a philosopher who is director and senior research scholar of the Institute for Philosophy and Public Policy at the University of Maryland, is critical of what he describes as formal policy analysis to the extent that it is based on the theory of welfare economics and its applied methodology of cost-benefit analysis. Practitioners of applied welfare economics (such as one of the co-editors of this book) argue that one attractive feature of the applied welfare economics paradigm is that it allows one to define a public interest in economic efficiency that is based on the satisfaction of individual preferences. Sagoff, however, notes that if this is taken as the only standard for evaluating public policies, concerns about public policies based on moral, cultural, or social grounds have no basis in formal policy analysis, because they have no rational basis for inclusion in the calculation of benefits and costs. Broadening the applied welfare paradigm to include concerns about equity or fairness does not help, according to Sagoff, because a number of important moral, cultural, or social values about policy have little or nothing to do with distributional equity. He goes on to argue that the only way in which such values will receive the weight that they are due is through a complex deliberative process. Formal policy analysis would continue to play a role in such a process, but as a form of objective inquiry about the consequences of different policies in relation to social goals that are accepted as given by the policy analyst, instead of as an application of applied welfare economics.

Chapter 8 by Douglas MacLean, a philosopher whose primary research interests are in moral and philosophical issues in risk analysis, also considers the case for using cost-benefit analysis, with its implied emphasis on economic efficiency as a social value, to evaluate public policies that affect life and limb and environmental quality, which are things that "many people believe cannot faithfully be served by thinking about them in a certain kind of economic way." MacClean strongly supports the proposition that cost-benefit analysis should never be used as the sole arbiter to decide whether society should or should not regulate private activities in the name of improving health and safety or the environment.

But a more fundamental question is whether cost-benefit analysis should have any role in the process of evaluating such regulations. The issue addressed by MacLean may be summarized as follows. Critics of using cost-benefit analysis often contend that it forces comparisons between items such as the value of human life and the monetary costs of regulations that cannot or should not be compared. Yet, common sense also tells us that there are limits to what people would be willing to spend to save human lives. The question is whether these perspectives can be reconciled in any kind of formal analysis. MacLean suggests that this may be possible, but only if practitioners of cost-benefit analysis are willing to move away from attempting to use market-like prices to evaluate "goods" such as quality of life that are not traded in the marketplace and are prepared to embed such cost-benefit analysis in a deliberative process that weighs a variety of different social values without attempting to arrive at a single bottom-line estimate of benefits and costs.

Chapters 9 through 12 focus centrally on respective problems of public policy and on the way in which the policy process has been affected by various social values. In Chapter 9, Gene D. Cohen, a gerontologist and director of a center on aging, is concerned with intergenerational equity, especially in the allocation of health care resources. In terms of Douglas MacLean's analysis of incompatible values in Chapter 8, Cohen finds no real incompatibilities between generational, or age group, values regarding resource allocations. It is a mistake, Cohen asserts, to frame the country's resource problems as an intergenerational conflict issue. The real problem concerns the gap between popular, media fed, misperceptions and myths concerning intergenerational conflicts (such as the myths that "kids don't care" or that there is a "growing generation gap") on the one hand, and, on the other, a burgeoning intergenerational consensus over values Cohen calls intergenerationalism. This emerging consensus involves social values that underlie the allocation of resources, even though distributive policies will affect age groups differentially.

Cohen seeks to expose widespread myths and mistaken beliefs about intergenerational conflict and to replace them with realities. Unless this is done, he notes, public debate will be distorted and public choice may well be prejudiced, involving among other injustices, the scapegoating of older adults.

One important feature of Cohen's argument, as well as those in the ensuing chapters, is evidence that there is no neat match between social values and corresponding public policy. Social values change or become reinterpreted over time. Moreover, a policy or program may be supported by different, overlapping, or even conflicting values. Cohen reminds us that Medicare, which is now widely viewed as serving the special interests of the elderly, was initially a family-in-mind program, strongly supported by family values to protect families from the burdens of excessive medical costs.

The social historian Edward D. Berkowitz argues in Chapter 10 that no set of values has had universal appeal in connection with social welfare policy, but that social welfare policies have instead been shaped by an ongoing tension between several different social values. Should social welfare policies reflect the will of the majority, or should the majority instead put its trust in experts to deal with the needs of those less fortunate? Should the social welfare system simply provide enough money to meet the needs of the poor without attempting to better their circumstances, or should it provide the poor with the means and incentives to improve their economic well-being? Berkowitz provides a rich account of how social welfare policies have, at various points in U.S. history, been designed to reflect these conflicting values, and just as important, how the importance of these values in defining the debate about social welfare policy has shifted back and forth over time. A dominant theme of the essay is that observed administrative features of the social welfare system, which at times seem incoherent, can be traced to attempts to implement social welfare policies consistent with these shifting and conflicting social values about what a social welfare system is supposed to accomplish.

Cynthia Harrison, a professor of history and women's studies, maintains in Chapter 11 that, although social values emphasizing virtue have consistently been associated with women since the founding of the Republic, the meanings and uses of "virtue" have undergone radical change. Early ideology assigned to women a special civilizing function in upholding and inculcating virtue within the home and family. Later, notions of women's "virtue" were used to justify policies of exclusion, presumably to protect women (who had an atrophied moral capacity), and then to argue, inconsistently, for women's participation—in the antialcohol and settlement house movements, for example—because, as political outsiders, women had fewer opportunities to be corrupted.

Harrison notes that now, at the end of the twentieth century, some policy makers are defining work for wages as the essential component of virtuous mothering for poor mothers receiving public assistance, while continuing to applaud the ideal of full-time home care for children for predominantly white, middle-class mothers. In addition, in response to feminists' efforts to eliminate the internal contradiction between protection of women's special relationship to children and equal access for women to public life, some contemporary proponents of so-called family values (i.e., traditional male-dominant family values) have revived the centuries old notion that the central function of women ("women's burden") is to civilize men by restoring the traditional roles and prerequisites of fatherhood.

Although policy issues concerning women, children, and families traditionally have been framed in terms of values, Harrison points out that major changes in federal policy, such as implementations of provisions of the President's Commission on the Status of Women and of the Civil Rights Act of 1964 have preceded rather than followed major shifts in public values. Family structure and women's behavior have changed most in response to economic imperatives. Moreover, continuing to treat policy debates such as those over aid to families with dependent children, national health insurance, and guaranteed child support as contests over values and virtues masks the political agendas of conservative and liberal constituencies and diverts attention from rational economic decision-making. Harrison concludes, "We may need now less talk about values and more about economics."

In Chapter 12, Eric T. Juengst, a biomedical ethicist, focuses on genetic engineering and our ethical obligations to future generations. Within this context, Juengst is most concerned to illustrate how *not* to integrate social values into our science policies regarding genetic engineering, by showing how an increasingly popular and influential approach to international genetic research policy—the common heritage view—is conceptually flawed and socially dangerous.

Juengst's argument attempts to show how values supporting a position for public decision and intended to safeguard our way of life, paradoxically, may lead to policies that ultimately undermine that way of life. Thus, in addition to being based on false conceptions of genes as resources and of genetic engineering, Juengst believes that advocates of the common heritage view unwittingly risk supporting eugenic programs and practices leading to discrimination, precisely the kinds of outcome advocates of the common heritage view oppose as erosive of the freedom and dignity of the individual.

The most important ethical issue raised by genetic engineering, Juengst asserts, concerns the risk of unjust distributions of the benefits of the new technologies among future generations. Given the benefits of phenotypic prevention and genotypic prevention, it will be the "unengineered"—those who could most benefit but have least access to these therapies—who will be especially disadvantaged. Consequently, because it is the range of human capacities that is valuable in our common genetic heritage, the critical principle in regulating new gene therapies must address equal opportunities for reaping the benefits of genetic engineering in human flourishing.

The book concludes with a commentary on the papers offered at the end of the conference by Kenneth F. Schaffner, The George Washington University Professor of Medical Humanities. Despite the wide range of disciplinary perspectives in the papers, Shaffner is able to identify several interrelated themes that recur. In many respects, these themes raise questions rather than answer them. Can the attempt to identify universal values that apply in a wide range of policy settings, which is appealing analytically, be reconciled with the unavoidable pluralism of values that exist in practice? Can different values be made commensurable? Does the satisfaction of preferences provide a logically consistent framework for weighing different values in the policy process? Inevitably, the richness and complexity of social values make such questions difficult if not impossible to answer. But, the central role of social values in policy discourse demands that those who practice the art and craft of policy analysis ask and critically reflect on these questions, even if (perhaps because) easy answers are not forthcoming.

NOTES

1. David L. Weimer and Aidan R. Vining, *Policy Analysis Concepts and Practice* (Englewood Cliffs, NJ: Prentice-Hall, 1992), 1, 12.

2. Ibid., 13.

3. Ibid., p. 16.

A Framework for Democracy, Social Values, and Public Policy

Milton M. Carrow

In the historical perspective of past millenia, modern democratic governments are new and fragile. Because of such newness, their underpinnings are only beginning to be understood. Not long ago, it was assumed that the establishment of a democratic structure, by constitution or otherwise, based on consent of the people with the guarantees of freedom, justice, and equality, was sufficient to assure the development of a flourishing democratic society. Recent history has shown this not to be true. Recognizing attributes and practices accepted in particular societies, not necessarily provided for by law or constitution, is of vital importance for assuring the survival of democracies.

In the United States, which represents the embodiment of democratic structure and constitutional rights, we are confronted with problems that can erode these basic components. Fortunately, there is now widespread recognition of the incipient dangers to our democratic institutions. Scholars are probing the destructive forces and methods for alleviating them, civic institutions are engaged in a variety of efforts to overcome them, the general public is manifesting frustration about them, and politicians are scrambling to mollify their constituents.

In this chapter, I briefly review certain historical aspects of democracies, especially how fragile they have been, the erosive trends in U.S. democratic institutions, certain noninstitutional attributes that are essential for successful societies, and some of the thinking about and civic responses to our flagging democratic institutions.

WHERE DEMOCRACIES HAVE FAILED

From a historical perspective, democracies are fragile and only recently have they been fully developed. The premodern history of democracies indicates not only how vulnerable they were but also how rare. The first, the Greek city-state of Athens, lasted fewer than 200 years. Donald Kagan recently retraced the origins of Greek democratic institutions to some time before 500 B.C. and reminded us that their most significant development occurred under the leadership of Pericles after he was elected in 463 B.C. as one of the governing generals.

Pericles was instrumental in establishing a constitution that gave direct power to its citizens in assembly, where decisions were made by a majority vote, public officials were selected by lot for short terms of office, and which provided for close control of such officials. It is true, of course, that women, slaves, and aliens could not become citizens, but U.S. democracy did not start much better (women, for one, did not get the right to vote until 1920). It is also worth noting that Pericles' reforms were strongly resisted and that his great leadership was shown by his ability to persuade the citizens to do what they were not disposed to do but who, nevertheless, reelected him from year to year.[1]

More than two thousand years passed before democracy reemerged. During those years governments were despotic and strongly monarchical, many dynasties lasting far longer than 200 years. The American and French Revolutions and the adoption of the U.S. Constitution in 1789 gave birth to the modern era of democracy. Except for the United States and several small cantons in Switzerland,[2] there followed a volatile succession of the rise and fall of democratic governments. (English democratic institutions developed in gradual stages until the middle of the nineteenth century.) In 1921, after the First World War, James Bryce, in his classic work *Modern Democracies* optimistically declared: "Within the hundred years that now lie behind us what changes have passed upon the world! Nearly all the monarchies of the Old World have been turned into democracies. . . . There are now more than one hundred representative assemblies at work all over the earth legislating for self-governing communities. . . . A not less significant change has been the universal acceptance of democracy as the normal and natural form of government."[3] We recall, of course, that President Wilson, in his message to Congress when the United States entered the First World War, stated that the aim was to "make the world safe for democracy."

Even as Bryce wrote, the challenge to the new democratic governments had set in, beginning with the Bolshevik overthrow of the Kerensky government in Russia in 1917. As William E. Rappard pointed out in 1938, "Not only have most of the new liberal constitutions collapsed like the light huts of an American mining town, with whose mushroom growth their spread compared, but the cyclone of the authoritarian reaction which passed over the world has even shaken the institutions of democracy where they were older." In addition to Russia, he indicated that the other major nations with emerging democratic institutions that succumbed to dictatorial regimes by 1938 were Italy, Germany, Poland, Spain, and Japan. He did say, however, that "none of those states which in the nineteenth century had been led by a gradual process of evolution to adopt democratic institutions and in which such institutions had been working and developing normally for several generations have heretofore fallen prey to post-war dictators."[4]

According to a more recent study by Michael W. Doyle, whose findings were updated by Francis Fukuyama, between 1919 and 1940 the number of democracies declined from twenty-five to thirteen. The losses (mostly Second World War casualties) included France, Belgium, Netherlands, Denmark, Piedmont/Italy, Norway, Austria,

West Germany, East Germany, Poland, Czechoslovakia, Estonia, Chile, and Argentina. The number increased by 1960 to thirty-six, restoring, among others, France, Belgium, Netherlands, Denmark, Piedmont/Italy, Norway, Austria, West Germany, and Chile. The number dropped again by 1975 to thirty, including Greece, Chile, Brazil, Uruguay, Bolivia, Peru, Ecuador, El Salvador, and the Philippines. However, a new surge of democracies, a total of sixty, became established between 1975 and 1990.[5]

WHY DEMOCRACIES FAIL

Despite the differences in the circumstances in each of the countries where democracy failed, certain general aspects have been noted. High on the list was lack of experience in the populace with the democratic structure of popular government and with the institutions of liberty and equality. Closely related was a nonparticipatory and dispirited citizenry. Of overriding importance was a lack of high-quality leadership that could deal with divided legislators and disenchanted citizens. Norman L. Stamps, in 1958, described some of these as "executive impotence," "party stalemate . . . party deadlock in the legislature," "lack of agreement on fundamental matters," "political inexperience and exploitation," and "demoralization and feeling of futility."[6]

In his commentary on Greek democracy, Kagan said that successful democracies met three conditions: (1) is "to have a set of good institutions"; (2) is "to have a body of citizens who possess a good understanding of the principles of democracy, or who at least have developed a character consistent with the democratic way of life"; and (3) is to have "a high quality of leadership, at least at critical moments."[7]

Some of the reasons for failure, as listed above, appear relevant to the present state of democracy in the United States, such as "lack of agreement on fundamental matters," "lack of high quality of leadership," and "demoralization and feeling of futility." There are even deeper trends that should be of concern. If U.S. democracy, in its structural aspects, represents a government with the consent of the governed and with certain inalienable rights as promised by the Declaration of Independence and the Bill of Rights, then current trends show it to be at risk. It is common knowledge that opinion polls indicate that voting and nonvoting citizens believe that many, if not most, of their representatives are more responsive to special interests rather than citizen interests, their sources of campaign funds, and spend inordinate amounts of time to assure the security of their jobs and its perks. Citizens are also said to believe that policies adopted by their representatives on such problems as health care, deficits, environment, crime, disintegration of localities, and others do not reflect a reasonable consensus of what citizens want. If true, these hardly add up to a government with the consent of the governed.

Regarding the status of our inalienable rights, it is true that U.S. citizens have the greatest range of freedoms (free press, free speech, freedom of religion, freedom to assemble) in human history. This may, in fact, be the shining light on the road to the survival of U.S. democracy. However, equality in its several manifestations is in a tormented condition. In terms of equal opportunity, income, and equity, the rich are getting richer and the poor poorer, the middle class is carrying the burden of support and hurting, and women and minorities are struggling for fair economic recognition.

The great ideals of the melting pot and e pluribus unum are being threatened. The recent challengers, political "correctness" and multiculturalism on the one hand and a resurgence of libertarianism on the other have had a shattering impact on the presumed unifying forces of learning in the colleges and universities with repercussions beyond them. Unlike the frontier days when people from diverse cultures were readily absorbed into U.S. democracy, today's entrants are facing increasing racial and economic barriers. Angry confrontations among white, ethnic, Latino, and African-American communities, rooted in economic and discriminatory disparities, are increasing and are an ever present tinder box for violence. These and similar manifestations present dire challenges to our inalienable rights and its ideal of neighborly cultural diversity.[8]

UNDERLYING ATTRIBUTES OF SUCCESSFUL DEMOCRACIES AND SOCIETIES

As the above described circumstances indicate, successful democracies need more than simply a structure of democratic institutions such as a constitution, unrestricted voting rights, representative government, and so on. As several recent studies have shown, we need to examine the history, attitudes, and motivations of the people in particular societies to ascertain why some communities become successful democracies and others do not. The recent work by Robert Putnam, *Making Democracy Work*, is a striking example.[9] He describes how in the 1970s, a major government reorganization was undertaken in Italy, whereby twenty new regional governments were established with essentially identical constitutional structures and mandates. Putnam and his associates decided that this provided an excellent opportunity to examine the "conditions for creating strong, responsive, effective representative institutions." They followed such developments for more than twenty years, and Putnam later summarized his findings as follows:

> As we expected, some of the new governments proved to be dismal failures— inefficient, lethargic, and corrupt. Others have been remarkably successful, however, creating innovative day care programs and job training centers, promoting investment and economic development, pioneering environmental standards and family clinics—managing the public's business efficiently and satisfying their constituents.
>
> What could account for these stark differences in quality of government? Some seemingly obvious answers turned out to be irrelevant. Party politics or ideology makes little difference. Affluence and prosperity have no direct effect. Instead, the best predictor is one that Alexis de Tocqueville might have expected. Strong traditions of civic engagement—voter turnout, newspaper readership, membership in choral societies and literary circles, Lions Clubs, and soccer clubs—are the hallmarks of a successful region.[10]

These civic attributes he called social capital. "The social capital embodied in norms and networks of civic engagement," he said, "seems to be a precondition for economic development, as well as for effective government." [11]

A view of how society works indicating that not all social capital is moral, was presented several years earlier by Jon Elster in his seminal study entitled *The Cement of Society*. He sought to identify the attributes of what he called social order, particularly "that of stable, regular, predictable patterns of behavior and that of cooperative behavior."[12] He distinguished three varieties of human motivation: "(a) envy, (b) opportunism, or self-interest with guile, and (c) codes of honour, or the ability to make credible threats and promises. Each of these has been taken to provide the 'cement of society,' without which chaos and anarchy would prevail."[13]

I found one of Elster's arguments especially intriguing, namely, "that opportunism glues people together, using corruption and bribery as the vehicle of the argument."[14] I was struck by how this applied to the criminal trial of Italy's prime minister, Giulio Andreotti. He was the country's dominant politician for forty years and was accused of being the patron of the Sicilian Mafia during that time. Nevertheless, "Andreotti helped shepherd the country from an agricultural backwater ravaged by war into one of the world's leading industrial democracies. . . . Patronage and ever-expanding government spending greased the creaky wheels of government as the system produced featherbedding, graft and favored treatment for business."[15]

Another similar example was the trial of two former presidents of South Korea, Roh Tai Woo and Chun Doo Hwan, and assorted business leaders. "Political corruption has been a way of life in this country for decades, fueled by 30 years of authoritarian rule. For years, those leaders presided over Korea's rise from economic weakling to a world-class economy, choosing which corporations and sectors to promote."[16]

RECLAIMING U.S. DEMOCRATIC IDEALS, IDEAS, AND PRACTICES

It is common for scholars and others to refer to the 1830 book by Alexis de Tocqueville, *Democracy in America*, which identifies voluntarism in community activities as a significant source of the strength of U.S. democracy. There is renewed recognition of this attribute.

After the 1996 presidential election and President Clinton's call, in his inaugural address, for a nonpartisan effort to promote community service, the idea of voluntarism was embraced by the leaders of both major parties as a means to that end. President Clinton and former President George Bush as well as former Presidents Jimmy Carter and Gerald Ford, with former First Lady Nancy Reagan standing in for ailing former President Ronald Reagan, agreed to hold a three-day summit meeting on voluntary community service in Philadelphia in April, 1997 to be headed by General Colin L. Powell.[17]

Such a "summit" effort, aside from its immediate political implications, reflects the cumulative effect of a long series of studies and volunteer efforts seeking to correct what have been perceived as destructive trends in our democratic institutions. One such negative perception, stemming from a cautionary note in the de Tocqueville book, was that the strong individualism de Tocqueville saw in the U.S. character could undermine freedom. In a widely recognized book, *Habits of the Heart* (a phrase from de Tocqueville), Robert Bellah and his colleagues focused their research on individualism in middle-class American life. They found that "this individualism may have grown cancerous—that it may be destroying those social integuements that Tocqueville saw as moderating its more destructive potentialities, that it may be threatening the survival of freedom itself."[18]

Individualism, individual rights, personal responsibility, civic duty, social order, community rights and responsibilities, as well as voluntarism have been intensively examined in recent years. Liberals, conservatives, libertarians, communitarians, in their various extremist or moderate stances, have been attempting to stake out policy positions relating to all of these societal elements. The lines of difference are far from clear. Politically, the debates focus on the extent to which the government should intervene in the economy and on social issues. Libertarians want to get government out of all economic and social activity, maintaining that private action can achieve better results than government intervention.[19] Although, fortunately, we do not have an equally extreme authoritarian movement, a newly invigorated communitarian movement supports limitations on individual rights in favor of social order and community rights. Its most prolific exponent currently is Amitai Etzioni whose book *The New Golden Rule* espouses a new communitarianism that seeks to establish an equilibrium between social order and personal autonomy. He states that "the communitarian paradigm entails a profound commitment to moral order that is basically voluntary, and to a social order that is well balanced with socially secured autonomy— the new golden rule."[20]

The emphasis on personal responsibility, as a departure from the nurturing state, is represented by the controversial welfare law enacted in 1996 by the 104th Congress, which, among other things provided for termination of welfare benefits after five years. On the volunteer front are the pleas and proposals for increased engagement of citizens in civic responsibilities. Benjamin Barber, in his book *Strong Democracy* said, "Strong democracy requires unmediated self-government by an engaged citizenry. It requires institutions that will involve individuals at both the neighborhood and national level in common talk, common decision-making and political judgment, and common action."[21] A similar argument, identified as civic virtue, one that is "attentive to the civic strand of freedom," is made in Michael Sandel's book *Democracy's Discontent*:

> A politics attentive to the civic strand of freedom might try "to restrict the sphere of life in which money matters" and shore up the public spaces that gather people together in common experiences and form the habits of citizenship. Such a politics would worry less about the distribution of income as such, and more "about rebuilding, preserving, and strengthening community institutions in which income is irrelevant, about preventing their corruption by the forces of the market." It would encourage "class-mixing institutions" like public schools, libraries, parks, community centers, public transportation, and national service. Although such policies might also be favored by welfare-state liberals, the emphasis and justification would differ. A more civic-minded liberalism would seek communal provision less for the sake of distributive justice than for the sake of affirming membership and forming the civic identity of rich and poor alike.[22]

Alongside these efforts there have been, in fact, in the course of the last decade, an extensive series of volunteer activities with the objective of encouraging and enlisting citizens to participate in community and public affairs. One of the most prominent is the National Issues Forums and Study Groups sponsored by the Kettering Foundation, which has involved more than 5,000 civic and educational organizations throughout the United States to discuss prepared papers on current issues such as crime and welfare (three topics each year). The groups are provided with possible options for resolving the issues and are guided by trained facilitators to attempt to arrive at some consensus. David Mathews, the president of the Kettering Foundation, has described the rationale and successes of these efforts in his book *Politics for the People*.[23] Another central source for supporting, encouraging, and disseminating information about the growing number of volunteer focus groups and study circles is the Study Circles Resource Center, which publishes a newsletter describing community-wide programs around the United States.[24]

Finally, an intriguing perception of the future of citizen participation has been offered by Lawrence Grossman, a former president of Public Broadcasting Service and of NBC News. In his book *The Electronic Republic*, he maintains that "the electronic republic opens the way for the public at large to become the actual fourth branch of government."[25] He explains how

[t]his democratic political transformation is being propelled largely by two developments—the two hundred-year-long march toward political equality for all citizens and the explosive growth of new telecommunications media, the remarkable convergence of television, telephone, satellites, cable, and personal computers. This is the first generation of citizens who can see, hear, and judge their own political leaders simultaneously and instantaneously. It is also the first generation of political leaders who can address the entire population and receive instant feedback about what the people think and want. Interactive telecommunications increasingly give ordinary citizens immediate access to the major political decisions that affect their lives and property.[26]

The Focus on Social Values in Policymaking

The influences, attributes and developments I noted above demonstrate the growing recognition of the danger of relying on the structural framework of democracies as the primary source for their continued or potential success. To appreciate the fragility of democracies, we need only to observe the current struggles in Russia, the new states that formerly were part of the Soviet Union, in Poland, and Bosnia to realize that constitutions, popular elections, and representative government do not of themselves assure the maintenance and success of democratic government.

The studies on social capital and social order have alerted us to the fact that we must look to underlying attributes of the individuals and groups in our societies to determine whether democratic institutions can be successfully maintained. The renewed interest in voluntarism and the growth of citizen participation movements manifests a recognition of the importance of such attributes.

The role of social values in public policymaking in our democracy may be narrower than the subjects already discussed, but the principles they illustrate are germane. They demonstrate that we must look beyond the conventional considerations that dominate public policy discourse to determine what really underlies our public policies. Is it sufficient to say that government costs too much or that we don't spend enough? Or that government needlessly invades personal lives? Or that, in social welfare areas, for example, that the states can govern better than the federal government? Or that taxes are too high or insufficient to cover essential functions? Or that providing for the disadvantaged or minorities is either a community responsibility or creates dependence instead of self-reliance? The cost-benefit arguments that dominate such issues leave the disputants hopelessly in disagreement.

What, then, are the operative factors that influence these stances held by individuals and groups? Underlying them, I believe, are the social values of individual citizens that do or do not flow through the governing process to those who make public policy. What these social values are, where they originate, how and why they may change, how they are affected by social and economic trends, how they affect the governing institutions as well as how they are applied in major policy areas are some of the subjects in the chapters that follow.

I believe that an understanding of the social values that underlie public policy is essential for promoting the success of our democratic institutions. We may find that some of the values reflected in public policies are not conducive to an effective democratic government. Or we may find that the social values of most citizens are not incorporated in public policies. Or we may find that they are. With such awareness, I believe, we can be much clearer in directing or efforts to sustain and improve our democratic institutions.

NOTES

1. Donald Kagan, *Pericles of Athens and the Birth of Democracy* (New York: Free Press, 1991). See Francis Fukuyama, *The End of History and the Last Man* (New York: Free Press, 1992), 48, who said "that before 1776 there was not a single one (liberal democracy) in existence anywhere in the world. (The democracy of Periclean Athens does not qualify, because it did not systematically protect individual rights.)." But see Josiah Ober, *The Athenian Revolution: Essays on Ancient Greek Democracy and Political Theory* (Princeton: Princeton University Press, 1996), 4, "Athenian democracy is remarkable because it was the real thing—in classical Athens the demos (the mass of ordinary adult male natives) was the true political authority. Though political leadership was a key element in the workings of Athenian government . . . there was no behind-the-scenes oligarchy of bureaucrats, dealmakers, landlords, warlords, or aristocrats."

2. Jonathan Steinberg, *Why Switzerland?* (New York: Cambridge University Press, 1973).

3. James Bryce, *Modern Democracies* (New York: Macmillan, 1921), 1: 3–4. Bryce's definition of democracy was narrower than current notions of "liberal democracy." He said:

In this book I use the word (democracy) in its old and strict sense, as denoting a government in which the will of the majority of qualified citizens rules, taking the qualified citizens to constitute the great bulk of inhabitants, say, roughly at least three-fourths, so that the physical force of the citizens coincides (broadly speaking) with their voting power. . . . Democracy is supposed to be the product and guardian both of

Equality and Liberty, being so consecrated by its relationship to both these precious possessions as to be almost above criticism. Historically no doubt the three have been intimately connected, yet they are separable in theory and have sometimes been separated in practice. (Ibid., 22)

4. William E. Rappard, *The Crisis of Democracy* (Chicago: University of Chicago Press, 1938), 5–6, 69.

5. Michael W. Doyle, "Kant, Liberal Legacies, and Foreign Affairs, "*Philosophy & Public Affairs* 12 (summer 1983): 209–212. Fukuyama, *End of History*, 49–50. The numbers in these two studies don't exactly coincide and there are qualifications described in both Doyle's and Fukuyama's footnotes. However, the scenario is obvious.

6. Norman L. Stamps, "Empirical Causes of Dictatorship," in *Why Democracies Fail* (South Bend, IN: University of Notre Dame Press, 1957).

7. Kagan, *Pericles of Athens*, 3.

8. Arthur M. Schlesinger, Jr., *The Disuniting of America* (New York: W. W. Norton, 1992). Also Benjamin Barber, *Strong Democracy: Participatory Politics for a New Age* (Berkeley: University of California Press, 1984). For a trenchant analysis of the failings in American democratic ideals "[a]t a time when democratic ideals seem ascendant abroad," see Michael J. Sandel, *Democracy's Discontent: America in Search of a Public Philosophy* (Cambridge: Harvard University Press, Belknap Press, 1996), 3.

9. Robert D. Putnam, *Making Democracy Work: Civic Traditions in Modern Italy* (Princeton, NJ: Princeton University Press, 1993).

10. Robert D. Putnam, "Social Capital and the Prosperous Community," *Wingspread Journal* (autumn 1995): 4–5.

11. Ibid. According to James Coleman, the term "social capital" was first introduced in 1977 by G. Lowry. Coleman expanded extensively on the concept. James S. Coleman, *Foundations of Social Theory* (Cambridge: Harvard University Press, Belknap Press, 1990), 300 et seq.

12. Jon Elster, *The Cement of Society: A Study of Social Order* (Cambridge: Cambridge University Press, 1989), 1.

13. Ibid., 250–251.

14. Ibid., 264.

15. *The Washington Post*, September 27, 1995, p. A26. Also reported in the *New York Times*, p. A1, on the same day.

16. *The Washington Post*, December 6, 1995, p. A30. For an account of the background leading to the trial and conviction of the presidents and business leaders, see "Can S. Korea Do Business Without Bribes?" *The Washington Post*, October 6, 1996, p. H1 and December 17, 1996.

17. *New York Times*, January 25, 1997, p. A1; and *The Washington Post*, January 25, 1997, p. A1.

18. Robert N. Bellah, Richard Madsden, William M. Sullivan, Ann Swidler, and Steven M. Tipton, *Habits of the Heart, Individualism and Commitment in American Life* (New York: Harper and Row, Perennial Library, 1986, first published in 1985 by University of California Press), vii.

In our interviews, it became clear that for most of those with whom we spoke, the touchstones of truth and goodness lie in individual experience and intimate relationships. Both the social situations of middle class life and the vocabularies of everyday language predispose toward private sources of meaning. . . . Americans, it would seem, are genuinely ambivalent about public life, and this ambivalence makes it difficult to address the problems confronting us as a whole. (Ibid., 250)

19. Charles Murray, *What It Means to Be a Libertarian: A Personal Interpretation* (New York: Broadway Books, 1996).

20. Amitai Etzioni, *The New Golden Rule: Community and Morality in a Democratic Society* (New York: Basic Books, 1996), 257.

21. Benjamin Barber, *Strong Democracy: Participatory Politics for a New Age* (Berkeley: University of California Press, 1984), 261.

22. Sandel, *Democracy's Discontent*, 332–333. For a collection of essays on citizen activities see Don E. Eberly, ed., *Building a Community of Citizens: Civil Society in the 21st Century* (Lanham: University Press of America, 1994).

23. David Mathews, *Politics For the People Finding a Responsible Public Voice* (Urbana: University of Illinois Press, 1994).

24. Study Circles Resource Center, a Project of the Topsfield Foundation, P.O. Box 203, Rt. 169, Pomfret, CT 06258. A "database" of national projects engaged in civic and community activities is provided in *Wingspread Journal* 17, no. 3 (autumn 1995): 12, published by The Johnson Foundation, Inc. Racine, Wisconsin 53401–0547. For a historical description of study circles, their origin in the United States, their proliferation in Sweden, and their resurgence in the United States, see Leonard P. Oliver, *Study Circles: Coming Together for Personal Growth and Social Change* (Washington, DC: Seven Locks Press, 1987).

25. Lawrence K. Grossman, *The Electronic Republic* (New York: Penguin Books, 1996), 189.

26. Ibid., 4. Grossman does not ignore the potential problems of this electronically motivated citizenry. In Chapter 8, "The Perils and Promise of the Electronic Republic," he points to the concentration of media ownership and control, the distorting influence of money and other concerns, the professionalization of politics, the rise of interest politics, and the dumbing down of the quality of information (ibid., 165 et seq.).

2

The Origin of Social Values

Jennifer Trusted

I take the view that social values do vary; they depend on two factors: (1) basic and absolute moral principles common to all human beings, which transcend particular circumstances and appeals to consequences; and (2) various and differing moral values or conventions established by different societies. These are not common to all human beings; they are supported by the social values of a particular society.

For many people, the moral conventions and supporting social values of their own society are taken as fundamental moral principles. They are held as sacrosanct and are accepted as the basis for ultimate moral judgments. There is no doubt that moral conventions and social values are important but they cannot be regarded as sacrosanct. This is clear since social values and moral conventions of *other* societies are often criticized. Ultimately then, all such values and conventions, including our own, are subject to critical examination in the light of the basic principles. This chapter defends the thesis of absolute moral principles and shows how they establish criteria for assessing social values and the dependent moral conventions.

MORALITY MATTERS

First, all human beings (save for a few psychopaths) do have a moral sense; the words "right" and "wrong" are morally significant and important. We can and do make moral judgments and we know the meaning of moral responsibility. Moreover, it is no more possible to *explain* the meaning of morality to someone who has no moral sense than it is to explain the meaning of pain to someone who lacks pain nerves or the meaning of color to someone who is color-blind.

Even philosophical determinists (I do not take them to be psychopaths) regard themselves and others as being able to make moral choices in many situations. Here I do not discuss the philosophical (and in my opinion the metaphysical) problems of free will. Human beings can be morally evaluated as responsible agents who are, at least to some extent, free to choose how to act. This is not to say that our capacity to make moral judgments and, a fortiori, our ability to act morally can be exercised without help. Like other innate capacities, our understanding of morality and our making of moral judgments must be elicited through education.

Our moral capacity can be compared with our innate capacity to speak and our innate capacity to carry out simple arithmetical calculations.[1] These too must be elicited: we need to hear others talking in order to learn to talk ourselves, and we need some instruction in order to manipulate numbers. Likewise, we need to observe others making moral choices and to experience examples of moral behavior if our innate ability to make moral judgments is to be developed. If a child receives no moral education then he or she will not be morally aware; just as an isolated child fails to learn to speak. Unfortunately, it does not seem possible to compensate for time lost; it is likely that education must be early if a latent innate capacity is to develop. There is therefore a strong case for moral education in schools though there are obvious dangers here. We do not want young children to be programmed to conform with the current social mores. However, just because a policy has dangers it does not follow that it must or should be rejected.

Of course morally aware human beings do not necessarily *act* morally: they can and do make mistakes, they may have genuine doubts as to what to do, or they may decide to act entirely in their own self-interest (short term, sometimes long term). The last is the paradigm of immorality: when we know very well what we ought to do but do not do it. Allied to this, though clearly less damaging, is to act rightly but for the wrong reason.

Even though immoral behavior is all too common it does not follow that most people are unaware of moral principles. We may not accept Aristotle's thesis, "Every art and every investigation and similarly every action and pursuit, is aimed at some good. Hence the Good has been rightly defined as 'that at which all things aim,' "[2] for we may not agree that the truly wise will *necessarily* be virtuous. But most of us would acknowledge the desirability of virtue and, at least in theory, we would like to act virtuosly. As Kant wrote: "There is no one, not even the most hardened scoundrel—provided only he is accustomed to use reason in other ways—who, when presented with examples of honesty in purpose, of faithfulness to good maxims, of sympathy, and of kindness towards all . . . does not wish that he too might be a man of like spirit."[3]

BASIC MORAL PRINCIPLES

There have been many suggestions as to the nature of the Good but they have a common element: that morality must be a social matter and must relate to consideration of the interests of others. Kant's two maxims express this: "Act in such a way that you always treat humanity, whether in your own person or in the person of any other, never simply as a means, but always at the same time as an end,"[4] and "I ought never to act except in such a way that I can also will that my maxim should become a universal law."[5]

Thus moral behavior is incompatible with egoism (since egoism implies that self-interest is paramount). In addition, since moral principles entail a universal law, they are absolute. It should be noted that though moral principles rule out egoism, morality is not incompatible with self-respect; indeed one can maintain that an important reason for acting morally, and certainly the reason we would *like* to act morally, is to maintain our self-respect.

To take account of the interest of others just as we take account of our own interest is a general (and basic) principle of morality. But how do we justify our confident belief that morality is important and that self-respect entails acting morally? Why do we have the feeling that even though we do not always live up to our ideals, we ought to act morally?

THE INFLUENCE OF RELIGIOUS BELIEF?

One explanation of our innate moral sense depends on appeal to religious belief. In the West, until recently at least, morality was often related to some form of Christian belief but other religions also provide a basis for moral standards in other societies. Many people would go so far as to maintain that morality and religion are inextricably joined. That position is not supported here and many philosophers and theologians have explicitly rejected direct religious support for morality from any creed, but this is not to say that religion has had no influence on moral conventions and social values. Indeed it cannot be denied that all major religions are concerned with morality.

PRIMITIVE SOCIETIES: SHAME AND GUILT

Eric Dodds considers that in primitive societies the highest good was not possession of a quiet conscience but the enjoyment of public esteem.[6] So it was only wrong to do something that incurred public censure and a deed could not be immoral if it were not discovered. This is what Dodds calls a shame culture and shame is not necessarily indicative of what we would call moral awareness. But with the development of religion, that is, veneration of a God (or gods) interested in each individual, emerges the belief that any wrongdoing will be observed by the deity and that wrong behavior will bring divine punishment. Dodds says this stage represents a guilt culture.

But does even a sense of guilt, as opposed to shame, necessarily entail a moral sense? One might say that fear of being found out by God (or by one's fellows) makes morality a matter of prudence. The only difference is that divine retribution (in this world or the next) will be more certain.

> In the corrupted curents of this world
> Offence's gilded hand may shove by justice,
> And 'tis often seen the wicked prize itself
> Buys out the law: but 'tis not so above;
> There is no *shuffling*, there the action lies
> In his true nature, and we ourselves compell'd
> Even to the teeth and forehead of our faults
> To give in evidence.[7]

But even if we concede that acting morally may be motivated by prudence as much as by self-respect, and this is an interesting topic, it is irrelevant to a discussion of what moral principles are.

THE RELATIVIST VIEW

There is no originality in pointing out that the religious criteria and religious justification of absolute moral standards have been questioned at least for several hundred years. Hume argued that there were no absolute standards and that insofar as moral judgments were more than subjective statements they must refer to what the *community* (and this would include its accepted religious beliefs) thought was disgraceful or commendable (illegal or legal). That view has been developed to promote the thesis that all our moral intuitions of absolute right and wrong are chimeras and that moral judgments can only be made relative to particular societies and particular religious beliefs. It is argued that what we take to be an intuitive moral sense is merely the result of social conditioning, that is, our moral principles are those of our society.

REBUTTAL OF THE RELATIVIST VIEW

Yet that view is clearly wrong, for undoubtedly it makes sense to say, This is legal or Society holds this to be commendable or This is what the Holy Writing decrees, but I (or we) think it is immoral. Remember the song about the son of the cannibal chief who maintained, "Eating people is wrong." We find the song amusing because we agree with the son but it is illogical to condemn one moral convention just by appeal to another convention. Thus though current moral conventions clearly reflect current social values the only firm grounds for accepting or rejecting them must be by appeal to an absolute morality, that is, by appeal to some transcendent universal moral principle or principles.

ABSOLUTE PRINCIPLES

I suggest that there are two absolute moral principles, absolute at all times and in all places: keeping trust and benevolence. I think that they are absolute because they are part of our genetic inheritance. Of course the view that there is an absolute morality, based on fundamental principles, is not *incompatible* with the belief that our moral capacity is a divine gift. Perhaps some present-day aversion to the acceptance of the existence of objective and absolute moral principles stems from fear of religious superstition. But although absolutism is not incompatible with certain religious beliefs, there is no reason to suppose that human moral sense is necessarily a gift bestowed by God. I propose a purely secular account of the rise of morality in terms of natural selection.

EMERGENCE OF MORALITY THROUGH NATURAL SELECTION

Like many animals we live in social groups, and cooperative behavior among members of the group must increase the chances of the group's (and therefore the species') survival. Since cooperation requires that the interest of others be considered there is also, at least in human societies, the presupposition that other people are autonomous and worthy of respect. This entails treating all people, including one's own person, as ends in themselves rather than as mere means to some extraneous desire: "Now I say that man, and in general every rational being, *exists as an end in himself, not merely as a means for arbitrary* use by this or that will: all his actions, whether they are directed to himself or to other rational beings, must always be viewed *at the same time as an end.*"[8]

However, the argument for altruism (i.e., cooperation rather than egoism) developing by natural selection meets the objection that natural selection is not a selection of species but a selection of genes carried by individuals. It would seem that if one member of a species has genes tending to make him or her behave altruistically (sacrificing his or her own interests to those of others) that individual is less likely to survive.

This objection can be countered because natural selection is ultimately based on the genes themselves. Therefore, provided the individual survives long enough to reproduce (children and the young are notoriously egotistical) the gene (or genes) he or she carries can be transmitted to the next generation. Since a gene carrying a trait for altruism promotes cooperation it will tend to promote survival of the species. Thus such genes will give an evolutionary advantage and will therefore spread through the species.[9] Robert Paul Churchill, one of the editors, has pointed out that any individual's altruism is especially likely to enhance the reproductive chances of his or her siblings and this will help to ensure that the gene goes to the next generation even if the individual herself does not reproduce. It is worth stressing that this evolved morality is certainly *not* a matter of prudence as far as the individual is concerned, though, in a metaphorical sense, it could be regarded as species prudence.

Thus moral awareness and moral behavior is not to be taken as external to human nature, rather, they have both evolved as *part of* human nature so as to promote the survival and flourishing of our species. I suggest we are guided by the two absolute moral principles, keeping trust and benevolence. Keeping trust is a necessary requirement for the very existence of any human society—there is honor even among thieves—for no group can cohere unless its members can rely on each other. Therefore each member of the society should honor his or her social obligations. Primarily benevolence is love and affection for one's own kind and entails a *wish* for the well-being of other human beings.[10] It can be regarded as supplementing a *duty* to keep faith and treat others as ends in themselves, with a *desire* to keep faith. Benevolence entails a positive impulse to do more than bare duty requires.

Keeping Trust and Benevolence

The absolute moral principle of keeping trust and respecting others is the fulfilling of obligations (explicit and implicit). It is doing one's duty and carries with it the principle of justice (fair-dealing). Particular duties and obligations are accepted as a matter of course in a given society and arise from its established customs. As indicated above, there is always an accepted code of justice and fair dealing in any human society.

Each member is expected to behave in certain ways in certain situations, and this may be a result of formal laws and contracts or of less formal conventions. But the *moral* force of such obligations rests on the absolute moral principle of keeping trust.

I must stress that we do not first become aware of the basic principles and then embody them in a particular moral code, rather we learn the content of morality from the behavior we observe. It follows that what we first recognize as Good (a result of the development of our innate moral capacity) is profoundly influenced by our social (often including religious) values. We may think these values are absolute; it is the sophisticated who come to appreciate that the moral conventions of their own society are not *basic* and absolute moral principles.

Have I been too naive in asserting that benevolence (wishing well to one's own kind) is a fundamental and absolute moral principle? I think not. Admittedly, we have all too numerous cases of both principles being ignored or flouted but it does not follow that they are not acknowledged and that there is no moral uneasiness when conduct is not in accord with the principles.

In fact there can be no clear distinction between obligation and benevolence. For example, to say we ought to help those in distress may be justified by appeal to duty rather than to kindness; for are there not occasions when we have a duty to be benevolent? We must also recognize that, though there can be sensible debate as to whether we ever have a moral obligation to be benevolent, as well as sensible debate on obligations in particular circumstances, there is no doubt that we have a general duty *not* to be malevolent. Thus it can be argued that there is only one fundamental and ultimate principle—keeping trust—and that benevolence should be regarded as the negative of malevolence and be treated as part of duty. However there are so many examples of actions that merit praise because they transcend what is normally taken as duty and certainly transcend what is legally required, that it is probably more helpful to consider benevolence as a separate moral principle. To be benevolent is to show an active concern for the interest of others, more than is required or even expected by our fellows. We can show benevolence to people to whom we have no special obligations and to creatures who do not have rights.

MORAL CONVENTIONS AND SOCIAL VALUES

In any stable society people rely on their routine expectations being fulfilled; mutual moral duty arises as a result of this reliance. But since what constitutes keeping trust is closely related to the customs and conventions of each society, and since these can be very different, the kind of behavior that is expected and is morally required will be different in different societies. I call the moral values of a given society its social values. "Social values" is a less misleading term than "moral values" since the latter implies that they transcend social custom (which they do not) and that they are sacrosanct (which they are not).

Observation of alien societies and records of laws and customs in the same society at different times plainly show that social values are diverse and even that they can conflict. In addition we know from direct experience that current social values in our own society are and have been questioned and indeed changed. Those changes can and do lead to formal changes through the law. (Later I take as a case study changes in our attitude to the family.) We may personally be in doubt as to the validity of some of the social values we were brought up to accept. Nevertheless one reason why social values and their supporting moral conventions are commonly thought to be more fundamental than they really are, and hence why certain values are erroneously thought to be absolute, is that moral teaching in childhood has a very great influence on us all.

Of course, some duties seem almost universal: in most human societies it is taken for granted that parents shall protect their infant children and cater for their needs but the *kind* of care expected depends on the moral conventions. In certain Polynesian societies many parental services are undertaken by aunts and uncles. In ancient Greece weak or deformed infants (and sometimes healthy female infants) were left to die on hillsides; (it is interesting that the ancient Greeks were reluctant to kill the babies directly) hence the survival of Oedipus and Paris. Children were also sacrificed by parents for the benefit of society (Iphegenia) and we should remember that Abraham was prepared to sacrifice Isaac on God's command.

In primitive societies there were special obligations to any person sheltering an enemy (even if by chance) under one's roof. Wagner expresses this in his libretto of *Die Walkuri* when Hunding discovers the identity of Siegmund:

> My house will shelter you
> you, Wolf-cub, for today.
> For this night I put you up.
> But with stout weapons
> arm yourself tomorrow
> choose the day for fighting,
> You must pay for those deaths.[11]

Much more was the obligation to kinsmen and to one's king or liege lord. Macbeth was fully aware of his duty to Duncan:

> He's here in double trust
> First as I am his kinsman and his subject
> Strong both against the deed; then as his host
> Who should against his murderer shut the door
> Not bear the knife myself.[12]

In our own society we have general obligations based on conventions and we may also incur special obligations through legal contracts or, more informally, through promising. There used to be obligations relating to marriage but, as we shall see in the case study, conventions here have changed.

Subcultures

There are also subcultures within societies whose members have special moral conventions and who respect codes of behavior that are different from the codes of the parent culture, for example vegetarians, Jehovah's Witnesses, Mormons, and the Greens. The case of the Greens illustrates how the moral conventions of a subculture can come to dominate, that is, its values become generally accepted and may become formalized as new laws are enacted or old ones repealed.

Examples of different, even what we might regard as bizarre, moral codes of a culture or a subculture are noncounter examples to the universal acceptance of the principle of keeping trust and consideration of the interest of others. They are examples of the different ways in which the basic principles are interpreted and implemented. Changing circumstances such as those brought about by technology, increased psychological knowledge of human nature, changing opinions of what is fair shares and proper reward will alter our interpretations and will alter our codes of behavior by altering our moral conventions and social values. Nonmoral factors are relevant because they influence our notions of what is possible and, indeed, what is probable. For example, the development of powerful telephoto camera lenses and of bugging equipment have changed values connected with personal privacy.

Thus the view that there is a basic moral principle of trust which justifies and indeed requires consideration of the interests of others does not entail that any particular moral convention and code of conduct must be absolutely and permanently morally right or wrong. Rather it entails that we look at our moral conventions critically because, first, they determine what we value and how we think we ought to behave (our social values). We need to be vigilant and when a code is questioned it is necessary to make a careful assessment. We cannot assume that the old ways must be best any more than we can assume that the new ways must be better. Changes in social values may emerge imperceptibly or they may arise through active campaigning.

But an appreciation of the dependent nature of all social values will encourage critical examination of the moral conventions explicitly or implicitly supporting any change occurring or proposed. This is particularly important in relation to changes which become formally embodied in new laws. If we bear in mind that moral conventions are not sacrosanct we shall be in a better position to assess their merits (and demerits) and to give clear and cogent criticism. I want to suggest, finally, that assessment criteria should depend on the basic principles and not on appeal to various kinds of consequentialist standards.

CONSEQUENTIALISM

Consequentialists hold that moral judgments are statements that can be judged true or false by appeal to observed or potentially observable or putative consequences. By far the most well-known consequentialist theory is utilitarianism, promoted by Jeremy Benthan and John Stuart Mill nearly two hundred years ago. The basic premise is that it is *self-evident* that everyone desires happiness and that everyone wishes to avoid unhappiness. Thus actions that increase the general happiness (or decrease unhappiness) are morally good and actions that decrease happiness (or increase unhappiness)) are morally bad. A modern form of utilitarianism formulated to avoid difficulties associated with defining happiness is based on appeal to human flourishing or to human preferences. Egalitarianism is another less popular consequentialist theory based on appeal to justice (fair shares) rather than happiness, or preference or flourishing.

The Legal Aspect

First it must be acknowledged that in seeking change (and hopefully improvement) in social values, consideration of consequences can be helpful; thus utilitarianism (or a modern form) is presupposed in much economic and political planning. But appeal to any form of consequentialism, though it may be convenient, can also be dangerous.

One very great practical danger is the likelihood that consequences are often unknown so that predictions of good effects can be dramatically misleading or wrong. Hence actions (and new laws) that are truly believed to promote human well-being turn out to have no effect or to do more harm than good. For example, in the United Kingdom laws restricting rents and giving security to tenants have resulted in a dearth of decent accommodation for letting because landlords were not prepared to carry the burden of property at low rents. Likewise a social policy of building high-rise flats in place of slums failed because the elevators were vandalized and ceased to operate, there was no safe place for children to play, and stairs, entrance halls, and external corridors became sordid and dangerous. Even the new low-rise housing, also built to replace slums, with regulations to reduce the risks of vandalism and crime, did not bring the happiness envisioned. George Orwell's language is too emotive and probably exaggerates the dreariness but there was no doubt that the social planning was a failure:

> They are built "in a ruthlessly inhuman manner" and are "soulless," with, for example, "dismal sham-Tudor pubs." The estates are replete with petty restrictions on such things as the decoration of houses and the keeping of pets, restrictions which witness the fact that "owing to the peculiar temper of our time," in order to secure slum-dwellers decent housing "it is also considered necessary to rob them of the last vestiges of their liberty."[13]

But a more serious reason for hesitancy in appealing solely to utilitarian consequences is that it can lead to promoting or at least to condoning laws and policies that we intuitively find unacceptable. Why are they unacceptable? Because they are not compatible with the basic principles: keeping trust and benevolence. Consequentialist laws and policies can lead to disregard for individual preferences, such as the compulsory purchase of houses to build new roads and occasionally to carnage such as the bombings of Hiroshima[14] or the wholesale shooting (by the police) of children in Mexico City. Stuart Hampshire writes:

> When the generally respected barriers of impermissible conduct are once crossed, and when no different unconditional barriers within the same areas of conduct are put in their place, then the special, apparently superstitious, value attached to the preservation of human life will be questioned . . . it is not clear that the taking of lives can be marked and evaluated on a common scale on

which increases of pleasure and diminutions of suffering are also measured. This is the suggested discontinuity which a utilitarian must deny.[15]

As Hampshire implies, there are various dispositions—spontaneous affections, justice, loyalty, particular concern for one's own children—which can be hard to justify if we take a strict utilitarian view.

One way in which utilitarians have coped with this is by asserting that in the long run such dispositions will produce states of affairs which do promote general happiness (human flourishing). Moral intuitions should be regarded as *devices* for generating certain actions, not as being intrinsically meritorious. As Williams says, this is how it may be seen looking at it from the outside, a sort of moral high ground, but it is not necessarily the way agents themselves view their own dispositions.[16] From the inside the dispositions seem good per se, and they are *not* regarded just as instruments to realize the greater good. They are *not* seen merely as dispositions for action but dispositions of belief and judgment.

Moreover utilitarians *need* the agents to view their dispositions in this way and not to look on them as mere instruments for action. This leads to a position where the utilitarian elite uphold a moral theory which they keep from the masses, who must act directly in accord with their spontaneous dispositions. The utilitarian instrumental justification must be kept secret from all but the chosen few. There should also be secrecy when an action which would appear unjust (not in accord with our spontaneous dispositions) must (on utilitarian grounds) be carried out for the general good. Sidgwick said:

> The Utilitarian conclusion, carefully stated, would seem to be this; that the opinion that secrecy may render an action right which would not otherwise be so should itself be kept comparatively secret; and similarly it seems expedient that the doctrine that esoteric morality is expedient should itself be kept esoteric. Or, if this concealment be difficult to maintain, it may be desirable that Common Sense should repudiate the doctrines which it is expedient to confine to an enlightened few. And thus a Utilitarian may reasonably desire, on Utilitarian principles, that some of his conclusions should be rejected by mankind generally; or even that the vulgar should keep aloof from his system as a whole, in so far as the inevitable indefiniteness and complexity of its calculations render it likely to lead to bad results in theirs hands.[17]

On this kind of account utilitarianism indeed emerges as the morality of an elite. Williams argues that theoretical utilitarian-type reasonings are themselves only sustained by some sense of the moral shape of the world as provided by everyday dispositions. He is arguing for a reconsideration of moral intuitions. There are dangers in relying on intuition: a confusion of social values with moral principles, but it is still true that the criticism of a utilitarian or preference ethics is cogent and it is as cogent for lawmakers and politicians as for private individuals.

Another criticism which also rests on accusation of a kind of elitism, namely a tendency for preference ethics to embody a form of paternalism is offered by Hausman.

This is also related to personal and social-policy problems. Hausman suggests that we identify any person's well-being (flourishing, happiness) with the extent to which his or her preferences are satisfied.[18] Then it will be morally right to act so as to maximize preferences. He makes the acceptable qualification that these must be rational and informed preferences but they must be *the individual's* preferences if a morally unacceptable paternalism is to be avoided. Finding out what these preferences are involves great practical difficulties and these are increased when we allow that people's preferences change and their ranking of their preferences also changes.

But even if we set all practical difficulties aside there is another difficulty which, Hausman argues, makes satisfaction of preferences *morally* unacceptable. It is morally unacceptable because different people have different expectations and it will be easier to satisfy people with low expectations. Hausman quotes Peter Hammod: "Consider some undemanding person who achieves his upper limit at a low level of consumption. Do we normalize that person's utility scale so that it has the same upper and lower bounds as that of a greedy person? If so, and if we distribute good to each individual so that each achieves, say, 90% of maximum utility . . . then the greedy person is likely to be given much more than one feels he deserves."[19] Hausman points out that this consequence has been directly appealed to by Rawls: "[G]reat social utility results from educating people to have simple desires and to be easily satisfied . . . such persons . . . are pleased with less and so presumably can be brought closer to their highest utility,"[20] and he adds: "If utility is just an index of the extent to which individuals' preferences are satisfied and their preferences are perfectly satisfied, then the individuals must be equally well off."[21] But this cannot be fair, or morally right and Hausman concludes that "welfare or well-being is not the satisfaction of preferences."[22]

The Brave New World

A preference satisfaction criterion of human well-being in fact *invites* a programming (an education) which will morally justify producing people who are easily satisfied. Huxley's *Brave New World* is a satirical attack on utilitarianism. In the *Brave New World* human zygotes are matured in bottles suitably treated to produce people of different calibre—alphas, betas, gammas, deltas, and epsilons—who are further conditioned to fulfill a social function and to enjoy the work to which they will be assigned. In the first passage the director of the embryo plant is showing students (all alphas) one production process:

> Hot tunnels alternated with cool tunnels. Coolness was wedded to discomfort in the form of hard x-rays. By the time they were decanted the embryos had a horror of cold. They were predestined to emigrate to the tropics, to be miners and acetate silk spinners and steel workers. Later their minds would be made to endorse the judgment of their bodies. "We condition them to thrive on heat. . . . Our colleagues upstairs will teach them to love it."
>
> "And that," put in the Director sententiously, "that is the secret of happiness and virtue—liking what you've *got* to do. All conditioning aims at that: making people like their inescapable destiny."[23]

There is no doubt that here people are being treated as ends to promote social order and the important thing to note is that this is justified by consequentialist ethics—as it was in Stalin's Russia and Mao's China.

In the second passage two alphas note the puff of smoke which indicates a cremation and discuss the life of the unknown individual who has died:

> "'I suppose Epsilons don't really mind being Epsilons,'" she said aloud.
> "Of course they don't. How can they? They don't know what it's like being anything else. We'd mind of course. But then we've been differently conditioned. Besides we start with a different heredity." He sighed. Then in a resolutely cheerful voice, "Anyhow . . . there's one thing we can be certain of whoever he may have been, he was happy when he was alive. Everybody's happy now."
> "Yes, everybody's happy now," echoed Lenina. They had heard the words repeated a hundred and fifty times every night for twelve years.[24]

A direct attack on utilitarian and preference ethics is made by Professor Anthony O'Hear, who argues that suffering and weakness are an intrinsic part of human life so that manipulative programming undermines respect for our fellows:

> I am claiming that suffering and weakness are central and essential aspects of human life, and that most of what we find admirable in human life involves in some part an acceptance of suffering and the conquest of evil. (I am not of course saying that we should not strive to eliminate suffering as far as we can; but rather that we should, at the same time, strive to come to terms with its inevitability) . . . whatever else it would be, a totally rational and pleasant life, without suffering and wickedness, would not be a human life.[25]

It is only by appeal to the basic and absolute principles that we can find sure *moral* guidance. Following a consequentialist ethic leads to corruption of basic moral values and following from that a degeneration of social values.

CASE STUDY—THE FAMILY AND CHANGES IN SOCIAL VALUES

There are three aspects to this case study[26]: (1) What changes have there been in social values? (2) How are we to assess those changes in relation to the basic moral principles? and (3) Can we relate changes in values to changes in the moral and social climate and pass some judgment on them?

It will be enough to consider changes in the Western World during this century. Though the discussion could be enlarged to include changing values in much earlier times. The following changes reflect general social attitudes of the present day. Many are subject to criticism but they can all be considered as serious, albeit sometimes debateable values. At the start of the twentieth century many of these values would have been rejected out of hand.

First, there are entirely new attitudes to the position of women in society, to their education and participation in professional work, to their political rights (enfranchisement) and their participation in government at all levels, to their sexual freedom and the abandonment of a double standard of sexual morality. Thus women do not have to regard marriage as the only desirable way of life and women are accorded the same sexual freedom as men. (It does not follow that sexual license is condoned but rather that any moral restraints apply to both men and women.) Second, and perhaps as a consequence of changes in the position of women, contraception has become morally acceptable.[27] Third, divorce is no longer a disgrace. Fourth, the state is seen as having a much deeper duty to provide for those in need. Fifth, one-parent families are accepted, perhaps not as a norm, but no longer as a tragedy (widowhood) or as a consequence of evil living. Many women are choosing not to marry because they see men as irresponsible fathers; as (often very young) mothers they look to the state to provide what, in former times would be expected from a husband.

Sixth, it has come to be accepted that professional experts: teachers, doctors, and nurses may give better advice on rearing children than can parents. Paternalism by the parents is replaced by paternalism by state-funded experts. Seventh, children are seen to have rights, and tyranny in the family (and within the school) is regarded as being as reprehensible as political tyranny.

These are relatively new social values and they support new moral conventions, but in order to criticize them constructively they need to be assessed in relation to the basic principles.

Assessment in Relation to Basic Principles

I suggest that in relation to the position of women, there can be little doubt that the changes occurring can be fully justified by appeal to the principle of keeping trust and not treating others as mere means. There can be no moral justification for treating women as means to enhance the lives of men. But it does not follow that now both sexes (as opposed to just men) have no moral responsibilities vis-à-vis reproduction.

In relation to the second point I shall be contentious and state unambiguously that I do not think that any moral principle is involved. I suggest that earlier and indeed current moral censure of contraception is based on the view that it deprived potential people of life. I maintain that claims for the moral right of hypothetical or potential people to exist are invalid.

There may be some abrogation of trust in the third point, divorce no longer a disgrace, because the repudiation of an agreed commitment, whether on account of adultery or some other factor, can be seen as a breach of trust. It is clear that there are moral problems when only one spouse wishes to end the marriage. The position is further complicated by children.

In relation to the duties of the state, many political philosophers have argued that there is a social contract with the state which must therefore care for and protect its citizens. This is a moral convention, not a basic principle, but if it is accepted, then the state must keep trust. Do we need to modify this convention? In democracies the state is the citizenry, but is our current view of its duties (our duties) inappropriate?

This brings us to the problem of one-parent families. Though present moral conventions mean that one cannot now assert that women and men should be morally required to marry in order to procreate we must still see the rearing of children as an important social value and hold that parents (father as well as mother) should play a part in this. Such a view need not exclude the help of professional care givers because the absolute principle of keeping trust (from which care of children derives) does not and has not required that parents alone are concerned. The rights of children are dependent on the principle of keeping trust but I would say that they are also supported by the principle of benevolence since young children themselves do not have duties.

Judgments

It should be clear that when we come to practical issues judgment is not easy. The merit of bearing basic principles in mind is that we are less likely to give a knee-jerk judgment based on our current moral conventions and social values. There is need for critical assessment of those conventions and values not only in relation to moral absolutes but also in relation to external facts and past history.

What was the family situation like in 1900? Was the two-parent family the norm? Did couples then stay together till death? Was there less abandonment of children? How much child abuse was there? How much wife abuse? To what extent is family life important to us? Do most human beings need family ties? Are such bonds not just fetters but also lifelines? What has been the influence of the fact that many people move to live in several different communities during their lives? Could this be an important factor in what is seen as social malaise in the loosening of family ties? Is there in fact a social malaise worse than ninety years ago? Do we look at the past through rose-tinted glasses? Were people then any better morally than we are today?

Practical moral questions are not easy to answer, but the first step in dealing with them is to appreciate this and to become critically aware of the moral conventions and social values to which we commonly appeal. We must learn to assess their worth anew in the light of the absolute and basic moral principles.

NOTES

1. I discuss this more fully in *Moral Principles and Social Values* (London: Routledge and Kegan Paul, 1987), 7–9.

2. Aristotle, *Ethics*, trans. J. A. K. Thomson, revised Hugh Tredennick (Harmondsworth: Penguin, 1976), 63.

3. Immanuel Kant, *The Moral Law*, trans. H. J. Paton (London: Hutchinson, 1976), 114–115.

4. Ibid., 67.

5. Ibid., 91.

6. Eric Dodds, *The Greeks and the Irrational* (Cambridge: Cambridge University Press, 1951), passim.

7. William Shakespeare, *Hamlet*, Act III, Sc.iii.

8. Kant, *Moral Law*, 90; Kant's emphasis.

9. Peter Singer, *The Expanding Circle* (New York: Oxford University Press, 1983), 9 et seq.

10. Benevolence can also extend to care and concern for other species; it has been argued that our concern for animal welfare is better justified by appeal to benevolence than by appeal to animal rights.

11. Richard Wagner, *Die Walkurie*, Act I, Sc. ii, libretto trans. William Mann (EMI Records, 1972).

12. William Shakespeare, *Macbeth*, Act I, Sc. vii.

13. George Orwell, quoted by D. Thomas in *Naturalism and Social Science* (New York: Oxford University Press, 1979), 34.

14. When the bomb was exploded the long-term effects of nuclear fallout were not known, so here we have an example of fallible prediction as well as a disregard of basic moral principles.

15. Stuart Hampshire, *Ethics* (Oxford: Blackwell, 1957), 194.

16. Bernard Williams, "The Point of View of the Universe: Sidgwick and the Ambitions of Ethics" in *Making Sense of Humanity* (Cambridge: Cambridge University Press, 1995), 164.

17. Ibid., 166.

18. Daniel Hausman, "The Impossibility of Interpersonal Utility Comparisons," *Mind* 415 (July 1995): 473–489.

19. Ibid., 483.

20. Ibid., 484.

21. Ibid., 485.

22. Ibid., 486.

23. Aldous Huxley, *Brave New World*, Chapter 1.

24. Ibid., Chapter 5.

25. Anthony O'Hear, *Experience, Explanation and Faith* (London: Routledge and Kegan Paul, 1984), 82.

26. For much of the material in this case study I am indebted to Mary Midgley and Judith Hughes and their paper, "Trouble with Families," in *Applied Ethics*, ed. Brenda Almond (Oxford: Blackwell, 1995), 17–32.

27. There are other factors which have led to tolerance and even approval of contraception, for example new techniques, population problems, and a decline in a religious ethic which regards sex as only morally permissible if it is associated with procreation.

3

The Wellsprings of Social Values

James L. Peacock

This chapter addresses two questions: Do social values change as a result of changes in economic, social, and environmental conditions? and Can adopted policies induce changes in social values? Obviously, the answer to the first question affects the answer to the second. To the degree that values are fixed genetically by biological inheritance, as opposed to environmentally determined, the impact of policy on values is limited unless that policy includes gene therapy. The Human Genome project and others address this issue, and physical or biological anthropology is involved here. As a social or cultural anthropologist, my focus is on social and cultural rather than biological wellsprings of values.

What are values? Values are defined by Kluckhohn and Strodtbeck (1961) as conceptions of the desirable, that is, values are ideas but also ideals; they conceive of "oughts" and "ought-nots," good and bad; they define morality and they entail conscience (as well as external sanctions such as hellfire and damnation, or other supernatural rewards and punishments if they are associated with religion).

Talcott Parsons (1951) distinguished values from norms: values define broad, general conceptions of the desirable; norms are more specific. Values are exemplified by conceptions of the good Christian, the good Buddhist, the good American, the good person. Norms are the rules and laws that specify what you should and should not do to fulfill these values. When Robert E. Lee was president of Washington College, now Washington and Lee, a student asked him, "What are the rules of the college?" Lee replied, "There is but one rule: Be a gentleman." He was asked about norms; he responded with a value. Of course, Lee would need a broader answer today, since Washington and Lee enrolls both men and women and values have perhaps changed.

What are the wellsprings of values? The human condition is one. Are there values that are intrinsic to being human, values that are found among all humans everywhere? One such value appears to be having values themselves. All human societies appear to have values, to have conceptions of right and wrong, good and bad, against which they measure behavior. While individuals whom we call psychopaths or sufferers from character disorders may seem to lack values, these people are considered exceptions and problematical. And while particular societies, like Colin Turnbull's Ik, may seem to be rather amoral, the evidence supports the generalization that values are a human characteristic.

Are particular values panhuman? Anthropologists have suggested, for example, that the taboo against murder and the taboo against incest are essentially universal values, although various societies permit exceptions under special circumstances. If having values and particular values are panhuman features, this might suggest some biological basis—something common to the species *Homo sapiens*. But one could also argue that values generally and certain particular values are simply functionally necessary for societies in their human mode to survive—that without a value against murder, life would be nasty, brutish, and short. Doubtless, both arguments are true, but rather than pursue them, I turn to the values that most specifically affect policy, namely the values that vary among societies, cultures, or subcultures.

Anthropologists were among the first to emphasize such variation, under the slogan Cultural Relativism. Needless to say, one cannot be totally relativistic in analyzing values; if nothing else, one's own values enter analysis of others. In any case, we must not be paralyzed by the various biases that inevitably enter our analysis. Let us try to step back and view values globally, noting variation and associated conditions.

WHAT ARE THE WELLSPRINGS OR CONDITIONS OF VARIATION IN VALUES?

Anthropologists and other social scientists have followed essentially two lines of analysis. The first derives from such thinkers as Durkheim, Marx, and Freud, and might be termed causal-functional. The argument is that values derive from functional needs and processes of society. These include economic, ecological, political, and psychological functions and needs. Society needs to feed itself, defend itself, adapt to the environment, and handle tensions, fears, and so forth. The processes by which it accomplishes these tasks mold its values, and values are in the service of processes.

The second line of analysis derives from thinkers such as Max Weber, and might be termed logico-meaningful. The argument is that values cannot be reduced to social, political, and economic processes, but instead are part of the human quest for meaning. Human beings seek conceptual frameworks—systems of ideas, symbols, and beliefs—to order and to make sense out of existence. Such frameworks or systems are important in themselves, aside from their social, economic, political, or even psychological roots and functions. These frameworks of meaning (Weber termed them *Sinnzusammenver-hang*) mold values, which in turn mold social processes.

The classical work that exemplifies the first position is Emile Durkheim's *The Elementary Forms of Religious Life* (1912). Durkheim argues that society is the model and source of belief and thought. Thus, social classes give rise to conceptual classes—classification—which among other things define values.

The classical work to exemplify the second position is Max Weber's *The Protestant Ethic and the Spirit of Capitalism* (1985). Weber argues that Calvinist theology was the source of a certain set of values, the Protestant ethic, and that these values in turn inspired the spirit of capitalism, which brought about various social and economic changes.

Now, these two classics go back to the early years of this century. Yet the works and the issues they raise remain central. In the September 22, 1995, issue of the *Times Literary Supplement*, for example, Richard Sennet discusses Weber's Protestant ethic argument in relation to contemporary society. Weber remains alive in a spectrum of thinkers ranging from Foucault to Gingrich.

Anthropologists and others have advanced the Weberian arguments—not so much in fundamental conception, as in application to hundreds of complex situations throughout the world. This chapter concentrates on the Weberian argument but reflects on it in light of world events and scholarly developments since Weber wrote. To summarize the essence of the Weberian argument—the so-called Weber Thesis— remember that this argument, stated in Weber's *Gesammelte Aufzatze zur Religionssoziologie* contains not only the chapters translated as "The Protestant Ethic and the Spirit of Capitalism" but also the chapters comparing Asian religions, translated as "The Religion of China" and "The Religion of India," and the chapters translated as yet another book, "Ancient Judaism."

The larger argument has a positive and a negative aspect. It treats Protestant theology, grounded in the prophetic tradition of Judaism, as a crucial positive source of those values known as the Protestant ethic, a work ethic grounded in Calvinism, as explained below. This Protestant ethic is a positive factor engendering the complex of values known as the spirit of capitalism, which in turn inspires, at a certain point in history, attitudes and behaviors and institutions conducive to capitalism as well as to other rationalizing trends. By comparison, Asian religions such as Hinduism and Confucianism are treated as negative factors in the genesis of capitalism and associated values, though positive in sustaining values of social order.

In more detail, the argument can be summarized as follows. Early Calvinism taught that everyone was either damned to eternal suffering or saved eternally, and no one could know whether one was damned or saved. Seeking evidence or signs that one was saved, Calvinists came to emphasize incessant work as evidence. This work ethic, theologically based, is the essence of the Protestant ethic. Even though Calvinists often condemned wealth itself, the values and attitudes engendered by Calvinism, manifested in the Protestant ethic, encouraged capitalism. The spirit of capitalism, bolstered by the Protestant ethic, gained expression not only in individual behavior but also in institutions—the bureaucracies, market systems, and legal systems of capitalistic society. Weber termed these the Iron Cage, which persist today independent of the religious impulse that was their wellspring.

In contrast to the transcendentalism of Protestantism, China and India were traditionally centered on the social order—in China the clan or family, in India the caste. The prevailing religions sustained this social order. In China, Confucianism was at the core. Confucianism is an extremely rational religion oriented toward buttressing traditional society. The Confucian gentleman, the mandarin, finds his calling in propriety—in properly carrying out his ritual duties, in respecting the classics, in obeying the rules of his office, and thus in sustaining the given social order.

In India, Hinduism plays a similar role in a different way. The key Hindu concepts are *dharma* and *karma. Dharma* is the law of one's caste. One law is to avoid mixing of castes, thus one should not marry into another caste. *Karma* is the law of the cosmos. Bad action in this life brings rebirth into a lower station in the next life, perhaps even rebirth into a lower form, such as an insect. Violating dharma brings bad karma. To marry up in this life threatens that one will move down in the next, for example. This illustrates, Weber argued, how Hinduism discouraged values of social mobility and social reform and thus sustained the given social order.

Both Confucianism and Hinduism offered escape from the social order. This was through mystical, other-worldly paths such as Yoga, Taoism, and Buddhism. These did not threaten or change the social order, but simply offered otherworldly alternatives to it. Thus, through meditation one could obtain Nirvana.

Calvinism and the Protestant ethic, by comparison, combined an otherworldly vision—the Kingdom of God—with a worldly and inferior reality—the Kingdom of Man. Calvinism called for this world, the Kingdom of Man, to be changed and reformed in the image of the other world, the Kingdom of God. The Protestant ethic brought forward the prophetic spirit of ancient Judaism and instilled a discontent with the given order and an incessant drive to change and reform it. Thus the source of modern values, Calvinism, institutionalizes anti-institutionalization, making change the one constant.

This is Weber's argument, distilled into bare bones, almost stereotypes. What can it teach us about the wellspring of values? It is still the most sustained and comprehensive treatment of this topic. Weber even considers, economist that he was, most of the political, geographic, social, economic, and material factors that come into the first type of argument noted above, the processual. But, in conclusion, his abiding conviction is that the logico-meaningful patterns, grounded in religion, whether Protestant ethic or Asian or other, were the wellsprings of values that endure and are pervasive in guiding, inspiring, and limiting the development of societies.

What can we add to the Weberian argument, now that three-quarters of a century has passed since he died in 1920? Much has happened in the world of affairs and much has happened in the world of scholarship. In affairs: the Second World War, the end of colonialism in the third world, new nations, the rise of Asia as an economic force, and globalism. In scholarship: fieldwork, so that anthropologists and others enjoy sustained, first-hand immersion in the societies, Asian and other, that Weber knew only second-hand through libraries. Also, Weber's own work has inspired a whole industry of critique and application.

What have we learned? East Asia—Japan, China, Korea, Singapore—has exploded capitalistically, seemingly shattering Weber's description of Asia as socially conservative. Yet many would argue that despite these economic changes, the cultural values endure, grounded in deep frames. In Gananath Obeysekere's phrase, summing up Yoko Tsui's analysis, Japan is a "conserving" culture (American Anthropological Association, 1993). Others would note that the East Asian capitalistic developments differ from Western early capitalism in being centralized, topdown. These nations offer experiments in wellsprings of values other than the Protestant ethic—for example, government policy deliberately geared toward value change, whether China's cultural revolution or Singapore's city-state autocracy not unlike Calvin's Geneva. Yet, as Bellah noted long ago, East Asian development was spurred by an analogue to the Protestant ethic expressed collectively more than individualistically, as in the West.

South and Southeast Asia are different again. Indonesia is one of the most surprising to me, perhaps because it is where I have been most deeply immersed. Thirty-five years ago, when Clifford Geertz (1976) had just published his Weber-inspired *Religion of Java*, he characterized Java as being dominated by Hinduistic values emphasizing hierarchy and harmony, inner as well as social and cultural harmony. Thirty-three years ago, my wife and I lived in Sukarnoist Indonesia on the eve of "the year of living dangerously," which brought the Gestapu massacre and the advent of Suharto. Though living in a Communist-led slum community hinting of revolution, I felt that the values noted by Geertz were deeply grounded in Java; they seemed eternal. So did the shamble in which the economy was mired then.

Today, what has happened in Indonesia? The growth rate is 7 percent. Minister of Technology Habibi is planning a hundred-million-dollar airplane factory in Mobile, Alabama, reversing the direction of colonization. And what of those eternal values? Here is a brief case study. My wife and I lived with two families, each for roughly half of our year 1962–63, in Surabaya. The first was poor and lived in a slum; the second was wealthy. The first had twelve children, two of whom were dead of TB within a year or two of our departure. One of the twelve came to the United States, got an engineering degree, married a Philippine woman, and had a son. He graduated from the North Carolina School of Math and Science, from Brown University in engineering, and is getting an MBA from Duke while working very successfully for an environmental engineering firm. His pattern resembles that of the East Asian success story. The wealthy family had a smaller number of children, who have become bankers, a physician, and a chemist and remain in Indonesia. Their grandsons have received university degrees in the United States. One of them, visiting us prior to going to work in a business in Singapore, borrowed Clifford Geertz's book on Java, saying he needed to reacquaint himself with his culture since his mother wanted to arrange a marriage with a Javanese woman, and he needed to remember the values.

What do these stories say? They remind us that values are not eternal, archetypal, that they are constructed, at least more so than I imagined when first encountering them in their seemingly eternal otherness. Yet I still believe that these values remain deeply there; and, in subtle ways that I treasure, I see even in the two grandsons the heritage of their grandparents, still rooted in their own culture. In saying this, one must be careful not to be racist—to refuse to admit that individuals of a given ethnic and cultural background can deeply and radically transform their own values and virtually amputate those of their forebears.

Let me conclude by turning to a more familiar case—ourselves, the United States. Weber saw America, epitomized by Ben Franklin, as quintessentially Protestant ethic and spirit of capitalism. The connection between the two was suggested, incidentally, when Weber visited his first cousins in 1904 in Mt. Airy, North Carolina, and witnessed a baptism. He asked why anybody would subject himself to such an icy immersion and was told, "He's about to open a bank" (Shils and Mills, 1949).

For the United States, the dominant values that Weber and Weberians emphasize is what Parsons (1982) terms "institutional individualism" and "instrumental activism." The first term emphasizes that society is a means or instrument toward individual ends, though individuals organize into voluntary institutions to achieve these ends. The second term emphasizes the value of activism as opposed to fatalism. Further, Parsons emphasized the endurance of such values even when particular norms or styles of life would seem to have changed. He wrote about America: "We do hold that there is and has been a single well-integrated value system institutionalized in the society which has 'evolved' but has not been drastically changed" (1982, 327).

As with Asia, so with the United States. Since Parsons made his major contributions in the 1950s, we have experienced the Vietnam War and the 1960s, and also a great influx of immigrants, including Asians. Many contemporary Americans who place a strong emphasis on diversity argue in favor of multiculturalism and against the sort of core values Parsons asserts. We can tell our own stories of children and grandchildren: generational change. How profound are these changes, and what do they say about wellsprings of values?

The wellspring itself, Protestantism, has changed. Mainline denominations have diminished, new sects, including fundamentalist ones, have expanded, and diversity of religion has increased, in part owing to the immigration of Buddhists, Muslims, and others and in part owing to new currents of thought. Many Americans have become less conventionally religious, though the United States remains remarkably religious when compared to other Western nations.

Structural changes, too, undermine values. Buyouts and layoffs, for example, undermine the work ethic, though the value may endure as Katherine Newman (1988) notes in *Falling from Grace*, which finds that Americans who lose their jobs tend to blame themselves for being unproductive. The American dream dims with stultifying bureaucracy. The town, the farm, the central city give way to the suburb, and community is corroded; the family yields to the single-parent household and anchors are seemingly lost.

Diverse cultures challenge core values. Conceptions of time, for example, among Native Americans or other minorities clash with Protestant ethic visions of future-orientation, plans, careers. The patriarchal bias of the Protestant ethic is challenged by female patterns of life history which emphasize relationships over narrowly defined goal-orientation. The New England, Northeastern version of the Protestant ethic, which has been the classic and prevailing vision for America is challenged by the Sunbelt and Biblebelt version, in company with that region regaining economic vitality. And, of course, paradoxes abound in the Southeast which, as someone says, seems too southern to be Protestant just as Ireland is too northern to be Catholic. The South is usefully viewed as the northernmost extension of the Caribbean and of Latin America, but with a European majority superimposed on a plantation heritage—not to mention multiple cultures ranging from African to Appalachian, and now Asian, Hispanic, Caribbean, and others. In further ways, the Southwest differs from the historically core American values, owing to Native American and Hispanic cultures.

Projected against these experiences, diversities, real conditions, and life worlds, the core values appear abstract and unreal—constructs manufactured by puritan pioneers or by elite ancestors and far removed from life today. On the other hand, the values endure, manifesting themselves at deep levels even among groups whose homeland and native tradition may have manifested other values. Rebellion and release often manifest the values rebelled against, as when Americans work so hard at playing, ascetically seeking hedonism. Bellah et al. (1985) argues in *Habits of the Heart* that therapy often extends capitalist values into what is intended as a cure of such values. Consumerism, as Veblen showed long ago, parallels the productive ethic: one strives to consume.

Obviously, an issue for us is the nature and the extent of the diversities, changes, and rebellions, whether in Asia or the West. Do they fundamentally contradict core values, or are they lower-level variations continuing to affirm the core at basic levels? Conversely, one must ask whether calls to reaffirm the core in fact construct new values. Such a question should be addressed to Newt Gingrich's call for the original American values, for example, which, in his vision, border on individualistic anarchy. Transnational, global integration dilutes values such as the Protestant ethic, mixing East, West, North, and South. But it also spreads such values; this is shown in symptoms—workaholism, anorexia, and the like are increasingly international.

CAN POLICY TRANSFORM VALUES?

The Weberian argument implies, first, that values derive from religious or other definitions of meaning, and, second, that they are pervasive and enduring. In reflecting on this argument, we have noticed changes derive from socioeconomic processes and history, but also note how values endure so that the old structures the seemingly new, and, indeed, is the source of the new.

If we follow the Weberian or neo-Weberian tack, our policy would be to affect values through affecting religion or the like: we would missionize or at least do moral education. Yet liberal and democratic values in our own society question such a path; it is brainwashing, we say, proselytizing; it undermines individual freedom. Therefore, we might favor less controlling techniques, such as providing economic incentives and hoping that, in time, the values would change to fit changes in behavior. Other societies—such as China, Russia, or South Africa—blink less at directly working on hearts and minds.

Weber would call for us to look sharply at our seemingly value-neutral policies and discern the unstated religiosities they reflect—perhaps not to disavow them, but at least to make explicit what values they imply.

A second strategy is not to create culture ourselves, but to support indigenous movements or initiatives that bid to transform core values. Following Weberian or neo-Weberian arguments, these must contain some vision that transcends the present social and cultural order, yet also engage that order—be anchored in the other world, so to speak, but work on this world. Had there been AID or Ford or Rockefeller foundations in seventeenth-century England, and had Weber been a consultant, the Protestant sects would have qualified for support.[1] Today, such groups might include fundamentalist or evangelical movements such as Muhammadijah in Indonesia, Pentecostals everywhere, some of the new religions in Japan, and self-help movements among blacks ranging from Rastifarians to Islam.

We would, if we follow Weber, support their initiative. Actually, lists of nongovernment organizations supported by U.S. foundations include hundreds of grassroots movements, though they tend not, I think, to include sectarian ones. And one imagines that government and private agencies are cautious about supporting movements that are opposed to the prevailing governments, which sectarian movements tend to be. They also tend to be exclusionist, sometimes violent, hard headed, zealous, almost by definition, and charismatic, to use another of Weber's words, hence destructive of received orders, whether bureaucratic or traditional. Further, the kinds of movements and initiatives Weber found to be wellsprings of value were also rationalistic, methodical, systematic, which is true of many contemporary sects from Mormons to Jehovah's Witnesses; they are thus effective, hence dangerous.

Such worries apply, of course, to seemingly secular movements as well. An example is the information revolution, whose leaders range from Bill Gates to Newt Gingrich. Replacement of teacher-student relations by computers would destroy a cultural value sustained since the Paleolithic and force a process of thinking constrained by electronics rather than open to patterns of thought and language characteristic of human beings. Here the zeal of quasi-religion and of politics is fueled by the greed and power of business. More humane are National Endowment of the Humanities Chair Sheldon Hackney's National Conversations with Americans, dialogues in search of common values that they share or freely choose to affirm. Is this a better way?

So a policy that seeks to transform values, either by actions of the policy makers, by supporting initiatives of others or by dialogue and participational processes, must deal with powerful, explosive forces. Wisdom is essential, for timidity and over-caution in support of established neutrals risks no results at all while instigating transformative movements can destroy the heritage of millennia while instituting values that endure for centuries.

NOTE

1. This proposal was made hypothetically but subsequently has been carried out, I am told. Susan Berresford, President of the Ford Foundation, tells me that Ford is now supporting certain religious organizations including specifically Muslim "pesantren" (schools) in Indonesia which combine grassroots leadership and ethical/spiritual commitments with socially progressive programs such as family planning. Although I had, coincidentally, suggested something like this to a Ford representative in Jakarta following my fieldwork with Muhammadiyah in 1970, it appears that Ford arrived at this decision independently, following an argument rather like the Weberian one noted here. Ford is making the development of values a piece of its social policy.

REFERENCES

American Anthropological Association. 1993. Symposium on "Ritual." Washington, DC.

Bellah, Robert. 1957. *Tokugawa Religion*. Glencoe, IL: Free Press.

Bellah, Robert, Richard Madsen, William Sullivan, Ann Swidler, and Steven M. Tipton. 1985. *Habits of the Heart: Individualism and Commitment in American Life*. Berkeley: University of California Press.

Durkheim, Emile. 1912. *The Elementary Forms of Religious Life*. Translated by V. W. Swain. London: Allen and Unwin.

Geertz, Clifford. 1966. *Person, Time, and Conduct in Bali: An Essay in Cultural Analysis*. New Haven: Yale University Press.

Geertz, Clifford. 1976. *Religion of Java*. Chicago: University of Chicago Press.

Kluckhohn, Florence, and Fred Strodtbeck. 1961. *Variations in Value Orientations*. Evanston, IL: Row, Peterson.

Newman, Katherine. 1988. *Falling from Grace: The Experience of Downward Mobility in the American Middle Class*. New York: Free Press.

Parsons, Talcott. 1951. *Toward a General Theory of Action*. Cambridge: Harvard University Press.

Parsons, Talcott. 1982. "American Values and American Society." In *On Institutions and Social Evolution*. Chicago: University of Chicago Press.

Shils, Edward, and C. Wright Mills, eds. 1949. *Max Weber*. Freeport: Free Press.

Weber, Max. 1952a. *Ancient Judaism*. Translated and edited by Hans H. Gerth and Don Martindale. Glencoe, IL: Free Press.

Weber, Max. 1952b. *Religion of China: Confucianism and Taoism*. Glencoe: IL: Free Press.

Weber, Max. 1958. *Religion of India: The Sociology of Hinduism and Buddhism*. Glencoe, IL: Free Press.

Weber, Max. 1972. *Gesammelte Aufzatze zur Relgionssoziologie*. Tubingen, Germany: Mohr.

Weber, Max. 1985. *The Protestant Ethic and the Spirit of Capitalism*. New York: Unwin Paperbacks.

4

American Democratic Institutions and Social Values

Timothy Brennan

In the last few years, there have been a number of intriguing and important efforts to institute research and practical programs to cure what many perceive to be a serious flaw that had arisen in the U.S. public policy machinery during the 1980s. This concern, as I understand it, was primarily related to the budget-cutting (except for defense), tax-cutting (especially for the rich), "guns, not butter" free-market philosophy of the Reagan presidency. The Gingrich quasipresidency and the Contract With America appear to highlight that same perceived flaw in the process.

To perhaps oversimplify, the alleged flaw is that the policies as designed, advanced, and implemented seem severely disconnected from the values that the citizens purportedly hold. In this view, either the system is unresponsive to values, or, if it responds, it is unable to resolve conflicts among them. Those issues where private values make it into the public sphere, most notably abortion and gun control, are characterized by an uncivilized inability to achieve common ground. Most serious injustices, such as homelessness, racism, and poverty are left to fester.

There have been numerous effective, articulate, and insightful advocates of this view. The 1985 book *Habits of the Heart* offers multiple examples of the character of persons as reflected in their everyday lives.[1] It suggests that the failure of this character to resound in the public sphere was, in large measure, the fault of the growth of large organizations, government predilection to put those organizations ahead of people, and media "more interested in the charisma of politicians and the dramatic conflicts between them than in their positions on policy issues."[2] William Sullivan, following the lead of de Tocqueville, attributes a decline in civic awareness to the ascendancy of stultifying corporate bureaucracy and the decline of civic associations.[3]

Other critics of the current separation between public policy and privately held values direct our attention to the individualism that found a political voice in the Reagan era. In reminding us of the need to couple rights with responsibility, the communitarian movement, led by Amitai Etzioni, has drawn our attention to the role of modes of explanation, primarily from economics, that purport to place all action within the rubric of self-interest and deny "the moral dimension" to behavior.[4] Jane Mansbridge finds that political processes will not function well if driven by self-centered interests rather than public spirit.[5] More recently, Stephen Carter has identified legal and political norms that serve to alienate the religious, and to some significant degree the values dependent upon their beliefs, from the public sphere.[6]

The core premises underlying these complementary contentions, perhaps put in an unfairly stark way, are that (1) we find ourselves in the midst of a social crisis, which has come about because (2) good people are the overwhelmed victims of the negligence (at best) or malfeasance (at worst) of bad institutions—big government, corporations, the media. Many share the negative evaluations of social policy and concerns regarding the dearth of values in the public sphere that follow from these premises. We all should sympathize to some degree with the concerns that have led to the diagnoses, discussions, and prescriptions offered by the aforementioned authors and their like-minded colleagues.

INSTITUTIONAL FAILURE OR INDIVIDUAL FAILINGS?

Despite sympathy with these concerns, I find it difficult to share the premises that underlie these analyses. To put my differences as starkly as the premises, the crucial question is whether the lack of social consciousness in public policy is because the policy institutions fail to reflect underlying social values held by the body politic, or because they faithfully reflect the absence of social values in the body politic. In short, is the problem in our institutions or in ourselves? My sense is that most of the social critics discussed above see our institutions as the primary problem, where I see the fault in ourselves.

Many who disagree with the first premise, that society is facing a crisis, are likely to accuse those voicing these concerns as being alarmists and pessimists. These critics of the critics believe that there is too much focus on the supposedly small part of the economic glass that happens to be empty rather than the supposedly large part that is full. The critics of the critics also may interpret concern with a lack of social value in the public sphere as a thinly disguised elitist and paternalistic disparagement of the choices the body politic happens to make. I accept the crisis premise as a working hypothesis, but in disagreeing with the second premise, that the fault lies in the bad performance of political and economic institutions, I view those taking the "institutions at fault" perspective as hugely and perhaps dangerously optimistic.

Optimism seems an odd accusation to direct at those devoting so much energy to raising awareness of society's ills and to devising and advocating cures. However, it is our differences regarding the diagnosis and hence the cost and effectiveness of the remedies that make the question I asked earlier more than idle academic chatter. Essentially, the reason I see the "institutions at fault" view as optimistic is that, whatever the costs of fixing or replacing institutions, those tasks are much easier to undertake than it is to fix or replace individuals. To fix institutional performance we can pass some laws (campaign reform, progressive taxation), subsidize some practices (e.g., public radio, town meetings), and offer some programs (catastrophic health insurance, education, nutrition support).

Even optimistic solutions such as these seem hopelessly expensive and out of kilter with the prevailing mood. But their cost pales before the costs of restoring civic consciousness in our policy institutions by restoring civic consciousness in the public at large. Those costs are not the only direct ones having to do with family reinforcement and education. We also would have to realize that a fix directed at individual beliefs will not be quick, even if we suppose that it is functionally or politically feasible at all. Not only does this suggest that it could take decades rather than mere months or years before repairs become effective, absent some unanticipated catalyst or leader, but, if the "pessimistic" diagnosis is correct, we might have to accept the tragedy of having to write off some generations of citizens who managed to come of age without acquiring an internal sense of social responsibility.

WHY GETTING IT RIGHT MATTERS

It is popular to blame the decline in social values on the cultural revolution of the late 1960s, but I would hope that the strong sense of social involvement of those years is as remembered as the hedonism. Some might blame economics, but in only their wildest dreams do economists wield that kind of power.[7] Some place blame on the Reagan era, but the harm of that time does not appear to arise from the implementation of policies that ran counter to the public's values. Many of the policies of that administration, and the willingness to raise the empirical question of whether government does better than markets in achieving social goals, were continuations of policies initiated by his predecessor, Jimmy Carter, surely one of the most ethically attuned presidents in our history.

Rather than setting public policies apart from civic virtue, the harm of the Reagan era was more likely in convincing people that self-interest was all the civic virtue they needed, setting individualism as the standard in the public sphere. The legacy of the 1980s is not that institutions veered from the path, but that the path itself was rerouted toward the wealth of each and away from the welfare of all. Were it as easy to convince the hearts and minds of the body politic that society should be judged by, say, Rawlsian standards of how well the worst off among us are doing, as it was to get the public to reject such matters, I would not be so concerned.[8] My fear, however, is that internalization of civic virtue is like a boulder on top of a hill. Once tipped off, it may be very difficult to put back.

Focusing our attention on institutional reform may divert attention from the hard but necessary efforts to fix the problem. By definition of the problem, whether because social consciousness is not widespread or because institutions fail to transmit it to policy makers, effective concern with public value is an exceptionally scarce resource. We lack the luxury of enough energy to fix both institutions and individuals, and if we guess wrong, we may have too little left over to change course. The wrong course of action may play into the hands of those who prefer the status quo, who would be happy to let us squander efforts in the direction of institutional reform, if those efforts will leave the underlying problem unexamined and uncorrected.[9]

For these reasons, it is important to do what we can to answer the institutional failure versus individual failure question for the present democratic institutions in the United States. After a short review of the reasons why individual responsibility rather than institutional failure seems to be at fault, I will review various theoretical reasons why we might and might not believe that our economic, electoral, and governmental institutions produce outcomes corresponding to the social values held by their constituent individuals. Failures are not hard to find, but only to identify them would beg the political and philosophical question of whether we want liberal, democratic institutions to be responsive to our values. John Rawls, William Galston, and Thomas Nagel among others have raised this question, and a look at the reasons for a negative answer is important.[10] Most important, however, is that complaining about institutions, when individuals are at fault, may be one of the most socially consequential errors we can make, if we believe that the public sector should take more than the self-interest of the secure majority into account.

WHY FOCUS ON INDIVIDUALS RATHER THAN INSTITUTIONS

Suggestions from Economics

How one might gather evidence to show that public policies diverge from social values may be less an exercise in empirical research and more one of heuristic interpretation. Making this showing would appear, at least, to require that one be able to discover public values independent from policy choices. Looking at economics illustrates the difficulty. It is a commonplace among economists that markets, absent some independently demonstrable failure associated with monopoly-like power, unpriced side-effects, or informational differences, lead to outcomes that, in some degree, maximize something they call economic or, worse, social welfare. This boils down to a claim that markets provide those goods and services to each consumer that make them as well off as they can be, given the value of the labor and resources that they have to trade for these goods.

Now, imagine how one would test this proposition. In theory, one would find out what people want, find out what markets give them, and see whether the two were the same. This requires that we have a way to ascertain what maximizes a person's welfare that is independent of his or her market choices.[11] If one is methodologically committed to the view that what people say is an inherently inferior indicator of their preferences than what they buy—because talk is meaningless unless they put their money where their mouths are—then there is no independent measure, and the empirical test becomes impossible.[12] Since substantive tests of correlations between independent satisfaction measures and market performance are unavailable, one is forced to take a procedural perspective, looking for credible market failures that preclude value-maximizing outcomes.

Market failures are important in understanding why market outcomes may fail to reflect social values. But one reason to doubt the disposition to blame institutional failures rather than individual failings for the ills of society is that so many of the "institutions as bad" arguments are applied to situations where no market failure is apparent. How many of us have heard critics blame prurient, violent, or merely mediocre movies and television programs on the studios and networks instead of the viewers?[13] Sensationalist journalism or trashy novels on the publishing business? Poor nutrition on the food industry? Low-quality goods on the manufacturing sector? In all of these cases, if consumers valued better movies, in-depth news coverage, more nutritious food, or higher quality products, by more than it costs to produce them, firms would line up for the chance at the attendant profits. Even a monopolist faces the same qualitative tradeoff between the per-unit cost of product improvements and the willingness of consumers to pay more for them. Consequently, even assuming that the data would back the assertions that industries are performing poorly relative to some scale of goodness or value, laments of discord between public choice and private value are weakened by being associated with claims in situations where the discrepancy is not plausible.

Suggestions from Politics

This guilt by association need not apply. The mechanisms under which public policies are chosen may be more prone to failures than those associated with private consumption. Votes, unlike dollars, cannot be allocated in bits and pieces for particular public goods; one has to vote for candidates as indivisible entireties. Among other consequences, simple voting rules cannot register how much one prefers candidate A to candidate B, thus keeping intensity of preference from influencing electoral outcomes.

This insight might cause us to doubt whether political processes would reflect underlying values. However, there are a variety of arguments for the proposition that electoral processes and the statutory law that follows from them, tend to reflect underlying preferences as well as other institutions. Wittman notes that candidates compete for votes and survive only if they are relatively faithful agents of the electorate.[14] He goes on to argue that information on the benefits and costs of political programs is widely available, eliminating various forms of alleged systemic bias, and that political processes promote efficient rearrangements to maximize value.[15] Tiebout has long been cited in support of the proposition that if local public officials do not do what the voters want, the voters will "vote with their feet," moving to jurisdictions that provide a more preferred combination of taxes and public goods.[16] In comparing statutory law to the allegedly more efficient common law, Rubin argues that the former like the latter is subject to marketlike forces, where those on one side of a position are more likely to see their position enacted if they are willing to pay more than those on the other side.[17]

Whether or not the political system is as responsive to privately held values as Rubin and Wittman predict is ultimately an empirical proposition.[18] One important datum that skeptics of the connection between privately held social values and public policy note is that the electoral process does not faithfully represent the views of the voting public. Two prominent pieces of data in the argument are that a substantial fraction of the public fails to vote and that the fraction of the public that does vote differs across socioeconomic groups. Voter participation has declined in recent elections, but less so than perhaps many realize. Since 1932, average voter turnout for presidential elections has been about 56.4 percent; since 1976, turnout averaged 52.9 percent, about a 6 percent drop from that average level, and less than one standard deviation from the mean.[19] If turnout is an indicator that the population has given up on the process, it would be hard to glean a significant increase in alienation from that datum.

It is worthwhile to focus on a particular election, and the 1984 presidential campaign between Ronald Reagan and Walter Mondale seems the best candidate. The reelection of Reagan, in which he won every state but the massively Democratic District of Columbia and Mondale's home state of Minnesota, would seem to be the nadir to those who perceive disregard for civic spirit in the public sector. But that very margin of victory and the clarity with which the candidates differentiated themselves from each other provide strong evidence that the outcome of that election and the policies that followed did not disregard the electorate, but rather faithfully represented the decline of civic spirit in the electorate. With perhaps the nontrivial exception of the Iran-Contra debacle, there is little reason to believe that Reagan's subsequent policy initiatives were accomplished by pulling the policy wool over the population's eyes.

Before jumping to this conclusion, we should look at the electoral data a little more closely. They do lend some support to the argument that those who voted did not represent the public at large. Based on census data using self-reporting of whether one voted, there were some groups whose participation rates were substantially below the average self-reported rate of 59.9 percent.[20] Potential voters who were young, Hispanic, unemployed, or failed to complete high school, were perhaps only half as likely to vote than the average.[21] In the other direction, being college educated, over forty-five, or living in the Midwest increased one's likelihood of voting by five or more percentage points.[22] These data suggest that had voting rates been the same across demographic groups, the election outcome might have been different. However, those groups with significantly smaller reported participation rates are also significantly smaller pieces of the voting age population.

The more crucial questions are probably whether the 47 percent of the voting age population who did not vote at all would have voted differently than those who did, and if so, whether a different set of policy outcomes would have prevailed. Perhaps polling data would support such a conclusion—but interpreting such a conclusion must be tempered. Had non-voters voted, we might have had a different income in that those voters might have cast votes promoting their own interests. But if the hypothesis at issue is whether elections underrepresent those endowed with civic virtue, the data probably prove the opposite. For if a minimally defining characteristic of the socially concerned citizen is that he or she votes, a low voter turnout would suggest that the outcome disproportionately overrepresents the views of that fraction of the electorate with such concerns. Accordingly, those who would argue that the Reagan revolution ran counter to the views of the electorate, including the electorate professing to be socially concerned, have an uphill fight.

The Local Activism Exception?

Perhaps we ought not expect civic virtue to manifest itself in national elections. Complex issues such as global warming, the budget deficit, and intervention in Bosnia may seem too distant or abstract for concerned citizens who lack the time to acquire the technical knowledge necessary to contribute to the debate. However, the response might continue, we can list case after case of community action where people chip in to support the schools, preserve open spaces, fight undesirable growth, promote neighborhood security, and so on.

To some extent, we each can benefit from these local activists' efforts without supporting them directly. Consequently, one might infer that there must be civic virtue out there, otherwise we would not see the level of participation we see. However, this fact need not provide much support for the proposition that civic virtue is locally effective. That some take the trouble to fight to promote local community values need not imply that there is a groundswell of support for those values. The assertion that civic consciousness plays a stronger role at the local level than at the national level is belied to some extent by the much lower turnout for local elections compared to national elections.[23]

The main reason to draw little optimism regarding widespread civic virtue from local activism follows from the underlying causes of that activism. Simply put, the primary fact that may make people more willing to take on local issues while sitting out national debates is that those local issues affect their self-interest so directly. One ought not take too much comfort in, say, neighborhood opposition to plans for commercial development or sports arenas, when their effects would be to cause a drop in value of homes in the neighborhood. Political action spurred by the "NIMBY" ("not-in-my-back-yard") syndrome provides little evidence that people really are willing to make nontrivial sacrifices to promote the general good. Efforts to block incinerators are no different than efforts to block homeless shelters, except that the former are easier to cloak in the garb of civic virtue.

THEORETICAL SUPPORT FOR INSTITUTIONAL FAILURE HYPOTHESES

Empirical support for the proposition that individuals rather than institutions are to blame for the paucity of social sensitivity in public policy making is unlikely to compel those whose personal experience leads to a more optimistic premise. One could add to these empirical findings general theoretical support for the proposition that, in U.S. democracy, institutions that make social decisions ultimately survive by being responsive to their economic or political constituents. Markets provide the driving force in the first case, and elections provide the primary driving force in the second. Turning to theory, however, opens ways in which the optimists may be able to make their case and find data to bolster their positions.

Market Failures

In theory, markets efficiently translate preferences into outcomes by rewarding those suppliers who can satisfy those preferences at least costs. Competing for sales should drive prices down to the point where the price for a desired good or service just covers the cost of the resources used to make and deliver it. These costs, in turn, reflect the amount others would be willing to pay for products that could have been made and delivered with those resources. In effect, one can view a market as a decentralized auction, where resources go into providing products to the highest bidder. But in practice, markets may not translate desires into outcomes so effectively. Consequently, market prices may not be good indicators of the values that citizens deem socially important. We ought not infer that it is better to provide more of X than more of Y to the public, just because the price of X exceeds that of Y. Willingness to pay need not be everything.[24]

The most familiar problems with markets are the familiar categories of market failure. There may be side effects or externalities where activities impose costs or deliver benefits that are not reflected in markets. The textbook example is polluted air. One ought not conclude that the value of clean air is negligible just because there appears to be no positive price anyone pays for it. A second category of market failures involves distortions of prices created by a failure of competition to drive prices of goods and services down to the opportunity costs of the resources used to produce them. While the high prices may reflect the value consumers place on having a less-than-competitive industry provide more of a good, those high prices come about because there is too little output.

Less familiar, yet perhaps more interesting, are factors that cause expressions of willingness to pay to diverge from the values persons actually place on goods, services, or activities. At the top of the list is the commonplace that expressed willingness to pay typically depends on ability to pay, that is, wealth. This will be especially true for goods or services crucial to well-being, if not survival, such as emergency health care and the basics of food, clothing, and shelter. The relatively poor may not be willing to pay much for these necessities, but that does not imply that they are less important than luxuries for which the wealthy are willing to pay a great deal.

In addition, a variety of information-related problems can plague the values nominally expressed in markets. People may not have the information they need to tell if goods and services will actually promote the ends they seek, whether in the private or public sphere. Markets are especially prone to fail if one side knows something the other does not, for example, when insurance against a disease is unavailable because insurance companies know that the only people who will end up purchasing it are those who know they already have they disease.[25] In addition, consumers may lack either the ability to make effective use of the information they have or the will to address desires that, in more reflective moments, they deem most important.

A final and admittedly problematic category is that the intended preferences of fully informed persons may not be correlated with any reasonable conception of social value. Merely "selfish" choices may fall in this category, although many of the things we do primarily for ourselves (and our families) are surely prima facie morally worthy, such as becoming educated, protecting our health, and pursuing our friendships. Conversely, preferences directed at social or community ends, such as racism, jingoism, and exclusionary zoning may be worthy of condemnation rather than praise. Just because something is valued by someone does not make it valuable to support or provide it.

This survey of reasons why market choices need not reflect social values is not necessarily exhaustive. Yet, it does suffice to show the need for a public sphere to complement markets in some cases, and perhaps substitute for them in others. Thus, looking to see if institutions rather than individuals are responsible for inadequate influence of social values in the public realm requires a look at the democratic processes and political institutions that exist to translate social values into the public sphere. It is worth remembering that income distribution, information-related problems, and the divergence between "valued by" and "valuable to" can infect not only market choices, but may disrupt the connections between electorate preferences and elections outcomes as well.

Voting

The 1950s saw two major contributions to the analysis of whether voting in democratic elections could reliably lead to public policies reflecting social values. Downs applied economic principles to the voting decision itself, concluding that the likelihood that one's vote could affect the outcome is so low that the benefits to an individual from voting would virtually always be less than the cost in time and trouble to vote.[26] On this account, our 50 to 55 percent voting rate is not something to lament in shame, but to applaud with wonder. Underlying the lament, however, is an implicit view that the costs of voting are not so great to outweigh a minimal sense of social responsibility.

From a process perspective, the dominant contribution was Arrow's so-called impossibility theorem, implying that no voting mechanism—majority rule, rank-order, or anything else—could mutually satisfy a set of apparently minimal conditions while avoiding dictatorship, that is, a situation under which only one person's vote counts.[27] There are as many interpretations of Arrow's theorem as there are interpreters. For me, the reason for the impossibility result is that we are asking a voting rule to work for virtually any set of public preferences, while being able to use only ordinal or ranking information and to take no account of intensity of preferences.

Accordingly, the two usual ways to get around the Arrow result are either to allow interpersonal comparisons of intensity of preference in some way or to look at settings where individual preferences for public policies or candidates are restricted to conform to a pattern of some kind. For preference restrictions, the convention is to represent the views of the electorate along a single dimension, say from liberal to conservative. The voters are assumed to prefer candidates whose views are closer to theirs on the political spectrum, in the sense that if V is the voter, Candidate A is more conservative (liberal) than V, and Candidate B is even more conservative (liberal) than A, then V would vote for A over B. The terms "left" and "right" in political parlance reflect the idea that it does not do a great disservice to voters to align them in this way.

If voter preferences meet these criteria, and if two candidates are running, one will have an incentive to take a position just to the right (left) of the other, if the other is left (right) of the position held by that voter for whom 50 percent of the other voters are more conservative, and 50 percent of the others are more liberal—the median voter. The predicted result is that both candidates will gravitate to the position of this voter, leading to what political scientists call the "median voter rule." This rule says that the winning position in democratic, majority-rule, two-party elections will be that held by the median voter, and that both candidates will tend to take centrist positions.

When the median voter sets the political agenda, some may perceive that values are underrepresented in the policy process. If there are a substantial number of voters significantly left and right of the median, they are likely to feel unrepresented rather than part of a democratic compromise, since no candidate will feel it's worthwhile to represent their position. In a fragmented electorate, the majority of people may fit into these left or right "unrepresented" categories, leading to a polarized alienated public. From abortion rights and gun control to opinions regarding the O. J. Simpson verdict, examples abound.[28]

There is also an important possibility under which reforms to expand democracy in a two-party system may paradoxically inhibit rather than promote social consensus and cohesion. Suppose that the two parties are predominantly a right party and a left party. If the two parties each determine their candidates for office via a primary, the winners will tend to be the median of the right and the median of the left. In the meantime, the actual median voter, reflecting the rightmost of the left and the leftmost of the right, will be unrepresented in the subsequent general election between two polarized candidates. On the other hand, if party candidates are chosen by kingmakers, who take electoral success as well as party faithfulness into account in selecting candidates, one is more likely to get candidates closer to the median, helping to forge a consensus when most voters are in fact somewhere in the middle. Some of the recent complaints that parties are nominating candidates with extreme positions, and suggestions to form a third party to represent the middle majority, may reflect this dissatisfaction.[29]

Perhaps the most troubling circumstance in which the electoral process may seem to fail to reflect values is when voter values cannot be categorized along a right-to-left spectrum. In such cases, it is well known that one can get majority-rule voting cycles, in which position A would defeat B, B would defeat C, but C would defeat A.[30] For example, assume that during the Vietnam War the electorate could be divided into roughly three equal categories, with views as follows regarding the three alternative policies—withdraw (WD), pursue a limited war (LW), or undertake an all-out full fight (FF): Doves, as one might expect, preferred WD to LW, and LW to FF; Moderates preferred LW most, but they preferred a FF to WD, regarding abandonment as the least desirable alternative; and Hawks obviously preferred FF most of all, but preferred WD to LW, finding that unless one is going to fight a war all-out, one shouldn't fight it at all.

Imagine a series of elections in which first, a WD candidate is up against one endorsing LW. Then, WD beats LW, since only Moderates prefer LW to WD. Now, assume an FF Hawk is up against a WD Dove. The Moderates would side with the Hawks, leaving the Doves on the losing end, implying that FF beats WD. Now, imagine a Moderate endorser of LW up against an FF candidate. Only the Hawks would vote for the latter, so LW beats FF. Putting it all together gives LW beating FF, which beats WD, which beats LW, which beats . . . and on and on. This cycle not only is theoretically possible, but arguably may explain why the nation could not adopt a coherent set of values during an era where controversies and alienation from the acts of government seem far more profound than they may be today. Still, the problem is not that government was ignoring consensus values, but that there was insufficient consensus to generate policies consistent with the any set of values.

Markets for Policy: One Voter, Many Votes

Policy values are not set simply through elections every few years of representatives who directly carry out the policies they elected to support in their campaigns. The policy process is continuous rather than discrete; pressures operate on policy makers at all times, not just on election day. In addition, those continuously operating pressures are not constrained to fit the one man-one vote model. The currency of policy influence is less like ballots and more like dollars, where those desiring greater influence on the process can expend more time, effort, and money with reasonable hope of success.

Making the political process more market-like may improve matters, in the sense that the vote of one person who very strongly supports a candidate or policy cannot be simply canceled out by the vote of another only minimally against it. As already noted, Becker and Wittman offer arguments that democratic processes tend toward efficiency. Becker's primary point is that those who want the government to take a particular action will find the results more effective the more the government has to spend on the action and to mollify opponents. This implies that efficiency in achieving political ends complements political action and would be a goal sought through the political process as well as through markets.[31]

Viewing politics as an efficiency-driven market process raises the entire set of questions listed earlier as to whether market forces translate values into actions. In addition, Becker's model depends upon political actors being able to extract benefits in a lump sum way. In practice, those who seek to achieve benefits through the political process must manipulate a limited set of service-specific parameters such as how much we pay for education, how much housing we provide for the homeless, how much we subsidize health care, how we set prices for public utilities, or how carefully our police investigate crimes. It is when we look at political influence on those policy parameters that the most crucial distortions of the process come to light.

To those concerned that community-oriented values may get unduly little weight in public policies, it may seem ironic to note that the primary culprits are the vagaries associated with collective action. In economics, the leading analyses of these vagaries were by Olson and Stigler. Olson's contribution was to bring out the fact that a group's ability to exert political influence depends on its ability to organize itself, which in turn depends upon its ability to counteract free riding by its members.[32] Smaller groups such as trade associations of a few firms are not only likely to possess disproportionately great political power, but will often be able to overcome the diffuse, inchoate opposition of a vast majority.

Stigler incorporated these insights into models treating a regulator like any other economic agent interested in matters of direct self-interest, such as political support, rather than necessarily a benevolent interest in pursuing social values.[33] Because of the effects identified by Olson, this will manifest itself as a systemic regulatory bias in favor of concentrated, corporate interest at the expense of consumers.[34] Stigler's perspective complements less formal analyses of how the financial and media aspects of the political process may tend to promote the interest of wealthy minorities at the expense of poorer majorities.[35]

Consequently, those who doubt that policies reflect popular values have some good theoretical and empirical backing for their position. Unfortunately, the remedy specified by the underlying systemic failures is not more government, but less. To overcome the bias against the public at large, we would likely need to inculcate a strong sense of civic duty in persons, to encourage them to voice their values, and to ensure that the system responds to them.[36]

ARE VALUES GOOD FOR POLICY?

So far, the empirical evidence does not offer a great deal of support for the proposition that policy outcomes diverge from the consensus position on values. Market failure, voting paradoxes, and vagaries of the political influence process leave open plenty of theoretical doors. Many if not most of these problems result because values are in some degree spread over a wide range or are held in such a way to preclude an obvious or natural consensus. This raises the question of whether we want social values to play a role in our democratic policy processes.

That we might not want values to play much of a political role is hardly a radical idea. A defining tenet of the liberal theory underlying our political norms is that theories of the good, particularly moral theories, are not within the proper purview of state action.[37] According to liberalism, the exercise of political authority should ideally be neutral regarding conceptions of the good, with state action restricted only to ensure that individuals are at liberty to pursue what they believe the nature of the good to be. The intuition behind this belief comes out in the oft-made criticism of policy proposals on the grounds that they legislate morality.

Modern liberal thought offers at least three justifications for excluding conceptions of the good from the realm of public policy. Dworkin finds that liberal neutrality follows from the belief that for the government to regard each of us as free and equal, political decisions must leave all of us equally free to pursue our own visions of the good life. Rawls arrives at the same conclusion, arguing from the perspective of how risk averse persons would want to arrange social rules and institutions, assuming they did not know who they would be and which theories of the good they would espouse. A third, related view is that the only way a state can legitimately exert authoritative force over its citizens—ultimately, the acid test of a political theory—is by appealing to public reason, that is, based on premises and facts accessible to all. In particular, this requirement excludes privileged knowledge such as religious faith or intuitive conceptions of the good from public forums. Consequently, it limits the ability of the state to recognize or enforce values based on such knowledge.[38]

The public reason requirement does not and arguably should not preclude those motivated by faith or moral intuition from attempting to redirect public policy in accord with their values. Still, the bases for instituting and implementing such policies should meet the requirements of public reason.[39] As Nagel puts it, "It must be possible to present to others the basis of your beliefs, so that once you have done so, they have what you have, and can arrive at a judgment on the same basis.[40] To accomplish this end, Rawls argues "that in making these justifications [of public policies], we are to appeal only to presently accepted general beliefs and forms of reasoning found in common sense, and the methods and conclusions of science when these are not controversial."[41]

Efforts to support a value-neutral vision of liberalism have not been entirely persuasive. Alexander and Schwarzschild argue that Rawls's or Dworkin's visions of equality based upon distributions of primary goods or rights to purchase resources either lead to morally unappealing conclusions such as failure to compensate for handicaps, or collapse into non-neutral visions of liberalism based upon a vision of what best promotes human welfare.[42] Galston argues that the liberal vision of neutrality has made progressive politics unacceptable to those with traditional visions of the good including parental authority, patriotism, and specific outrage with respect to criminal conduct.[43] Rather than espouse neutrality, Galston argues that we should adopt a vision of liberalism as one embedded in and committed to virtues of freedom, rationality, social relationships, and development of our capacities.[44]

Rawls himself appears to have backed away from his original aspiration to ground political theory and justice in a contractually constructed Kantian moral theory, where the right of liberty and distributive justice takes priority over particular visions of the good. That aspiration itself demands more commitment to a particular ethical theory than he now believes appropriate for a theory of political legitimacy.[45] But in turning instead to what an overlapping consensus of reasonable comprehensive doctrines of an ethical or religious sort disposed to a fair system of cooperation would accept, he either begs the question of the meaning of "reasonable" or suggests, contrary to his intent, that liberalism and the requirement of public reason may not be neutral with respect to aims after all.[46] In the view of some critics, this attempt to achieve neutrality via appeal to reasonable comprehensive doctrines strips Rawls of the ability to invoke ethical arguments to support his conception of the just society, and thus reduces rather than enhances the persuasiveness of his vision.[47]

These retreats from the vision of liberal neutrality underlying U.S. democracy suggest that perhaps we ought to bring values more openly into public discourse. They provide strong support for the view that the ideology of liberal neutrality has allowed political discourse to reflect a particular yet unstated vision of the good, leading to bias in policies and alienation among those to whom other values, moral or religious, are important. Liberal neutrality remains the foundation for a number of compelling political commitments such as the First Amendment's protections for freedom of speech and separation of church and state. But while liberal theory tells us that values are too important to be left to the politicians, it may go too far to conclude that values are insufficiently important to bring to their attention.

WHERE TO GO FROM HERE

Despite numerous candidates for institutional failure, the fundamental cause of the paucity of principle in the political arena still seems to be with the values we have (or fail to have), not the inability of the system to reflect them. As the great philosopher Walt Kelly famously said through Pogo, "We have met the enemy, and they is us." This is not to say that market failures should go neglected, and that political reform is unimportant. In particular, campaign finance reform to deflate some of the advantages created by wealth and low costs of organization may restore both symbolic and functional correspondences between the views of the people and the actions of their government. But much as I would like to believe that a presumably quick but maddeningly delayed fix such as this would solve the problem, I cannot escape the sense that revolution of our values rather than reform of our institutions is necessary.

Perhaps the most academically interesting and practically important question is whether such a revolution is consistent with the traditional limitations on conscious public intrusion into the realm of value. To some extent, of course, efforts to inculcate values of social responsibility need not require government involvement, as value activists on the spectrum from Amitai Etzioni to William Bennett exemplify. But as with any public good, one can predict that such efforts will inevitably be undersupplied without overt public involvement.

Certainly, the government tries. A good example is the Federal Communications Commission's policies to promote minority ownership of broadcast licenses. While such a policy may secure a modicum of distributive justice or promote a bit of role modeling, the program makes sense primarily as one to ensure that a diverse set of viewpoints—one might say values—is available to inform the people and, thereby, to become reflected in social policies. However, our liberal neutrality provisions expressed in the First Amendment force the government to achieve an arguably worthy end through indirect and almost furtive methods.

This example exposes a more serious flaw with trying to fix value deficiencies with institutional reforms. No institutional fix, be it promoting venues for community deliberation, providing diverse content over the airwaves, or opening campaigns to the public at large, will accomplish much if hardly anyone attends, listens, or participates. Consequently, we need to look to policy initiatives that will reach the public and encourage attending, listening, and participating in ways that promote the kind of society in which we want to live.

I lack the expertise to be specific or concrete, but some broad recommendations seem like necessary steps. A first, advocated by Gutmann, would be to commit to ensure that all schools, public and private, teach the values necessary for democratic states to survive such as a deliberative character, including rejection of prejudice, respect for legitimate authority (while always retaining the obligation to question that authority), and the capacity to discriminate between sound and unsound moral and political claims.[48] A second, proposed by Putnam, would be to undertake efforts to reinvest in social capital, community networks, and civic norms that would reinforce democratic virtues.[49]

These recommendations do not involve quick fixes, assuming we can figure out how to accomplish them at all. Beyond the difficult empirical issues as to what educational methods promote deliberative character or which public policies might restore social capital, we have to recognize that character and capital are stocks. By their very nature, they cannot be rebuilt in a day. In addition, the rebuilding efforts may conflict with other core values such as freedom of speech and rights of parents to rear children as they see fit. Moreover, if there is a crisis in values, we face the difficult prospect of having to work toward those goals when the social and political wherewithal to undertake them is lacking. It may not exaggerate matters to note the unfortunate irony that if the perception that we have a problem were widespread, we would not have a problem.

A third recommendation, perhaps easier to achieve, may allow us to take one step in the restorative direction. Whether or not one believes that religious arguments are inconsistent with the standards of public reason, the proponents of traditional liberal neutrality may have accomplished too much by excluding ethics and visions of the good from the public sphere. This no more says that we want the state to find a conception of the good and enforce it, than it says that the government should choose our books, clothing, or dinners. In most cases, such choices are neither desirable nor necessary. But to exclude ethics from the discourse over policies that inherently involve the exercise of the power to take and to compel, and to pretend that such policies can be discussed and defended in ways that transcend ethics, is not only chimerical, but in the end contributes to the modernist trivializing of values that may have contributed to our present predicament.

The great achievement of recent political philosophy was to rescue ethics from its positivist exile. The recent moves to denigrate moral theory as too thin or abstract to apply to concrete problems, and to give up hope of achieving agreement on specific theories of what a good society should be, may be more than merely a cause for academic regret. They may be part of the mortar that keeps the walls of our individualistic neglect of each other from tumbling down.

NOTES

1. Robert Bellah, R. Madsen, W. Sullivan, A. Swidler, and S. Tipton, *Habits of the Heart* (Berkeley: University of California Press, 1985).

2. Ibid., 207.

3. Willam Sullivan, *Reconstructing Public Philosophy* (Berkeley: University of California Press, 1986).

4. Amitai Etzioni, *The Moral Dimension: Towards a New Economics* (New York: Free Press, 1988).

5. Jane Mansbridge, "Public Spirit in Political Systems," in *Values and Public Policy*, ed. Henry Aaron, T. Mann, and T. Taylor (Washington, DC: Brookings Institution, 1994).

6. Stephen Carter, *The Culture of Disbelief* (New York: Basic Books, 1993).

7. A more relevant consideration may be that for all the vices of economic efficiency as a policy criterion, it does force its advocates to think systematically rather than individualistically. Most policies designed to favor one group over another will, almost by definition, be inefficient, in that they give weight to something other than willingness to pay. Some of the problems with willingness to pay as a criterion for social policy are examined below.

8. John Rawls, *A Theory of Justice* (Cambridge, MA: Harvard University Press, 1971).

9. A story illustrating an analogous situation may be useful. During a symposium on telephone pricing, a member of the audience commended a speaker for recognizing the importance of "rights" in advocating subsidized phone rates for the poor. This struck me as basically stripping the term "rights" of any moral force, if applied in relatively trivial contexts. Moreover, knocking $10 a month off the cost of telephone service isn't going to help very many households cross the poverty line. If I wanted to make sure that nothing was really done about wealth inequity in the United States, I might try to get people to exhaust their limited political

capital by working on trivialities such as phone rates, thus leaving the tax code and capital asset ownership by and large safe for present and future plutocrats.

10. John Rawls, *Political Liberalism* (New York: Columbia University Press, 1993); William Galston, *Liberal Purposes: Goods, Virtues, and Diversity in the Liberal State* (Cambridge: Cambridge University Press, 1991); Thomas Nagel, "Moral Conflict and Political Legitimacy," *Philosophy and Public Affairs* 17 (1987): 227–237.

11. A very good discussion of this requirement is in A. Rosenberg, *Philosophy of Social Science* (Boulder, CO: Westview Press, 1988).

12. This difficulty can cause enormous problems regarding the provision of goods where there is no market or marketlike behavior trail from which preferences and values can be inferred. An excellent example is in calculating damages from an environmental disaster, such as the Exxon Valdez oil spill. In that case, economists are led against their disciplinary instincts to gather survey data, there being no travel, tourism, or other expenditures one could use to discover how much citizens who would never likely visit Prince William Sound would nonetheless be willing to give up to prevent future oil spills. These contingent valuation studies are quite controversial, notoriously dependent on how questions are worded and presented, and subject to differing ethical interpretation. However, were we to reject these surveys altogether because they are methodologically imperfect, we might be left with public policies that completely fail to take citizens' ecological values into account. See Paul Portney, "The Contingent Valuation Debate: Why Economists Should Care," *Journal of Economic Perspectives* 8 (fall 1994): 3–17.

13. Prior to the widespread availability of viewer-supported video programming (cable, satellite, video cassette rental), there was a market failure in conventional, advertiser-supported programs. Stations had no way to reap rewards, through direct program pricing, from those who place a high value on particular programs or on the absence of commercial interruptions. Timothy Brennan, "Economic Efficiency and Broadcast Content Regulation," *Federal Communications Law Journal* 35 (1983): 117–138.

14. Donald Wittman, "Why Democracies Produce Efficient Results," *Journal of Political Economy* 97 (1989): 1395–1424.

15. See also Gary Becker, "A Theory of Competition Among Pressure Groups for Political Influence," *Quarterly Journal of Economics* 98 (1983): 371–400.

16. Charles Tiebout, "A Pure Theory of Local Expenditure," *Journal of Political Economy* 64 (1956): 416–424. For a survey of criticism and empirical assessment of the Tiebout Hypothesis, see Dennis Mueller, *Public Choice II* (Cambridge: Cambridge University Press, 1989), 154–170.

17. Paul Rubin, "Common Law and Statute Law," *Journal of Legal Studies* 11 (1981): 205–223.

18. It is important to note that these arguments still retain the idea that values appropriate for the political realm can be expressed in "willingness-to-pay" terms. For discussions for and against this proposition, see Mark Sagoff, "Values and Preferences," *Ethics* 96 (1986): 301–316; Timothy Brennan, "The Futility of Multiple Utility," *Economics and Philosophy* 9 (1993): 155–164.

19. Calculated from data in the *Statistical Abstract of the U.S.* (Washington, DC: Government Printing Office, 1994), 288. There were only two elections since 1932 with turnouts less than one standard deviation from the mean. One of these elections where voter turnout may have made a difference is in Harry Truman's famous 1948 upset of Thomas Dewey; only 51.1 percent of the voting age population voted in that election. The other was the Bush-Dukakis campaign of 1988, which attracted a lower 50.1 percent. My unscientific explanation would be that neither candidate was particularly inspiring.

20. This figure should be compared with an actual turnout of 53.1 percent (*Statistical Abstract of the U.S.*, 1994, 287). This 6.8 percent difference is close to the average difference

between self-reported voting rates and actual voting rates in presidential elections since 1972 (calculated from data in *Statistical Abstract of the U.S.*, 1987, 244; 1994, 287).

21. Ibid. Self-reported participation rates were 36.7 percent for 18–20 year olds, 43.5 percent for 21–24 year olds, 32.6 percent for Hispanics of voting age, 42.9 percent for those completing less than eight years of school, 44.4 percent of those completing nine to eleven years of school, and 44 percent of those unemployed. The voting rate for African Americans was only about 5.6 percent below that of whites of voting age. Holding age, education, and employment status constant, blacks may have been more likely to vote than whites.

22. Ibid. Whether these groups voted more often, or were more prone to lie about voting on a census form, seems a fair point of contention.

23. According to one report, "[t]he turnout may be only 25 to 30 percent in the typical state and local election." Robert Lorch, *State and Local Politics: The Great Entanglement* (Englewood Cliffs, NJ: Prentice-Hall, 1992), 56. A weak indicator of this phenomenon is that voting for Congresspersons runs about 5 percent less than for presidents in same-year elections, despite that fact that one is already in the voting booth. *Statistical Abstract of the U.S.*, 1994, 289.

24. The following discussion draws heavily from Timothy Brennan, "Markets, Information, and Benevolence," *Economics and Philosophy* 10 (1994): 151–168. I leave aside here arguments claiming that there is a formal difference between social values and private preferences, which necessitates rejection of explanatory models such as neoclassical economics that rely on conceptions of rational agency and incorporate tradeoffs between narrow self-interest and other-directed concerns. For more, see Timothy Brennan, "A Methodological Assessment of Multiple Utility Frameworks," *Economics and Philosophy* 5 (1989): 189–208. A recent restatement of these tradeoffs is in C. Mills, "Goodness as Weapon," *Journal of Philosophy* 92 (1995): 485–499, esp. 488–489.

25. George Akerlof, "The Market For Lemons," *Quarterly Journal of Economics* 85 (1970): 488–500.

26. Anthony Downs, *An Economic Theory of Democracy* (New York: Harper and Row, 1957). A nice numerical illustration is in Russell Hardin, *Collective Action* (Baltimore: Johns Hopkins/Resources for the Future, 1982), 60–61.

27. Kenneth Arrow, *Social Choice and Individual Values* (New York: Wiley, 1951).

28. Disappointed social reformers are not the only ones who feel that the government is out of touch with their values. For a useful presentation of the value system tying together opposition to gun control, taxation, racial integration, and religious tolerance, see Gary Wills, "To Keep and Bear Arms," *New York Review of Books*, September 21, 1995, 62–73.

29. Bringing in a third candidate, however, can create more problems than it solves for decisions made via the ballot. It appears that if candidates from three parties can reposition themselves in competing for voters, there is no stable set of positions the candidates can take.

30. Mueller, *Public Choice*, 64.

31. Becker, "Competition Among Pressure Groups."

32. Mancur Olson, *The Logic of Collective Action* (Cambridge, MA: Harvard University Press, 1965). For further elaboration, see Hardin, *Collective Action*.

33. George Stigler, "The Theory of Economic Regulation," *Bell Journal of Economics and Management Science* 2 (1971): 137–146. An important theoretical elaboration of Stigler's argument is Sam Peltzman, "Towards a More General Theory of Regulation," *Journal of Law and Economics* 19 (1976): 211–240. A recent, detailed examination of "nonmarket failure" in the context of regulation is Charles Wolf, *Markets or Governments: Choosing Between Imperfect Alternatives* (Cambridge, MA: MIT Press, 1988), 57–87.

34. Typically, Stigler said it best: "The idealistic view of public regulation is deeply embedded in professional economic thought. So many economists, for example, have denounced the

Interstate Commerce Commission for its pro-railroad policies that this has become a cliché of the literature. This criticism seems to me exactly as appropriate as a criticism of the Great Atlantic and Pacific Tea Company for selling groceries, or as a criticism of a politician for currying political support." Stigler, "Economic Regulation," 144. Thanks to Stigler, the "is" in the beginning of this quote is now certainly a "was."

35. For the financial argument, see Michael Lind, *The New American Nation: The New Nationalism and the Fourth American Revolution* (New York: Free Press, 1995), quoted by Alan Ryan, "It Takes All Kinds," *New York Review of Books*, October 4, 1995, p. 32. The media access point is briefly discussed in Timothy Brennan, "The Fairness Doctrine as Public Policy," *Journal of Broadcasting and Electronic Media* 33 (1989): 419–440, esp. 427.

36. We also ought to consider whether the place to bring democratic values into public policy is, ironically, through our least democratic political institution, the judiciary. The argument that the promotion of core political values is and should be the proper responsibility of judges is most forcefully advocated by Ronald Dworkin. See, for example, Ronald Dworkin, "How Law is Like Literature," in Ronald Dworkin, A *Matter of Principle* (Cambridge, MA: Harvard University Press, 1985), 146–177.

37. Larry Alexander and Maimon Schwarzschild, "Liberalism, Neutrality, and Equality of Welfare vs. Equality of Resources," *Philosophy and Public Affairs* 16 (1987): 85–110.

38. Ronald Dworkin, "Liberalism," in A *Matter of Principle*, 181–204; Rawls, *Theory of Justice*; Nagel, "Moral Conflict." Ackerman espouses a "neutrality principle," claiming that no one can argue from the premise that "his conception of the good is superior to his fellow citizens'." Bruce Ackerman, "Political Liberalisms," *Journal of Philosophy* 91 (1994): 364–386, esp. 369. For criticism of the view that this intrinsically or effectively excludes religious values, see Carter, "Culture of Disbelief," 230–232.

39. Rawls, *Political Liberalism*, 213–224. Carter, "Culture of Disbelief," argues that religious interventions in the public sphere are important, citing the role of the clergy in the civil rights and antiwar movements of the 1960s. Religion undoubtedly gave those advocates the energy and conviction necessary to exert the tremendous effort and bear the costs necessary to espouse those sometimes fatally unpopular positions. But arguably the success and the legitimacy of those positions depended not on faith, but on the ability to show that those positions fit our nonsecular political ideals. Of course, if the success of those arguments depended upon their religious as opposed to secular appeals, then those finding these results desirable might have to recognize the severe social and moral cost in keeping religious arguments out of social discourse. See Galston, *Liberal Purposes*, 115, regarding the religious basis of arguments for the abolition of slavery.

40. Nagel, "Moral Conflict," 232.

41. Rawls, *Political Liberalism*, 224.

42. Alexander and Schwarzschild, "Liberalism, Neutrality."

43. Galston, *Liberal Purposes*, 14–18. A colleague pointed out to me that "neutral" and "neuter" have the same root, lending some philological support for the proposition that the neutrality doctrine makes policy institutions impotent.

44. Ibid., 173–182. Galston also argues that liberal theories are ultimately committed to Enlightenment visions of the good (92), and that the lines between "religious evidence" and "scientific evidence" are too fine to serve the "public reason" criterion (112).

45. Rawls, *Political Liberalism*, 11–14.

46. Bruce Brower, "The Limits of Public Reason," *Journal of Philosophy* 91 (1994): 5–26.

47. Brian Barry, "John Rawls and the Search for Stability," *Ethics* 105 (1995): 874–915.

48. Amy Gutmann, *Democratic Education* (Princeton: Princeton University Press, 1987), esp. 33–52. See also Richard Rosenblatt, "Teaching Johnny to Be Good," *The New York Times Magazine*, April 30, 1995, 36–41, et. seq.

49. Robert Putnam, "The Prosperous Community: Social Capital and Public Life," *The American Prospect* (spring 1993): 35–63. It should be noted that whether increases in social capital cause more responsiveness to social values in public institutions, or whether they are merely correlated with underlying dispositions among individuals to hold and act on social values, is a difficult question to answer.

5

Social Values and Public Policy:
A Contribution from a Religious Tradition

J. Bryan Hehir

This chapter is cast as a case study in two senses. First, it focuses on the role of religion in a modern democracy. Second, it uses one religious tradition, Roman Catholicism, to illustrate the broader question of religion and democracy. The analysis moves through three stages: first, it seeks to locate religious communities in the framework of the U.S. constitutional tradition; second, it examines how a given religious tradition engages the public policy debate; and third, it uses three issues to exemplify the intersection of religion, values, and policy formation in a democracy.

RELIGION AND POLITICS: THE AMERICAN WAY

The narrative about the relationship of religion and politics is as old as the recorded history of the Western political tradition. The narrative has its roots in the rich literature of the Hebrew scriptures in which prophets, priests, and kings struggled over the destiny of Israel and its convenental relationship with the God of Israel. A different chapter is recorded in the foundational texts of Western philosophy, where Greek and Roman authors located religion securely under the political authority of the polis or the empire.

The emergence of Christianity changed the structure and dynamic of the story. Jesus of Nazareth, recognized in his resurrection by many as Christ the Lord, was both solidly rooted in the teaching of the Hebrew Law and the Prophets and serenely indifferent to the political power of the Romans who occupied his homeland. While holding to the teaching of the prophets, his dominant message was that he was the bearer of a radically new power in history. The authors of the Christian scriptures described the new power in terms of a profound transformation of human history: like light in darkness, spirit vivifying flesh, leaven in the loaf. The imagery seeks to convey a sense that the human—human nature and history, human political and social institutions—is not to be destroyed or discarded, but changed down to its foundations.

In the political order the Christian faith accomplished a double transformation: Christian institutions and the Christian conscience.[1] The deeper reality, a spiritual power, was the shape of the Christian conscience. Its newness could be grasped by its differentiation from the accepted norm of the classical Greco-Roman world. Because the classical culture located religion *within* the political order, religious conviction never constituted a threat to political authority. The *possibility* of an ultimate conflict between religion and politics was foreign to the classical mind; if conflict emerged, the state was in possession. By opening a horizon of an order beyond the political, a transcendent order which stood beyond history ("the Kingdom"), Christian teaching created a new framework for conscience. The Christian citizen answered to two authorities, and in a case of conflict the logic of the Gospel took precedence over the logic of civil law. This change in the spiritual order of conscience was complemented by an institutional transformation. Not only did Christian teaching provide a different measurement of life for the citizen, but Christianity assumed an institutional life in society. In Augustine's statement of the case, both the earthly and heavenly cities had visible historical shape. Almost from its inception Christianity produced a voice and a presence which confronted the established power of the political order.

While Augustine's *City of God* is universally known as the statement of the Christian case in the face of temporal political authority, it could be argued that it was the letter of Pope Gelasius (496 A.D.) to the Roman emperor which established the structure of debate, conflict, and collaboration for the following millennium of political history in the West. Gelasius rooted all authority over human affairs in God, who in turn delegated spiritual authority to the church and temporal authority to the state. The dynamic of religion and politics was played out in the context of this framework through the seventeenth century. While the variations are fascinating, the details are not central to this narrative. What is central is the emergence of liberal democracy in the eighteenth century. The liberal tradition posed new challenges and new opportunities for the Christian tradition. Stephen Holmes has described the roots of modern liberalism as a struggle against aristocratic privilege and against religious persecution.[2] Central to the latter strategy was the separation of religion and state power: religion was to be stripped of state legitimation and free from state control.

The U.S. political tradition embodies the liberal heritage in the First Amendment to the Constitution. As Ronald Thiemann has recently argued, immense confusion is generated by describing the First Amendment in terms of separation of religion and politics, a term which never appears in the Constitution.[3] At the same time, it is clear that the new order of the U.S. polity, structured by the nonestablishment and free exercise clauses of the First Amendment, did constitute a decisive innovation in the ancient story of religion and politics. To grasp the context of the new order, which prevails in its basic structure in our time, it is necessary to look at religion through the lens of politics and law and then at the political-legal order through the lens of religion.

The first perspective might be called the political meaning of the First Amendment. It seeks to grasp the essential intent of the two clauses touching on religion without trying to capture the complex history of case law which flows from the amendment. It may also be called a political interpretation because it invokes three essential concepts from classical liberalism to explain the intent of the First Amendment.[4]

The legacy of the "separation" phrase is rooted in the nonestablishment clause; in political terms it means that religious communities should expect neither favoritism nor discrimination from organs of the state in pursuit of their religious ministry and civic duties. In this sense the First Amendment does make a clear distinction between the institutions of the state and religious institutions. The latter are neither directly supported by nor under the control of political power. It is the U.S. version of the Gelasian dictum. In this first dimension of the American solution one finds a central component of the liberal tradition: the limited state.

A second component is needed, however, to fill out the U.S. conception of religion and politics. Because the state is limited, the liberal tradition distinguishes between the realm of the state and civil society.[5] Much of what is socially important and influential resides not in the realm of the state, but beyond the state in the fabric of relationships, institutions, and associations which comprise civil society. Regarding religion, a crucial assertion emerges at this point: separation of religion from the state does not entail the separation of religion from civil society. The latter is the home for religious communities and institutions. Religion resides in the convictions and commitments of the citizenry. Just as the person, endowed with rights and duties, is antecedent to the state, so religion is prior to the state in its meaning, origin, and status.

Third, in the liberal tradition the role of religious communities in civil society is best understood as voluntary associations. These communities, which arise from the free choice of citizens, are distinct from the state in origin and purpose, yet they play an essential role in modern democratic societies. To be precise it is crucial to distinguish the civil or political status of religious groups as voluntary associations from their theological status. Some religious traditions (including Christian churches) are comfortable with a theological definition of voluntary associations, others find the phrase useful for civic denomination, but inadequate to define the religious meaning of the church.

Therefore, from the constitutional perspective in the United States, religion is to be neither favored nor controlled by the state, is to reside in civil society, and is expected to participate in society as a voluntary association with all the freedom and responsibility which such associations have in the life of liberal democracies. The political-legal perspective can be described as setting out how the state is constrained and how religious communities are situated in the sociopolitical order. It is a crucial component of the relationship of religion and politics. But it is not the whole story.

From the religious perspective it is essential in the Christian tradition to assert the freedom of the church. The phrase has roots in medieval Catholicism and strong resonances in Reformation Protestantism and implies that the ministry of the church is not conceived in the first instance by what the state permits, even if the state's definition is as broadly cast as the First Amendment. It is important to know what the state regards as permissible; it is imperative for the church to know what its religious heritage regards as obligatory.

In terms of what the Gospel imperative is for the church in its address to the political order, the Christian churches are not of a single mind.[6] Some see the principal role of the church as offering an alternative style of life to all prevailing secular standards; others place less emphasis on separation, but still expect the dominant voice of the church to be a critique of societal life; a third view (the dominant view in Catholicism and mainline Protestant churches) calls the church to a process of critical collaboration with the state, a search for common ground tempered by an awareness that agreement is not easily achieved that sometimes requires critique of the state and even outright opposition.

While a substantive review of the different positions taken would be a rich theological journey, it would move beyond the scope of this chapter. To focus on a religious understanding of the U.S. constitutional order, it is necessary to give primacy to a functional view of religion rather than a substantive survey of positions. Functionally, the religious communities in the United States have three arenas in which they can enter the democratic debate about values and social policy.

The first is within the religious community itself; here the constraints on state power are very severe and freedom of the religious community is very expansive. In this context the religious community influences social policy primarily by the way it schools the believing conscience and shapes a community of discourse, virtue, and way of life. The instrumentalities in fulfilling this ministry involve teaching, but they often go beyond teaching to an understanding of the formative influence of worship, sacramental life, and spiritual discipline. The emphasis in Catholicism on the combination of teaching and sacramental life is particularly strong, but some combination of intellectual and spiritual resources is evident in all the major Christian traditions.

The second arena of religious engagement is the sphere of civil society. Precisely because religious communities are voluntary associations, there is an invitation and expectation for them to engage the public policy debate in the realm of civil society. That invitation exists in spite of a recurrent theme which has been part of the liberal tradition and which surfaces periodically in U.S. political discourse. It is the view that the concept of religious freedom ought to be tied to the notion that religion is a private reality, a nonpublic dimension of life. Such a view can respect the personal significance of religion, its meaning for individuals and communities of belief, but it resists the idea that religion should have public significance. When this resistance is expressed, it is usually rooted in liberal memories and fears of religious conflict in society or the attempt of a single religious group to establish a public normative order in society.

The concept that religion belongs wholly in the private sphere of life is fatal for the social role of religion. Its logical outcome, which can be found in authoritarian states of the right and left, is that religion is confined to the sacristy and the influence of religion should be felt only within the sphere of the religious community. Even in the freer atmosphere of liberal political systems, a definition of religion as private in scope and meaning runs directly contrary to the basic Christian beliefs about the sovereignty of God, the Lordship of Christ and the meaning of much of the moral teaching of Christian faith.

Resisting the privatization of religion is a necessary role for religious communities in civil society, but it is hardly a sufficient understanding of this arena of discourse and action. To demonstrate the public significance of faith, religious communities are called to engage the public discourse about values and social policy in the realm of civil society. This is a different atmosphere than the world of the religious community. Pluralism—religious, philosophical, and political—is the norm in civil society. The church's freedom to teach and witness is not significantly different than in the arena of the religious community, but the constituency to which it speaks and the community in which it witnesses present more complex challenges to the voice and vision of religious witness. Civil society, however challenging, presents an extremely valuable resource for the social ministry of religious communities. In the realm of civil society major policy questions are defined and debated. The conversation of civil society is one step removed from the realm of policy choice, but it provides the context from which policy initiatives can be proposed, policy decisions can be reviewed, and constituencies can be mobilized to support or oppose existing measures of law or policy. Civil society also provides religious traditions with a setting in which direct appeal to religious values, principles, and rules is clearly understood as a legitimate exercise of religious freedom. The persuasiveness of such appeals is entirely dependent upon how effectively the resources of a religious tradition can be shaped to illuminate complex issues of facts and values, but the possibility of a religious appeal is virtually beyond dispute. Here again, different religious communities take diverse approaches to the possibilities offered in civil society, but the potential to influence within the realm of civil society is greater than and essentially different from the more stringently defined arena of law and making policy.

This third arena, the realm of the courts, the legislative and executive branches of government, is the source of coercive power in a democracy. Decisions made in these settings bind all equally. Hence the reasons supporting such decisions, particularly the normative reasons (as opposed to the assessment of empirical data) are of central importance to a pluralistic democracy. In this arena of discourse and decision, the U.S. constitutional order gives religious groups the same protection and scope of engagement as other nonprofit institutions. Neither the scope of activity nor the mode of participation is more restrictive of religious groups than other voluntary associations. Beyond the legal order, however, lie questions of what kind of rationale should undergird law or policy enforced by coercion. Opinions on this delicate question divide religious communities and the broader society as a whole. Many cite decisive appeals to religious conviction at key moments in the history of the country, for example, Lincoln's second inaugural address and Dr. King's speech at the Lincoln Memorial in 1963. Others distinguish these masterpieces of political-moral rhetoric from reasons which are intrinsic to specific policy proposals, arguing the latter must be more narrowly defined, cast in terms without specific religious reference.

The issues which are specifically at stake in the realm of law and policy choices are not constitutional ones (i.e., can religious groups speak and act, even using proposals drawn from their religious heritage). The issues involve how religious groups decide to use the political freedom assured by the Constitution in the realm beyond the church and beyond civil society. In other words even though they can invoke explicit religious reasons as the basis for law and policy, should they? This in turn raises the issue of what is persuasive in modern democracies. The vision of a Lincoln, the prophetic power of a King may serve as the background for law and policy, yet a pluralistic citizenry may require more precisely defined standards for measures which will bind all in the nation. From a constitutional perspective, religious groups are free to call upon any and all dimensions of their heritage in addressing values and social policy. From a theological perspective, how religious communities define their role in public life can restrict or enhance their mode of appeal. From a moral perspective, assessing what modes of argument are both illuminating and convincing to a pluralist society may be the final determination of how the religious voice is heard in the realm of law and policy.

ENGAGING U.S. DEMOCRATIC POLITY AND PROCESS: THE CATHOLIC STYLE

The religious voice in the United States is radically pluralistic. Precisely because of the protection afforded by the First Amendment and because of the diverse demographic pattern of its society, all major religious traditions of the world (and several variations of each theme) coexist in the United States. Historically the dominant influence has been exerted by the Judeo-Christian tradition, symbolized by the Hebrew and Christian scriptures of the Bible, but three comments are needed to situate this heritage in the contemporary social context.

First, "Christian" for much of the past two centuries has been synonymous with "Protestant," the latter being understood as mainline Protestantism. In the 1990s, "Protestant" must encompass the rise in strength, numbers, and public visibility of the Christian Right, evangelical churches which are both theologically and politically quite conservative.[7] Second, neither "Jewish" nor "Christian" captures the role of other religious traditions now visible across the landscape; the most significant example is the steadily increasing role of Islam. The major impact of Islam thus far has been in the growth of its membership; its public role is less well defined but appears certain to expand in the next decade. Third, an indication of how internal growth eventually leads to a more visible public role is the emergence of Roman Catholicism in the late twentieth century, playing a public role in a fashion quite different from its public role in the seventeenth through the early twentieth centuries. In this period "Christian" did mean "Protestant" in the United States, particularly in terms of the public life of the society. Catholic public influence took two forms: first, the role of Catholic laity in political life (usually this meant the Democratic Party) and second, selective and sporadic interventions of the Catholic hierarchy on questions affecting the Catholic community.

Since the 1960s the style of Catholic public engagement has changed; it has become more vocal and visible, more expansive in the range of questions addressed and more systematic in developing its public interventions vis-à-vis the state and civil society. The reasons for the change lie within the church and in its role in society. The Second Vatican Council (1962–1965) systematically transformed the public role of Catholicism, calling the church in every region of the world to a more explicit public witness; the ecumenical movement, originally a Protestant initiative, invited and influenced Catholic collaboration in the United States; finally, the evolution of Catholic participation in American life, involving growing numbers, a rising educational and social status and a stronger sense among the bishops of their social responsibility, reinforced both the impact of the Vatican Council and ecumenism.

To analyze Catholic participation in U.S. democracy and social policy debates is not to capture the full substance of Christian witness, much less to reflect the spectrum of interreligious witness. But specificity of subject allows a more detailed assessment of how a given religious tradition mobilizes its resources to engage a broader public in debate and decisions affecting the wider society. The resources mobilized are not unique to the Catholic tradition, but they are understood, shaped, and used in a distinctive fashion. Hence all the major religious traditions bring three principal resources to a democratic society, but each tradition (even *within* the Christian church) shapes these resources in a different way.

The resources are vision, structure, and community; the terms are not distinctively theological or religious, but I choose them to indicate at a general level the functional contributions of religion in a democracy. The more one specifies the meaning of vision or the role of structures in a religious tradition, the more one must keep in mind the pluralistic nature of U.S. religious communities.

Vision points to the intellectual component of a religious tradition. It focuses on the way in which ideas function within a religious community and the weight such ideas can have in the policy debate of a democratic society. Vision is about theology and philosophy; it is also about prophecy. The terms overlap but are not simply identical. Theology in the Christian tradition is systematic reflection on the content and meaning of faith; it usually involves a substantial philosophical component. Prophetic discourse always implies a theological position but often is not *expressed* in the precise organized manner of theological argument. The articulation of prophetic vision inevitably invokes theological discourse. The U.S. democratic polity has been addressed, confronted, and engaged in this century by a spectrum of theological and/or prophetic voices: the Reformation witness of Reinhold Niebuhr, the Neo-Thomism of John Courtney Murray, S. J., and the prophetic critique of Martin Luther King, Jr.

Vision in a religious tradition is usually a mix of convictions shaped by faith and moral values and principles which flow from faith. Traditions vary in the degree by which they stress the distinction of the religious and the moral components of their teaching. But the intellectual must be held in tandem with structure and community. Religious traditions cannot exist without ideas, but communities of faith are not purely intellectual. The vision of faith yields an institutional expression in society. Here again, pluralism is pervasive. Some traditions, like Roman Catholicism, invest heavily in social institutions (school, universities, health care institutions, social service agencies). Others place less emphasis on institutional witness and much more on personal witness. Few deny the value or necessity of *some* institutional presence. Finally, traditions vary widely in their size, geographical dispersion, and the criteria established for participation in the community. The "mass-church" model found in Catholicism and the major Protestant communities establishes definite standards for inclusion but is usually not rigorous about enforcement; sectarian models usually hold to strict standards of participation.

Roman Catholicism joins vision, structure, and community in the following fashion. The vision is broadly elaborated in both theological and philosophical categories which are expressed in both authoritive episcopal teaching and theological writing.[8] The vision is articulated in terms of doctrinal assertions of belief, systematic moral argument, canon law, and statements of social policy. The moral and social teaching in turn is embodied in the work of multiple social institutions cutting across society (e.g., Catholic schools, Catholic Charities, Catholic Health Care Association). The community of approximately 55 million Catholics is spread across the United States, is ethnically diverse, and manifests a good deal more pluralism in belief and practice than it did prior to the Second Vatican Council. Each element (intellectual, institutional, and communal) is important for democracy–social policy interests.[9]

Catholic social vision is best understood as a religiously rooted tradition whose social expression is often more philosophical than explicitly theological. The philosophy, in turn, has drawn heavily from the Natural Law tradition found in classical (Greek and Roman) sources and in Thomas Aquinas (1274 A.D.). Examples of Catholic religious and philosophical vision can be found in papal teaching and the statement of the Catholic bishops of the United States.[10]

The tradition combines a strong personalist emphasis with an equally strong interest in social structure. The human person is the basic norm for evaluating social systems and social policies. More precisely, each person is invested with a unique dignity which is rooted in the creative action of God and the eternal destiny toward which the person is ordained. Hence each person has transcendent significance precisely because of his or her humanity. This personal dignity must be preserved from violation and fostered so that it can find its full expression and worth. The protection and promotion of human dignity is measured by the way in which human rights and duties are observed in society. While contemporary Catholic teaching makes extensive use of human rights concepts, the incorporation of rights discourse into Catholic social thought has involved a long process of both engaging and rejecting aspects of the philosophy of rights which emerged in the eighteenth century.[11] Even today it is not possible to simply affirm an identity of content between the natural law and natural rights traditions.

The principal source of tension is not the concept of what a right is, but the prior notion of human nature which serves as the basis for rights claims. The anthropological basis of Catholic social vision joins human dignity to a strong social foundation. Personhood is social from its inception; the person is born into a social fabric which finds expression in three key communities of membership, relationship, and obligation: the family, civil society, and human society. In this conception there is less stress on the eighteenth-century tie of rights and individuality or autonomy, and much more emphasis on how a fabric of social duties is to be joined to a conception of human rights. In Catholic social teaching rights presuppose both duties and a fabric of social relationships within which the exercise of rights takes place. The stress on social nature leads to the concern for social structure. Social structure refers to two aspects of Catholic social vision: its conception of the state and its theory of justice.

The theory of the state has two dimensions: the role of the state within a nation and the role of sovereignty in international relations. In domestic policy Catholic teaching supports an activist but limited state. By activist I mean a conception of the state which asserts a broad range of normal responsibilities, particularly toward the poor and marginalized members of society. By limited, I mean a conception of the role of the state as the final guarantor of rights rather than the primary agent of social policy. The twofold view of the state is summarized in the principle of subsidiarity, a staple of Catholic social policy which has found broader usage in recent debates about the European Union.

The principle seeks to protect personal and communal freedom in society by preserving social space. It prescribes a method of social policy not a substantive outcome.[12] Specifically, it seeks to respond to social needs and to shape economic life by personal and group initiatives. The role of the state is to be a *subsidium*, an aid and support system for initiatives undertaken in the wider society. But the principle presumes and requires that unfulfilled human needs and basic social necessities must be met; hence if private initiatives or the action of social groups cannot meet these objectives, the state must assume these responsibilities. In brief, while the principle seeks to set limits on state power, it is not a laissez-faire conception of government. The activist state is as important as the limited state.

At the international level, Catholic teaching is again characterized by a polarity of assertions. On the one hand, the concept of state sovereignty is accepted as a principle of order in international life. On the other hand, the claims of sovereignty are limited in two ways. First, the wider human society is the context in which sovereignty is recognized; in moral terms the bonds of human community take precedence over the claims of sovereign states. The most visible example of the primacy of the preexisting moral obligations is found in the moral teaching on war. While Catholic teaching has been a home to the "just war" ethic for centuries, this doctrine not only legitimates a state's right to use force, it also sets specific limits to the exercise of the right.[13] The citizen who responds to the call of his or her state to take up arms does so within a framework of preexisting duties even to one's adversary. The sovereign state does not have the right to command any and all forms of violence. The citizen's conscience is bound by relationships which are beyond duty to one's state. Second, the bonds of human community, rooted in the social nature of the person, are the foundation for the structure of international human rights claims, which not only set limits to the exercise of state power but also create responsibilities for individuals and states toward those individuals and groups whose rights are being violated.

Structural arguments about the state permeate Catholic teaching; so do arguments about the multiple claims of justice in society. The teaching is rooted in Aristotle's ethic transmitted by Aquinas. In contemporary Catholic thought the theory of justice encompasses commutative, distributive, and social justice.[14] The first governs inter-personal relations; the second seeks to define just relationships between the state and members of society; the third, social justice, seeks to define the responsibilities of essential social institutions, starting with the state but expanding to address the role of law, the professions, unions, and major economic actors in society. Like the normative teaching on the state, the obligations of distributive and social justice apply within societies and across the relationships of states.[15] The logic of the teaching on justice is not strict egalitarianism. Rather it seeks to establish a floor of minimum necessities that is rooted in human dignity and defined in content by human rights claims. This minimum level of protection of rights (as liberties) and fulfillment of rights (as entitlement) becomes the basic standard that a just society should meet.

To summarize this survey of the component elements of Catholic social vision, it is grounded in human dignity, then articulated in terms of the rights and duties which express human dignity, realized in a fabric of social relationships which reach from the family through the nation to international society, and it involves both issues of personal moral responsibility and institutional responsibilities which are defined in terms of the state, the market, professional groups, and international institutions. How these broadly defined concepts take shape in specific cases can be illustrated in three areas of values and public policy that have been addressed by the church.

VALUES, PRINCIPLES, AND POLICY: ILLUSTRATIVE CASES

The full articulation of Catholic religious tradition, which has been synthesized here, is found in papal teaching of this century and recent major statements of the U.S. Catholic hierarchy.[16] One aspect of Catholic moral and social thought, which is often striking to external observers, is the range of issues and interests that it addresses. This range can be illustrated by taking three quite different dimensions of U.S. public policy debate to exemplify how religious-moral perspectives address the complexity of contemporary policy choices.

Safety Nets, Subsidiarity, and Solidarity

In the 1990s two major debates on social policy—in addition to the continuing debates on budget deficits and taxation—dominated the American political process: health care reform and welfare reform.[17] Taken together these two major issues of social policy assume the stature of a debate about the moral content of the social contract in the United States, at least in terms of how society conceives its responsibility to vulnerable sections of the population. The two issues, of course, differed in content and who was affected by their outcome. To some degree the welfare debate directly impacted those described by the Hebrew prophets as "the widows, the orphans and the aliens" in the land; in contemporary terms: women, children, and immigrants. Health care reform, in terms of the 40 million without health insurance, affects not only welfare families but the working poor, those whose work sporadically or are in situations where work and health insurance are not connected. Welfare, for all the controversy which surrounds it, is a small percentage of the federal budget; health care involves one-seventh of the gross domestic product (GDP). Welfare reform affected those with little or no access to the political process; health care reform catalyzed political involvement by some of the most powerful sectors of the U.S. political system. Delving into the details of either issue is beyond the scope of this chapter; the purpose here is to use these two issues as a way of defining how social obligations of justice are debated in U.S. society and in the framework of Catholic social teaching.

Faced with both issues Catholic teaching agreed with the need for reform in both welfare and health care and recognized that multiple values and interests had to be taken into account to define the questions adequately; but the Catholic voices (the U.S. Bishops Conference, Catholic Charities, Catholic Health Care Association) made clear choices about the priority of concern on both issues. In both cases they placed at the center of the policy debate the goal of meeting basic human needs. In health care it was extension of coverage to the uninsured; in welfare reform, the basic needs of children. These were the prime objectives but not the only concerns of the Catholic voices in the policy debate. On health care, the argument made for fundamental reform included opposition to funding for abortion as a health care entitlement, concerns about cost containment, and advocacy for retaining a health care system which was open to religiously based institutions. On welfare reform, concerns about the issues of personal responsibility, providing jobs for welfare recipients, and opposition to specific measures like the family cap provision (because of the conviction that the family cap benefit would intensify social pressures for abortions) were part of the broader public policy position of the church.

These two issues of social policy—health care and welfare—raised three issues for Catholic teaching. First, the priority of meeting the needs of the poor; the foundation of this moral concern is the strong emphasis on social obligation, which is at the heart of a natural law ethic. Recent Catholic teaching, however, has intensified the emphasis on meeting basic needs of the poor in two ways. First, John Paul II stresses the obligation of solidarity among members of society. The idea is not new in Catholic thought, but the preeminence given to it by the pope has reshaped traditional teaching. He describes it as a virtue, that is, a stable pattern of thought and action, which is particularly necessary in light of increasing socioeconomic interdependence in society. Solidarity is primarily expressed in "a firm and perservering determination to commit oneself to the common good of all and each individual because we are all really responsible for all."[18]

Second, solidarity's focus is further specified by the preferential option for the poor, an emphasis in Catholic teaching which first found expression in Latin America and has been incorporated into the universal teaching of the church. Solidarity calls for a sense of responsibility to all in society; the option for the poor calls for weighted attention to the poor without losing a universal perspective on social policy. Hence the primacy accorded in both welfare and health care to those who lack the minimum guarantees of basic human goods. Other policy goals are pursued in light of this primary concern.[19]

While society as a whole bears responsibility for the poor, the state's responsibilities are unique; this is the second theme arising from Catholic ethics. Some participants in the health and welfare debates assumed that the Catholic principle of subsidiarity would translate into rather wholehearted support for the privatization of social service. The judgment is too simple. It overlooks the strong conviction of Catholic teaching that the state has positive moral responsibilities to the poor. Some Catholic voices in health care reform advocated a single-payer system; none saw essential reform as possible without substantial federal involvement through funding and setting standards of care. While all Catholic advocates in the welfare debate wanted substantial change from the existing system, change never was understood as diminishing the state's basic role as the final support system for poor children and poor families. In its statement to Congress, the U.S. Catholic Bishops Conference said, "The national government cannot simply leave to others the task of overcoming poverty, which touches a fifth of our children and more than 30 million Americans of all ages."[20]

What then of subsidiarity? It continues to assert that the state should not be the sole or even principal agent of responding to human needs. But subsidiarity exists within a broader social vision shaped by solidarity and a strong normative conception of the state. Hence, subsidiarity seeks to preserve two criteria for social policy. First, a role for civil society and the institutions embedded in it as necessary participants in effective social policy; and second, subsidiarity is a principle which seeks comparative advantage among the institutions of society. Hence, in both health care and welfare policy subsidiarity presses policy analysis toward a testing of multiple public–private partnerships designed to fulfill the obligation of solidarity.

Human Rights and Military Intervention

In the years since the Cold War collapsed, the dominant problem of the use of force has become conflict within states rather than between states. While the Gulf War was a classical interstate conflict, there was much greater international consensus on what to do about it than there has been on decisions affecting Bosnia, Somalia, Rwanda, and other Central African conflicts.[21] Catholic teaching as summarized above, brings to these issues of internal conflict its policy perspective of an expansive conception of human rights, a doctrine of relative sovereignty, and a tightly constrained ethic of the use of force.[22] The human rights and relative sovereignty concepts are correlative. A strong human rights policy necessarily challenges notions of absolute sovereignty which limit the responsibilities of states and international institutions solely to the external behaviors of states. This idea has a long history in international relations but has never been accepted in Catholic thought because of the prior conception of an existing international community.

Giving human rights claims moral priority over the claims of state sovereignty is not a major step for Catholic thought. But legitimizing military action to prevent human rights violations is another issue. The concerns in Catholic teaching are twofold: (1) while maintaining an ethic which acknowledges the right of states to use force, the thrust of Catholic teaching since the 1950s has been to restrict previously accepted justifications of the use of force, and (2) while not supporting absolute claims of sovereignty of any state, recent papal teaching has also sought to secure the rights of small and weak states to self-determination, resisting any emerging patterns of neo-colonialism. This internal tension between an active stance in support of human rights and grave reservations about the use of military force was evident in Pope John Paul II's address regarding the Bosnian conflict. While condemning human rights violations, he quite explicitly refused to support military intervention before the U.N.-protected safe havens were violated. At that point he invoked the traditional "just war" ethic in support of international military action. It is unlikely, however, that official church policy will move in the direction of an expansive conception of using force to solve internal conflicts.

Bioethics and Social Consequences

Any observer of the U.S. political process or any analyst of John Paul II's pontificate knows that Catholic engagement with public policy debate is not limited to issues of domestic social policy or to international relations. Consistently visible on the Catholic agenda is a spectrum of bioethical issues. In the United States the dominant issue of the last twenty years has been abortion, but the intensity of that debate will likely be matched in the late 1990s by public debates about euthanasia and assisted suicide.[23] In American political discourse, the social policy positions of the Catholic church, both domestic and international, are interpreted as liberal, whereas the bioethical issues are uniformly seen as conservative.

In these designations little if any attention is ever given to concepts and principles which join social ethics and bioethics in Catholic teaching. It is this linkage that the late Cardinal Joseph Bernardin of Chicago spent much time and energy trying to highlight in public discourse during the last decade of his life. Concepts of human dignity, human rights, the sacredness of life, and the prohibition against the intended taking of innocent human life cut across Catholic teaching on war and euthanasia and on capital punishment and the social role of the state. Within the Catholic tradition the complementary nature of social and bioethical positions is an issue of major importance.

In the American public policy debate, the most salient point is how the stress on the social nature of the person and the social fabric of existence shapes an understanding of bioethics. Both abortion and assisted suicide debates have strong advocates of a moral vision shaped by personal autonomy, the right to privacy, and a conclusion that legislation on these questions is beyond the legitimate role of the state.

The differences in Catholic teaching are not only that it arrives at different conclusions than advocates of the right to abortion and/or assisted suicide, but that both positions are substantially influenced by a conception of the social meaning and consequences of both kinds of personal choice.[24] On assisted suicide, for example, in spite of its deeply personal meaning, the choice, if legitimated as common practice, is likely to have direct consequences on the role of the medical profession, the doctor–patient relationship, and—in an age of managed care—on the pressures that may arise to influence the personal choices of terminally ill patients. On issues of bioethics at the beginning and end of life Catholic teaching will not only argue against taking life, it will continue to stress the social meaning of how we think as a society about our responsibilities to all of life along the spectrum from conception to death.

The very specificity of these issues, on which other religious traditions have different positions, highlights how a religious tradition—in this case, Catholic—can engage a democratic society in debate and decision making. Because of the U.S. style of relating religion and politics, it is certain that the positions examined here will be both supported and contested but hardly ignored in the years ahead.

NOTES

1. The history is available in multiple sources. A concise statement is John C. Murray, "The Problem of Religious Freedom," *Theological Studies* (1964): 503–575, and *We Hold These Truths* (New York: Sheed and Wand, 1960), 197–217.

2. Stephen Holmes, "The Gatekeeper: John Rawls and the Limits of Tolerance," *New Republic*, October 11, 1993, p. 39.

3. Ronald Thiemann, *Religion in Public Life: A Dilemma for Democracy* (Washington, DC: Georgetown University Press, 1996), 42–71, 145–173.

4. I draw here from J. Bryan Hehir, "From Church-State to Religion and Politics: The Case of the U.S. Catholic Bishops, in *American Catholics*, ed., J. F. Kelly (Wilmington, DE: Michael Glazier, Inc. 1989), 51–71, and "The Church and the Political Order: The Role of the Catholic Bishops in the United States, in *The Church's Pubic Role*, ed. Dieter T. Hessel (Grand Rapids, MI: William B. Eerdmans, 1993), 180–186.

5. Murray, "The Problem of Religious Freedom," 520.

6. The classical study of different positions within the Christian tradition is Ernest Troeltsch, *The Social Teaching of the Christian Churches*, 2 vols. (New York: Harper and Row, 1960).

7. Again several sources chart the significance of the Christian Right: cf. Richard J. Neuhaus, *The Naked Public Square: Religion and Democracy in America* (Grand Rapids, MI: William B. Eerdmans, 1984), 38–54.

8. For an introduction of cf.: *Readings in Moral Theology No. 5: Official Catholic Social Teaching*, eds. Charles E. Curran and Richard A. McCormick (New York: Paulist Press, 1986); J. A. Coleman, ed. *One Hundred Years of Catholic Social Thought* (Maryknoll, NY: Orbis Books, 1991).

9. J. Bryan Hehir, "Religion and Politics in the 1980s and 1990s: Evaluating the Catholic Position and Potential" in *Action on Behalf of Justice* (Lansing, MI: Michigan Catholic Conference, 1989), 117–140.

10. David J. O'Brien and Thomas A. Shannon, eds., *Catholic Social Thought: The Documentary Heritage* (Maryknoll, NY: Orbis Books, 1992).

11. Cf. David Hollenbach, *Claims in Conflict: Retrieving and Renewing the Catholic Human Rights Tradition* (New York: Paulist Press, 1979).

12. O'Brien and Shannon, *Catholic Social Thought*, 60 (Pius XI's encyclical "Quadraqesimo Anno," 1931); and Hollenbach, *Claims in Conflict*, 157–163.

13. O'Brien and Shannon, *Catholic Social Thought*, 506–518 (National Conference of Catholic Bishops, Pastoral Letter, "The Challenge of Peace: God's Promise and Our Response").

14. O'Brien and Shannon, *Catholic Social Thought*, 595–596. (National Conference of Catholic Bishops, Pastoral Letter, "Economic Justice For All").

15. O'Brien and Shannon, *Catholic Social Thought*, 240–262 (Paul IV's encyclical, "Populorum Progressio," 1967).

16. Cf. ibid., and Hugh J. Nolan, ed., *Pastoral Letters of the United States Catholic Bishops*, 4 vols. (Washington, DC: U.S. Catholic Conference, 1984).

17. For description and commentary of cf. Daniel P. Moynihan, *Miles To Go: A Personal History of Social Policy* (Cambridge, MA: Harvard University Press, 1996), 26–63; David S. Broder and Haynes Johnson, *The System: The American Way of Politics at the Breaking Point* (Boston: Little, Brown, 1996).

18. O'Brien and Shannon, *Catholic Social Thought*, 421 (John Paul II's encyclical, "On Social Concern," 1987).

19. While concern for uninsured persons was at the heart of the U.S. bishops efforts on behalf of health care, they would not have supported legislation which included federal funding of abortion as part of a health care package.

20. U.S. Catholic Bishops Conference Testimony on Welfare Reform, *ORIGINS*, January 13, 1995, pp. 565–566.

21. To sample the explosion of writing on intervention in international conflicts, cf. Stephen J. Stedman, "The New Interventionists," *Foreign Affairs* 72 (1993): 1–17; and James Mayall, "Nonintervention, Self-Determination and the 'New World Order,' " *International Journal* 67 (1991): 421–429.

22. The human rights and sovereignty theories can be found in John XXII's encyclical, "Pacem In Terris" (1963) in O'Brien and Shannon, *Catholic Social Thought*, 131–162; the ethic on the use of force in "The Challenge of Peace," ibid., 492–518.

23. Cf. Daniel Callahan, "Vital Distinctions, Mortal Questions: Debating Euthanasia and Health Care Costs," *Commonweal*, July 15, 1998, pp. 397–404; Ezechiel Emmanuel, "Whose Right To Die?" *The Atlantic Monthly*, March 1997, pp. 73–79.

24. John Paul II, *Evangelium Vitae*, encyclical letter (Boston: St. Paul Books, 1995).

6

In Search of Identity:
Economics and Values

Arjo Klamer

When I was working in Washington D.C., I passed the same woman every day on my way home. Rain or shine, she wore a thick fur coat and a woolen hat. So now and then I gave her a quarter. In the evening I would spend a multiple amount on my children who certainly are much less needy than this woman.

My action shows what I really stand for, which of my values win out in real life. Preferences reveal themselves in the choices I make, economists would say. Accordingly, I apparently value the well-being of my own over that of an unknown person in spite of the far greater need of the latter. My superego responds to this with a sigh of despair and concurs with the progressive colleague who recognized the problem and concluded that we are all hypocrites betraying our values all the time. He was referring, of course, to the Christian and socialist values of compassion and equality which we passionately advocate in conversations with friends and students and at political occasions. Surely, my libertarian friends do not see my problem since they do not think I have a duty to share my well-earned income with the needy and since they question the very value of equality. But I do have a problem with the situation. According to my superego I am a hypocrite, but another self tells me to be a responsible father and to care for my children.

I am now living in the Netherlands, where a generous welfare system protects me more or less from confrontations with homeless and really poor people. The Dutch value solidarity with each other and express this in the political will to relinquish about 40 percent of all income to support government welfare programs. Admittedly, resistance toward this generosity is growing. Even in Dutch reality commitment to the value of solidarity has a limit. But there are yet no signs of an imminent tax revolt as we have seen in the United Kingdom and the United States. A Newt Gingrich is still inconceivable in Dutch politics. The Dutch hold on to their socialist and Christian values of compassion with their unfortunate fellow citizens.

The Dutch and Americans are more alike when it comes to their belief in equal opportunity for anyone regardless of race, sex, and age. Although I assess the U.S.

commitment to this value to be stronger—age is permitted as a discriminating factor in Dutch hiring and the Dutch sensitivity to racism and sexism is less developed than the American one—the great majority of the Dutch passionately declare that they oppose discriminatory practices. This commitment of both people notwithstanding, both countries discriminate on a massive scale. I refer of course to the discrimination on the basis of the passport that people carry. Only those who carry a Dutch passport can share in the Dutch generosity and can expect to make a living in the well-paying Dutch job market. The nationality that someone happens to have makes all the difference. Equality of opportunity goes as far as the border. Interestingly, this massive form of discrimination is not a major issue on the political agenda in the Netherlands or the United States. In the Netherlands, progressives support immigration and generous asylum programs for humanitarian reasons, not to combat discrimination. In the United States, libertarians are on their own in their fight against restrictions on immigration but they do this in the name of free-market principles, not compassion.

Does this mean that the Dutch, as well as the Americans, are as hypocritical as I allegedly am in my personal actions? After all, they say they believe one thing and do another. (What both people do in the form of development aid does not protect them from the charge. Their aid is, in proportion, less that the quarter that I handed now and then to the homeless person.) Just as in my personal case, the Dutch and American sense of equal opportunity applies to their own people only.

Dilemmas like these caused me to ponder the role of values in our lives. Something seemed amiss in the valuation of values by which we live. Then there is the contrast in values to which the examples allude. The Dutch and American societies appear to work with different values. Many studies bear the differences out. The obvious question to ask is how value systems affect economic performances. It is the question that motivated, for example, Max Weber's investigation into the religious sources for the capitalist spirit. His work spawned an extensive literature in which the very same question is pursued. Most recently, Francis Fukuyama rearticulated many of the findings in his much publicized book *Trust* (1995).

The issue of values, however, does not play in the economics literature even though economics appears very much involved. A plausible reason for this shortcoming is that economists customarily draw a distinction between facts and values or between positive and normative economics. The distinction serves to differentiate the scientific values that facts and values have in economics. Facts are to be valued as the focus of scientific inquiry (positive economics) whereas values are to be presumed given (normative economics). We scientists are allowed to get excited abour facts but we should be quiet about our values. Anyone interested in a study of values is referred to the sister social sciences or philosophy.[1] As those disciplines are considered less scientific, the implication is that such study is of lesser value than "serious" economic study. It follows that economists who want to explore the issue of values are doomed to violate deep-seated values in their profession.

This chapter is a report of my inquiry into the matter of values. As it began within the domain of economics it inevitably is self-conscious and still in the stage of justifying interest in the subject. I do not solve the dilemmas posed at the beginning, but I think I come close to an understanding as to why we must live with them.

CLASHING VALUES IN THE NAFTA DEBATE[2]

Since one of my challenges is to persuade economists that values are an issue to be taken seriously as a subject for economic inquiry, it makes sense to start at home, that is, at their own position in the world. The question to ask here is: What is the value of economics?

Economists customarily justify their research in terms of policy relevance. One grant proposal after another argues that the proposed research will be indispensable for policy makers; most academic articles conclude with a summary of the policy implications of their research. So it should be no exaggeration to posit that economists profess to share a strong belief in the value of policy relevance of economic work. Admittedly, this belief does not go unchallenged. Robert Lucas, the Nobel prize winner of 1995, questions whether economics in its current state is good enough to be relevant.[3] Other, especially theoretical, economists are cynical when it comes to the policy relevance of their research, and profess to value economics for economics's sake. To the outside world, however, economists stress, for very good reasons, the policy relevance. When Paul Krugman writes disparagingly about policy entrepreneurs and their abuse of economic knowledge, he quite explicitly affirms his belief in the political relevance of that knowledge.

The value of policy relevance squares with the enlightenment values of control and rational action. These are the values shared throughout scientific circles. Economists do economics because they aspire to rationalize economic policies, or, if not that, to prevent policy makers from stupidities. The end value is that of rationality based on scientific knowledge.[4]

We might congratulate economists with these values but how about a quick reality check? You would expect, for example, that people who value action that is informed by scientific findings, actually act that way. Economists themselves do not really. They have done their economics and believed in its policy relevance without ever conducting serious studies into the actual relevance of their work. We economists have no clue how the knowledge that we produce affects politics or any other realm of life, including our own. One expects that people who are able to become "scientific" about the rationality of marriage and suicide, such as economists frequently are, should at least get scientific about the rationality of getting scientific in their own discipline. Yet economists have been eager to study every conceivable human activity but their own. I know of no good academic research that traces and identifies the actual impact of academic research on policy decisions. Occasional anecdotal reports suggest a critical role for academic economists in the design of President Kennedy's economic policies in the 1960s and the deregulation of airlines and trucking in the late 1970s, but each such positive anecdote is matched by a negative one. None has the quality of a serious scientific study.[5] Economists tend to be content citing John Maynard Keynes's flippant remark that "[m]admen in authority, who hear voices in the air, are distilling their frenzy from some academic scribbler of a few years back," and stop there.[6]

More shocking than the absence of serious study is that economists implicitly have argued the irrelevance of what they do all along. Economic knowledge is after all not a factor in the economic models that economists have constructed of the world. That would suggest that economic knowledge does not matter in economies and hence is irrelevant. If economists are right in this respect, their actions become irrational. For what is the point of spending time and money on something of no relevance especially when relevance is the reason for doing that something? Like myself, the Dutch and U.S. economists are professing one set of values while living by other, unarticulated, ones.

One reason for this scientific, and possibly ethical, blindness on the part of economists might be their frustration when faced with reality. Academic economists are wont to complain about their limited role in public debate. In a recent book the widely acclaimed academic economist Paul Krugman expresses his frustration that "[t]he role of the economist who cares about policy can be dispiriting: one may spend years devising sophisticated theories or carefully testing ideas against the evidence, then find that politicians turn again and again to ideas that you thought had been discredited decades or even centuries ago, or make statements that are greatly contradicted by the facts."[7] Echoing these remarks, Alan Auerbach, another academic economist who actually spent time in politics as an economist for the Joint Committee on Taxation, is frustrated by (1) the "shorter time horizon" in Washington compared to academia, "with ideas being raised and discarded with more frequency than the occasional visits to Washington during my existence"; (2) the important role of lawyers; and (3) the disproportionate time spent on issues that affect only specific taxpayers versus the broader issues that concern an academic economist.[8] Furthermore, Stuart Eizenstat, who served as an advisor to President Carter, observed that "[e]conomists and politicians too frequently are like ships passing in the night, neither understanding the needs of the other."[9]

Initial Stage of the NAFTA Debate

I decided to have a look for myself and investigated the role of economics in the NAFTA debate. It appeared to be a good debate for academic economists. After all, when it comes to the issue of free trade, the bickering for which economists are so well known, effectively ceases. Free trade had been the rallying cry of Adam Smith and David Ricardo, the pioneers of modern economics, and it continues to be for an implicit majority of modern economists. In surveys, professional economists overwhelmingly support liberalization of trade and agree that tariffs and other protective measures are welfare reducing. So one would expect academic economists to grab NAFTA as an opportunity to rehash their case for free trade.

In many ways academic economists did so. They conducted empirical studies of the economic effects of NAFTA for the three participating nations, wrote reports for government agencies, organized and participated in numerous conferences and even more seminars, and talked with reporters. The activity was unusual for academics. Yet its effectiveness was dubious. Moreover, the connection between what academics say in public and what they say within the academic community is problematic. Even when academics appear to influence the public debate, that influence may not be because of their academic knowledge per se, but because of factors such as reputation, communicative skills, or simply the willingness or eagerness of the audience to hear the message. To paraphrase the late Chicago economist George Stigler, the public is willing to hear those economists who supply what they demand, ignoring the others.

In the case of NAFTA, various economists supplied the arguments that the government needed. In August 1991, the U.S. government requested that the International Trade Commission (ITC) investigate the findings of economic research into the economy-wide implications of NAFTA: "The Commission's investigation should be confined to studies recently completed or currently being developed that meet recognized academic standards for state of the art economy-wide policy modeling."[10] The ITC solicited twelve academic papers and reviewed them in a report which was sent on to the trade representative in May 1992.

All but one of the twelve papers present so-called computable general equilibrium (CGE) models. According to the executive summary, "CGE models are firmly grounded in economic theory, and embody microeconomic principles regarding firm and consumer behavior, national budget constraints, and the measurement of economic welfare."[11] Some focus on the economy-wide impact, others on specific sectors. They all find positive gains of NAFTA for each of the three countries, with the strongest gains for Mexico. As far as the United States is concerned they find positive changes in gross domestic product (GDP), employment, and real wage as the consequence of NAFTA. Evidence on the wages of low-skilled labor, however, appears to be mixed "with some studies showing decreases and others showing increases, although the real wage changes are all less than two percent."[12]

While the overview offers the studies as a body of knowledge to be accepted at face value, the subsequent discussion brings out their provisory nature. For example, "In most of the static models, it is assumed that labor is homogeneous, perfectly mobile between sectors within a country, and immobile internationally. While these assumptions are standard in trade theory, it would clearly be desirable to relax them to study a NAFTA."[13] The static character of most models gets mentioned, and so is the modeling of capital—always a tricky factor because of the time element that it embodies and the assumptions of perfect competition and constant returns to scale that some models make.

Indulgence into these issues is what characterizes the conversation among academics. Whereas everyday economists seek solutions, academics are trained to see and value problems. They are also trained to construct answers to those problems with the methods that their discipline prescribes, and, in turn, criticize the answers that others reached that way. This ritual is difficult for nonacademics to appreciate, but without it academic conversation would dry up and die out quickly. Because of it, successful academic conferences produce a sense of awe for the problems of representing things as they are and a recognition of how little we know. This does not sell well outside the academic community. The USITC report, therefore, stresses the unanimity of reports on the positive gains of NAFTA for the three countries.

The International Trade Commission did a follow-up study in 1992 at the request of congressional committees.[14] For this study the commission heard "testimony or received submission from almost 150 organizations (mostly agricultural), used a model developed by its own staff to estimate the effects on specific sectors," but also recalled the results of its previous study. Like the earlier one, this looks like a serious report, that is, it is in small print and it presents the usual caveats. The report points out, for example, that the studies the first report discusses do not take into account new provisions in the NAFTA agreement. In a footnote the reader is reminded that the model used by the commission itself is "only one of several means the Commission staff uses in providing assessments of the Agreement's impact for the Commission's consideration in adopting its final report."[15] It's difficult to ascertain how influential these reports have been. At any rate, the economists who conducted the studies for the ITC are rarely quoted or cited in the media.[16]

Among the many other reports that NAFTA generated, is a study by the Congressional Budget Office (CBO). Although the CBO is staffed with many economics Ph.D.s, it would be farfetched to call the study academic. The print is pretty large and, more importantly, the reader is spared the technical problems that the staff must have experienced in reaching its findings. Incidentally, the CBO finds "fairly small" gains for the United States and "contrary to some commonly expressed concerns . . . relatively little impact on jobs and the location of manufacturing.[17]

The Brookings Institute, always in the game to uphold an academic reputation while playing politics, also organized a NAFTA conference to contribute to the great debate with a publication of its own which heavily favors NAFTA, although a few dissenting economists are included. Among the dissenters is Jeff Faux, president of the Economic Policy Institute, who disparages the academic studies that support NAFTA and argues that NAFTA has bad distributive outcomes with especially bad outcomes for low-wage earners.

The print in this Brookings volume is as large as that in the CBO study. Neither Faux nor the others in the Brookings volume adopt the academic mode. They are more interested in advancing their opinions than sharing the problems in deriving and supporting them, as is the convention within the academic circle. The implied audience appears to be policy makers and other interested parties, not fellow academics. Here, the policy entrepreneurs are at work.[18]

The political intention—academic economists might prefer "manipulative" here—is even more obvious for the so-called academic study that has been cited most widely in the NAFTA debate and has had arguably the most impact on the proceedings.[19] This is a report by the Institute for International Economics authored by Hufbauer and Schott. It is presented in the form of a briefing book in large print. The academic impression is evoked through the use of tables and many numbers. The calculations in the report, however, do not withstand academic scrutiny, as many academic critics have pointed out.[20] All that does not matter. The reputation of the institute and its authors were sufficiently authoritative to lock one of its main "findings" in the collective mindset of everybody involved in the NAFTA debate, and that was the claim that NAFTA would generate 171,000 jobs for the United States. (Clinton would use a rounded figure of 200,000 jobs in his presentations.)

This is not to say that academic economists were relegated to the sidelines entirely. Especially influential was a letter signed by three hundred economists, including all of the American Nobel laureates. The press, the president, and political supporters of NAFTA regularly cited the support of the Nobel Prize winners. But they were the only academics that maintained some degree of visibility in the final stage of the debate, even though it was only in the form of lip service; none were cited by name, but as a group under the heading of laureates.

This lack of attention to their arguments was not for lack of trying on the part of economists; the activity that academics deployed in response to NAFTA was remarkable. But it is not clear how much of that activity was academic. The reports of the Brookings Institute and the Institute of International Economics suggest that academics were prepared to violate academic standards in order to get attention.

Accordingly, in the earlier stages of the NAFTA debate, with the political world barely paying attention and the staff government agencies in the position to reflect, academic studies stacked the deck in favor of the NAFTA agreement. Yet they showed that the impact on the U.S. economy was minimal. Paul Krugman declared NAFTA "economically trivial." His verdict of the debate was that "[t]he anti-NAFTA people are telling malicious whoppers. The pro-NAFTA side is telling little white lies."[21] Academic honesty compels academics to acknowledge that their research has shown the difficulty of knowing anything with a reasonable degree of certainty. If they know anything, it is that NAFTA does not make a big economic difference one way or the other.

So the conversation within the academic circle does not produce great drama and tends to have a dispiriting effect on those who are resolved to act. Not surprisingly, the academic values of disinterestedness and skepticism did not play well in the political arena. It seems that to be moved to act, politicians, as other people, need more than cold scientific calculation and analysis.

Special Interests

It was not only that economists failed to appeal to the imagination of the polity. Another formidable opponent was the power of special interests. In academia we turn our attention away from the hustle and bustle on the street and seek a distant vantage point that allows for abstraction from inessential factors and circumstances. Implicit in this move is the valuation of the general interest. The economic argument is about the effect of NAFTA on total employment, not on how NAFTA may affect the Simpson family in Detroit. In the public arena, the impact on the Simpson family can carry great weight especially when the media shows it. One good television picture is worth a thousand, possibly more, academic articles.

In the debate the academic argumentation proved to be no game for the force of special interests. Coming from a variety of races, ethnic groups, classes, and regions of the United States, perplexing and somewhat shocking unions were being created, with a clear line separating the pro- and anti-NAFTA forces. Comprising the pro-NAFTA forces were big businesses. The actors constituting the anti-NAFTA effort represented a more assorted lot. The more well known of the group, generally speaking, included certain environmentalists, labor unions, and specifically, two former presidential candidates, Ross Perot and Patrick Buchanan. Setting these diametrically opposed, both ideologically and personally, actors onto a stage to act out the unfolding drama of NAFTA was a fascinating process to witness.

That which is most interesting about the special interests was that it was they, not the administration, nor the economists, nor Congress who ultimately determined the terms and the direction of the NAFTA debate. Prior to the involvement of the special interests, the issues of labor, the environment, immigration, and enforcement, were rarely if ever considered. Furthermore, NAFTA represents the first time that such provisions have ever been included in a trade treaty, and this comes as a result of the special interest groups. Thus, the role that they play in the story of academic economists being crowded out of the debate is decidedly crucial. Most important, it is they who introduce and perpetuate the belittling of academic economists before the American public, effectively gutting this purely economic issue, free trade, and gambling its future on fear and on issues of seemingly little relevance to the free trade versus protectionism debate.

The anti-NAFTA forces perfected this process, basing their arguments upon discrediting and disproving economists and the economic arguments presented during the negotiation process. One of the leading members of this push is a policy entrepreneur himself, highly educated in the field of economics, who is currently the president of the Economic Policy Institute (EPI). In the EPI's briefing paper, "The Failed Case for NAFTA," Jeff Faux recognizes that "[n]o one, of course, can predict the future," yet, "we should always be suspicious of economists—who cannot tell us what interest rates will be next week—confidently predicting what the results will be years from now of a complex international deal for which there is no historic precedent."[22] Faux continues to degrade academic economists and economics throughout the paper questioning the unchallenged basis upon which the majority of economists support NAFTA; he continues in this manner, citing specific economists such as Cary Hufbauer of the Institute for International Economics in an attempt to discredit the work that they have done in support of the agreement.

Furthermore, in her comments on the floor of the House of Representatives, Congresswoman DeLauro questioned why a number of economists had come out in favor of the treaty. She wondered at how "[t]hose who push the treaty do not seem to understand . . . but then again, they don't stand to lose their jobs. They are our academics, corporate executives, economists, and editorialists." She pressed the point further by referring to acclaimed editorialist Abe Rosenthal, who said that "they [economists] have shown so little care, compassion, or understanding about the fears of working people who might lose their jobs—how they would howl if their own jobs were in danger." From these comments, the reader is clearly able to witness the hostility directed toward economists when the debate made its way to the spotlight. Not only were economists precluded from entering the debate other than covertly, their professional image was being tainted in the minds of the American public, an audience that was already doubtful of their effectiveness. In a sense, the NAFTA opposition used the debate as a whipping post for the academic economists. Anti-NAFTA social interests buried the reputation and the credibility of the academics and drowned the debate in the muddied and mired waters of "policy."

This in part is exemplified by comparative results of three different Gallup polls, in 1991, September 1992, and March 1993. The poll in 1991, conducted immediately following the commencement of negotiations, found that 83 percent of Americans favored a NAFTA which was similar to the already existing United States–Canada agreement. In September 1992, the heyday of the anti-NAFTA special interests, this figure of support dropped dramatically. In one short year, 57 percent of the public opposed NAFTA while only 33 percent supported the agreement. And if the pro-NAFTA forces thought it could only get worse, it did. By March 1993, 63 percent of Americans were opposed to NAFTA, while 31 percent were in favor.[23] These results, even allowing for a percentage error, were horrifying for the unorganized and ineffective pro-NAFTA forces; it would seem that their message was being lost on the American public, who was lending its support to call of fear of the "giant-sucking sound" from the south and the Save Your Job, Save Our Country: Why NAFTA Must Be Stopped—Now! campaign dictated by Perot and his followers. In fact, the future of NAFTA was characterized as volatile and tenuous until November 17, when the House of Representatives voted on the agreement. Although supporters of the agreement were able to clarify and relay to the public their approach beginning in September, the question Was it too little, too late? remained.

Although the reader is probably abreast of the end result, think back to that time of speculation and uncertainty surrounding those final months. By September of 1993, a *Wall Street Journal*–NBC News poll found that 36 percent of those surveyed opposed the agreement, while only 25 percent favored it, which left the number of Americans who were uncertain at 34 percent.[24] In an article entitled "Campaign to Sell Free Trade Pact Gets Off to Limp Start," these results were not reported as a sign of hope for the pro-NAFTA group. In fact, fewer people did not have an opinion, illustrating an American public uninterested and unmotivated to learn about NAFTA. Two weeks later, a slightly different poll released by Times-Mirror intimated slightly better results for supporters of the agreement. Of those Americans paying fairly close or very close attention to the agreement, 42 percent said they favored it, 31 percent said they opposed it, and 21 percent were undecided.[25] Again, these results did not bode well for the passage of NAFTA, especially since the individuals polled were relatively knowledgeable with the terms of the agreement.

The future was dismal and bleak for NAFTA, and many wondered if the treaty would ever get a fair shake. The supporters hoped for an opportunity to turn the tide of the debate, and their hopes were met, although in an unprecedented manner. To execute a direct offensive and answer the call of challenger Ross Perot, the White House agreed to engage itself, represented by Vice President Al Gore, in a debate on the popular CNN show, *Larry King Live*. After a day of negotiating the rules of the debate, the White House and Perot finalized the deal. Gore would square off against Perot, who had hitherto not been recognized as a legitimate opponent by the White House.

The debate ended up being about character. In front of a national television audience, Al Gore and Ross Perot became the issue themselves. Gore, generally considered a very stiff, stoic individual, shed those clothes for ones of wit and enthusiasm. Gore pointed out contradictions in Perot's earlier statements and the interests of the Perot family in the continuation of trade barriers between Mexico and the United States. While Perot made an emotional plea against the NAFTA treaty, alluding to job losses in the United States and the likely exploitation of unprotected Mexican workers by American corporations, Gore deflated the emotional plea by calling the character of the spokesman into doubt.

The debate did not introduce any new information or uncover otherwise unknown secrets about NAFTA that would sway an uncertain American public and uncertain Congress to one side or the other. No, it was the manner in which the arguments were presented and the men themselves which served as the point of definition. Gore's style was confident, aggressive, passionate, and steady. By contrast, Perot was defensive, seemingly irrational, and overly emotional. This dramatic difference rendered the subject they were to discuss secondary.

But Al Gore did more that night. His rhetoric was clearly geared to wrest the momentum away from special interests and elevate the debate to a higher level where general interests were at stake. He began one of his responses with a story of a family man in Tennessee who, after actually sitting down and reading the agreement, realized that it would benefit rather than hurt his small business. He went on to raise the stakes by stressing the unique opportunity that the treaty provided to the United States, adding the warning that if the Americans did not grab this chance, the Japanese would. He concluded by characterizing NAFTA as a choice between the "politics of fear and hope, past and future, pessimism and optimism, and the status quo and movement forward with confidence."

The public response suggested that Gore had successfully made the opposition suspect by making the individual who personified that position, Perot, suspect. Following the debate the White House "poured about 95 percent of its time and energy into the fight,"[26] holding a large press conference on November 10, where the president claimed, "I honestly believe we're going to win it now . . . and that's not just political puff." The real battle, however, would come in the House and in the Senate where a debate was scheduled on Thursday, following the Tuesday Gore-Perot debate. The battle was a grueling one spanning party politics, and up until the vote, nobody was certain of its outcome.

The Congressional Debate

In his submission of the NAFTA treaty to Congress, Clinton set the stage for the pro-NAFTA forces. He opened his (written) statement by offering NAFTA as an "agreement vital to the national interest and to our ability to compete in the global economy."[27] He continues in a similar vein throughout the message, referring to NAFTA as the first opportunity for the United States to enter such a treaty, a responsibility we cannot back down from. In his words: "America is a Nation built on hope and renewal. If the Congress honors this tradition and approves this agreement, it will help lead our country into the new era of prosperity and leadership that awaits us."[28] Thus Clinton tried to insert the values of national interest and pride into the debate. But he did not shun the economic argument depicting NAFTA as a "pro-growth, pro-jobs, pro-exports agreement"[29] which would help to increase environmental standards in Mexico, reduce tariffs, reduce drug trafficking, and allow the United States to challenge Mexico and Japan, two countries the pro-NAFTA side believed were carefully watching the course Congress would take.

In subsequent floor statements the majority and minority leaders mimicked the president's rhetoric. Like the president, then Senate Majority Leader George Mitchell placed emphasis on the historic opportunity that NAFTA provided the American people; he evoked American fears of the Japanese and their actions in case the United States did not approve the agreement. He added a few economic arguments and some numbers. Later in the proceedings he bypassed the economics, however, and stressed the national values at stake as follows: "This agreement will define the American role in the global economy and in world affairs well in to the 21st century. . . . We must have the courage and the confidence to lead this country into the next century. The Senate now will decide whether America will actively engage the challenges of this post-cold war period, or whether this Nation will reject new opportunities for the future."[30] Like Clinton, Mitchell directed the debate to the topic of the character of the American nation.

Then Senate Minority Leader Bob Dole ended up pursuing the same theme. Like Mitchell, he devoted portions of his earlier statements to economic arguments concerning America's productive capacity and NAFTA's role as a model for future American trade. But he shed this emphasis, especially in the Gore-Perot debate aftermath. In his final appeal to the American people, he expressed his desire to "talk straight" and stated that "[w]hen you sort out all the charts and charge, and now the countercharges, and all the predictions that the sky is falling, you cut right to the heart of the issue, NAFTA comes down to one word, and that is leadership. America has a choice. We can choose to be a leader in today's global economy . . . or we can pass the baton of leadership to Japan and Europe."[31]

Other characterizations were made by other Congresspersons, but in the end it was the line of argument established first by Clinton and then pursued by Democratic and Republican leaders in the Senate which set an example for the Congress. Although some deviated from this outline, they never strayed very far. In the end, the pro-NAFTA forces seemed to speak the same language and use the same rhetoric. Economics played a minor role. Senator Paul Simon alluded to the economics of the issue with the suggestion that "[a]ll we can do [by voting down NAFTA] is impoverish ourselves in the attempt."[32] Senators Carol Mosley-Braun and Pete Domenici offered a letter signed by hundreds of academic economists before Congress. But it was the story advocated and developed above which dominated the NAFTA debate and ultimately became victorious.

The rhetoric offered by the anti-NAFTA forces, which up until the debate in Congress was uniform, coherent, and consistent, began to disintegrate before the Congress. Although the same arguments seemed to be offered, they seemed less persuasive than they once were because they failed to address the appeals to the general interests of the American nation. On the House side, the lead opposition to the agreement came from Representatives Gephardt and Bonior. In his statements, Gephardt referred to workers rights in Mexico on a general level, decried the issue of enforcement, and, following a strategy that the NAFTA opponents developed late in the game, stated that he wanted a different NAFTA. "This is a new world in which we live," he stated. "We do not have to take second and third-best agreements. We can get good trade agreements."[33] He failed to provide the specifics, however.

The rhetorical approach and story that Bonior emphasized was one of enforcement and job loss. Thus, in itself, Bonior seemed to remain most consistent with the former story told by NAFTA opponents. In his statement, he questioned the sincerity of Mexico in entering the supplemental agreements by noting that "Jaime Serra, the Commerce Secretary in Mexico . . . told Mexican political, social, and economic leaders in Mexico in selling this treaty to them that they have nothing to fear basically in terms of the sanctions and the enforcement mechanisms in this treaty, because they are too cumbersome, they are too long, they are too difficult, and we are beyond that, we are safe, we do not have to worry about that."[34] Bonior echoed these arguments of fear with his dire prediction that taxes will be raised so that Americans can pay for all their jobs that have moved south of the border into Mexico. Like Gephardt, Bonior appealed to special and individual interests of the American people whereas Clinton, Mitchell, and Dole had moved ahead to a more general level.

In the Senate, the opposition was carried by Senators Craig and Riegle. Craig wrote a letter with Senator Kempthorne to President Clinton, emphasizing environmental questions, specifically the enforcement and conformity of standards between the United States and Mexico. In each of his preceding and succeeding statements, Craig restated these convictions. Riegle's approach was somewhat less defined. In his statement, Riegle addressed issues varying from labor to lobbying to domestic problems, concluding one such statement by stating that "[t]he NAFTA vote ought not to be for sale. We ought to turn out NAFTA and start over with a fresh negotiation that can look after the jobs and interests of working people and all people of this country."[35]

As has been implied by these two characterizations of the debate surrounding NAFTA, the advocates and opponents of the agreement operated in different modes. That is to say, that although the two forces were addressing the subject of NAFTA, their characterizations of the issues at stake were opposed. The difference reflects, I'd argue, a difference in values that are emphasized.

EVALUATION

Any economist will have noted that I have not followed the usual neoclassical economic heuristic in developing my argument. If I had done so, I most likely would have tried to identify initial conditions and by way of a well-specified algorithm—a maximization set-up—to determine the outcome, or product. The deviation from conventional practice is intentional because I think that a serious treatment of values in economics or politics calls for a process point of view, that is, an examination of the process of negotiation through which various values and arguments were played out against each other. The underlying hypothesis is that the process influences the outcome,[36] in which case it is impossible to explain the outcome at the outset, as neoclassical heuristics allow us to do, without consideration of the process. To see the epistemological impossibility of the neoclassical heuristic, imagine the situation in which participants in a debate have knowledge of a neoclassical model with which they could predict the outcome. Such a model would permit them to dispense with the debate altogether because the outcome would be known anyway or, in case the outcome has a stochastic dimension, they could flip coins. This does not make sense, because the process is too complex and too dependent on accidental factors and unforeseen circumstances to be dispensable. This makes the task of social scientist more complicated since we have to trace and interpret the process to make sense of the outcome, just as I have begun to do with the NAFTA debate. It calls into question the values of policy relevance for science and rational policy for government on which economics as a discipline appears to rest.

My reading of the process of the debate focuses on the contrast and conflict between the values that the various parties played out. In the initial stage administrators appeared to be interested in the truth. At least, so we may conclude from their readiness to consign academic studies of the economic impact of NAFTA. The academic economists who conducted these studies duly displayed the academic values of disinteredness, skepticism, intellectual integrity, abstract thinking, and analytical rigor. The fact that their studies were marginalized in the following political debate is indicative of the lack of public support of those values.

Michael Polanyi, the physical chemist turned economist turned philosopher, once noted that "the main influence of science on modern man has not been, as it is often supposed, through the advancement of technology; it has come rather, through the imaginative effects of science on our world view."[37] It is an interesting hypothesis but the case under consideration gives cause for doubt as to the extent of the influence. The resistance against science especially concerns the scientific way of thinking and the scientific attitude, that is, the values that define the character of the scientist. In the heat of the NAFTA debate the various parties turned away from academic economists frustrated and annoyed. The emotional reactions are indicative of a conflict in values. The values of disinteredness, intellectual integrity, analytical rigor, and problem-oriented thinking appeared to conflict with the values of specific interests that got emphasized in the political debate at that time. The politicians and unionists got frustrated with the scientific aloofness of the economists; they wanted to know whose side the economists were on. Recall the snide remark of Congresswoman DeLauro: "[t]hose who push the treaty do not seem to understand . . . but then again, they don't stand to lose their jobs. They are our academics, corporate executives, economists, and editorialists." Framing the academic argument in economics, however, does not allow for such personal values to be expressed.

The refusal of academics to choose sides betrays a romantic persona lurking behind the skeptical and disinterested facade. This persona imagines himself to be cosmopolitan in the true sense of the word, whose sole objective is to discover the truth for the sake of a better world. He is romantic because he aspires to transcend special interests and historical and cultural restrictions, and because he perceives himself to be at the service of the common good. Economists betray their romantic side in their models. Neoclassical economists at least portray everybody to pursue their own interest with only one exception: themselves. Consumers appear in pursuit of maximal utility, politicians go for votes, but economists stand outside the fray, observing, analyzing, and pointing out the optimal of the equilibrium for all. It is as if economists themselves have no other interest than the general interest and merely serve the end values of truth, efficiency, and at times equity.

Given their commitment to these general values it should not come as a surprise that economists balk when they are confronted with more particular values such as personal gain, power, nationalism, fairness, identity, honor, salvation, and social recognition. Whether the negotiations concern NAFTA, tax bills, welfare programs, or parking fees at the university, economists almost invariably become disgusted, upset, or otherwise emotionally disturbed at the process. Economists generally do not have a high opinion of the integrity and the economic sense of anyone but their own sort. So they balk, usually by sneering at power hungry politicians, ignorant students, and dense colleagues of the other departments. "They just don't get it" is the commonly heard phrase. (The irony is that in their models they nevertheless endow everybody with the highest rational powers.)[38] And indeed, the other parties at that moment do not share the values of disinterested truth and efficiency that economists implicitly proclaim with their arguments.

The posturing of economists in public, incidentally, becomes somewhat hypocritical when assessed in light of what goes on in their own world. Economists turn out to be like any other group or profession in the sense that they, too, abide by the very personal and social values that they reject in their scientific proclamations, values such as power, recognition, status, distinction, and possibly even wealth. The economist who sneers at power hungry politicians is in the meantime pursuing power in his own department and the profession where dirty politics is as much a reality as it is on Capitol Hill.

As Robert Merton pointed out some time ago, conflicting values are characteristic of the lives that scientists live.[39] Their grand values of disinteredness, communality, universalism, and skepticism easily clash with their personal and social values. Think of the interest of individual economists to get attention for their disinterested work, their battle for property rights to ideas that should be communal, and the lack of skepticism when it comes to the policy relevance of what they do.

The conflicts between personal and social values on one hand and general values on the other that characterize the world of economists may prove to be typical for any group, profession, community, or nation. They may account not only for the tension between economists and everybody else, but also for the dynamics of the NAFTA debate.

TOWARD AN ECONOMIC THEORY OF VALUES

I propose that the perspective to take is a socioeconomic one. In brief, the premise is that the overriding human desire is to belong. Accordingly, people tend to form groups; they tend to seek and sustain clubs, circles of friends, professions, corporations, organizations, churches, and families to get a sense of "we," as Etzioni calls it. Even libertarians, individualists by firm belief, have clubs and form families.

Much of what people do can be explained by their desire to belong; many personal and social values are determined by it. Think of fashion, the statement that the fish tie makes, the symbolism of the car one drives, the recognition and status that we seek, the importance of being heard, and the romanticization of intimate relationships. The crucial importance of belonging, of a sense of community, furthermore dictates values of responsibility and care for one's own. You can't imagine how upset my wife would be if I had followed Zacharias's example and given away half of our possessions to that poor woman on the streets of Washington, D.C. You can imagine what the Dutch would do if their government would live up to its human values and opened its borders to anyone who wanted to share in Dutch prosperity.

Because these conflicts cannot be resolved, we learn to cope with them. Usually, we suppress them, but when we negotiate a free trade treaty, try a national hero for murder, discuss parking fees, or find a really poor person in our path, the conflict comes out in the open forcing a process of negotiation.

Conventional economics is not equipped to deal with these processes. The distinction between normal and metapreferences does not provide insight into the conflicts that we have to master in our lives. Constrained maximization set-ups cannot accommodate the uncertainties and complexities of the processes of negotiations in which people engage. I prefer an interpretative approach, like I have pursued here. Hard conclusions are not in order. I have not solved my problem, yet I do understand it a little better. Consequently, I feel less hypocritical than I did when I began this exploration.

NOTES

1. To be fair, normative concerns find an outlet in welfare economics. In that field, however, philosophers and their philosophical arguments dominate. The main focus is on the topic of justice for which Rawls and Nozick, both philosophers, have provided the key arguments. Amarta Sen is arguably the main economic player in this field. But this literature does not deal with values per se.

2. The following discussion of NAFTA is based on a paper I wrote with Jennifer Meehan (Klamer and Meehan, 1997).

3. See, for example, the conversation with Lucas in Klamer (1983).

4. Rokeach (1973) distinguishes end values from instrumental values. End values concern a desirable end like truth, a comfortable life, and wealth; instrumental values are about behavior like honesty, sincerity, and generosity.

5. There have been studies of the role of economists in political life and public institutions (cf. Coats, 1986). Their main weakness is the dubious assumption that the presence of an economist signifies an impact of economic knowledge. Economic Ph.Ds, like the Mexican President Carlos Salinas and the Greek Premier Andreas Papandreou, may very well put their academic knowledge on the back burner and begin to think as politicians do. Our research suggests that they cannot avoid switching modes, and that there is a rhetorical gap between the academic and political modes.

6. Keynes, 1936, 383.

7. Krugman, 1994, 292.

8. Auerbach, 1992, 239.

9. Eizenstat, 1992, 71.

10. USITC, 1992, A2.

11. Ibid., v.

12. Ibid., vi.

13. Ibid., 3.

14. USITC, 1993.

15. Ibid., 1–4.

16. According to a search with the Lexus system.

17. According to a search with the Lexus system.

18. See Paul Krugman (1994) for the concept.

19. According to a search with the Lexus system.

20. According to a search with the Lexus system.

21. *New York Times*, September 17, 1993, p. A1.

22. Faux, 1993, 1.

23. Judis, *New Republic*, 1993, p. 32.

24. Broder and Gerstenzang, "Campaign to Sell," *Los Angeles Times*, September 16, 1993.

25. Gerstenzang, *Los Angeles Times*, October 1, 1993.

26. Steven Roberts, *US News*, 1994, 24.

27. Clinton, 1994, H8872.

28. Clinton, 1994, H8873.

29. Clinton, 1994, H8872.

30. Mitchell, 1993, S16702.

31. Dole, 1993, S16703.

32. Simon, 1993, S15797.

33. Gephardt, 1993, H9809.

34. Bonior, 1993, H9822.

35. Riegle, 1993, S15535.

36. See for example Langlois, 1986, and Lavoie, 1990.

37. Polanyi, 1958, x.

38. The contrasts between academic and everyday economics is further explored in Klamer and Leonard (1992) and Cordes, Leonard, and Klamer (1994).

39. Merton, 1973.

REFERENCES

Anderson, Elizabeth. 1993. *Value in Ethics and Economics*. Cambridge: Harvard University Press.

Auerbach, Alan. 1992. "Taxes and Spending in the Age of Deficits: A View from Washington and Academe." *National Tax Journal* (September): 239–241.

Bonior, David. 1993. *Congressional Record*. November 16, H9822.

Bonior, David. 1993. "Dump this NAFTA Now." *Congressional Record*. November 9, H8940.1

Choate, Pat, and Ross Perot. 1991. *Save Your Job, Save Our Country: Why NAFTA Must Be Stopped Now*. New York: Hyperion.

Clinton, William. 1994. *Congressional Record*. H8872.

Clinton, William. 1994. *Congressional Record*. H8873.

Coats, A. W., ed. 1986. *Economists in International Agencies*. New York: Praeger.

Cohn, Bob, and Howard Fineman. 1993. "Big Brawl." *Newsweek*, November 15, pp. 26–30.

Cordes, Joseph J., Arjo Klamer, and Thomas C. Leonard. 1994. "Academic Rhetoric in the Policy Arena: The Case of the Capital Gains Taxation." *Eastern Economic Journal*, 19 (fall): 459–479.

DeLauro, Rosa. 1993. *Congressional Record*. November 16, H9807.

Dole, Robert. 1993. *Congressional Record*. November 4, S15107–S15108.

Dole, Robert. 1993. *Congressional Record*. November 20, S16702–S16703.

Dole, Robert. 1993. "The North American Free-Trade Agreement." *Congressional Record*. November 16, S15699.

Domenici, Pete. 1993. "NAFTA." *Congressional Record*. November 10, S15518–S15519.

Dorgan, Byron. 1993. "Getting a Word in Edgewise on NAFTA." *Congressional Record*. November 8, S15257.

Eizenstat, Stuart. "Economists and White House Decisions." *Journal of Economic Perspectives* (summer): 65–72.

Etzioni, Amitai. 1988. *The Moral Dimension.* New York: Free Press.

Faux, Jeff. 1993. "The Failed Case for NAFTA." *Economic Policy Institute Briefing Paper.* June.

Fukuyama, Francis. 1995. *Trust: The Social Virtues and the Creation of Prosperity.* New York: Free Press.

Gephardt, Richard. 1993. *Congressional Record.* November 16, H9809.

Gingrich, Newt. 1993. *Congressional Record.* November 18, H10124–H10126.

Hufbauer, Cary Clyde, Jeffrey Schott, and Philip L. Martin. 1993. *NAFTA Briefing Book.* Institute for International Economics.

Keynes, John Maynard. 1936. *The General Theory of Employment, Interest, and Money.* London: MacMillan.

Klamer, Arjo. 1983. *Conversations with Economists.* Totoma: Allenheld and Rowman.

Klamer, Arjo and Thomas C. Leonard. 1992. *Academic versus Everyday Rhetoric in Economics.* Unpublished, George Washington University.

Klamer, Arjo, and Jennifer Meehan. 1997. *The Crowding Out of Academic Economics: The Case of NAFTA.* In *The Production of Knowledge,* ed. Robert Garnett. Charlottesville: University of Virginia Press.

Krugman, Paul. 1994. *Peddling Prosperity.* New York: Norton.

Langlois, Richard, ed. 1986. *Economics as a Process.* New York: Cambridge University Press.

Lavoie, Don, ed. 1990. *Economics and Hermeneutics.* London: Routledge.

Merton, Robert. 1973. *The Sociology of Science: Theoretical and Empirical Investigations.* Chicago: University of Chicago Press.

Mitchell, George. 1993. *Congressional Record.* November 4, S15106–S15107.

Mitchell, George. 1993. "The North American Free-Trade Agreement." *Congressional Record.* November 20, S16701–S16702.

Molyneux, Guy. 1993. "Unified 'Opinion leaders' Best a Reluctant Public." *The Public Perspective.* January.

Mosley-Braun, Carol. 1993. "The North American Free-Trade Agreement." *Congressional Record.* November 5.

Polanyi, Michael. 1958. *Personal Knowledge.* London: Routledge & Kegan Paul.

Riegle, Donald. 1993. "NAFTA." *Congressional Record.* November 10, S15532.

Rokeach, Milton. 1973. *The Nature of Human Values.* New York: Free Press.

Rokeach, Milton, ed. 1979. *Understanding Human Values: Individual and Societal.* New York: Free Press.

Simon, Paul. 1993. "If NAFTA Loses." *Congressional Record.* November 16, S15797.

United States International Trade Commission. 1993. *Economy-wide Modeling of the Economic Implications of a FTA with Mexico and a NAFTA with Canada and Mexico.* USITC publication 2516.

United States International Trade Commission. 1993. *Potential Impact on the U.S. Economy and Selected Industries of the North American Free-Trade Agreement.* USITC publication 2596.

Weber, Max. 1930. *The Protestant Ethic and the Spirit of Capitalism.* London: George Allen & Unwin.

7

Policy Analysis and Social Values

Mark Sagoff

What role do social values play in formal policy analysis? This chapter argues that policy analysis that is rooted in welfare economics makes little room for social values. Policy analysis that takes this approach seeks to determine those environmental and other policies that will maximize the satisfaction of the preferences for which individuals are willing to pay rather than satisfying the goals or values of society as a whole. The only social value it pursues is overall utility, or social welfare defined in terms of the satisfaction of the preferences of those individuals.[1]

SOCIAL VALUES VS. PRIVATE PREFERENCES

Social values are those values ascribed directly to society as a whole, whether or not a majority of Americans at any moment agrees with them. When the Supreme Court found the racial segregation of public facilities unconstitutional, for example, the goal of racial integration became officially a public or social value or commitment, even though it may not have appealed to the majority of citizens. Evidence from the 1950s—the outrageous treatment of Paul Robeson, for example—suggests that the private or personal preference maps of a great many Americans (perhaps a majority) reflected ignorance, prejudice, fear, and hate. Social values, which are the moral goals to which we commit ourselves as a community, are by no means derived mathematically or mechanically from private desires, wants, prejudices, fears, and so on. Rather, they are determined through a complex and deliberative cultural, legal, and political process.

Policy analysis, at least according to standard accounts, seeks to satisfy private preferences, whatever they are, whether or not they are consistent with the principled social values or commitments of society. Its goal is to maximize social welfare or "utility" defined as the satisfaction of wants or preferences, taken as they come, on a willingness to pay basis. According to economist Alan Randall, this "mainstream economic approach is doggedly non-judgmental about people's preferences."[2]

Edith Stokey and Richard Zeckhauser, in their influential *Primer for Policy Analysis*, lay out the fundamental assumptions of this approach. They write that "the purpose of public decisions is to promote the welfare of society" and that "the welfare levels of the individual members of society are the building blocks for the welfare of society."[3] The measure of these "welfare levels" is found in the amounts individuals are willing to pay to satisfy their preferences. "In the United States we usually take the position that it is the individual's own preferences that count, that he is the best judge of his own welfare."[4]

Policy analysis and the theory of welfare economics on which it is based asserts "one fundamental ethical postulate"—that the preferences of individuals are to count in the allocation of resources.[5] "In this framework," economist Alan Randall notes, "preferences are treated as data of the most fundamental kind. Value, in the economic sense, is ultimately derived from individual preferences."[6] Environmental economist A. Myrick Freeman III explains this conception of economic value: "Since the benefits and costs are valued in terms of their effects on individuals' well-being, the terms 'economic value' and 'welfare change' can be used interchangeably. Society should make changes . . . only if the results are worth more in terms of individuals' welfare than what is given up by diverting resources and inputs from other uses."[7]

David Pearce, a prominent British environmental economist, argues that policy analysis seeks to benefit individuals by satisfying their preferences. He writes: "Economic values are about what people want. Something has economic value—is a benefit—if it satisfies individual preferences."[8] Three economists observe that "[e]conomic value for the society arises from individual preferences which are taken to be exogenously given."[9] Michael Bowes and John Krutilla similarly regard the goal of environmental policy to be a settled question: It is to allocate resources "to provide the greatest discounted net present value from the resulting flow of goods and services."[10]

The goal of utility maximization was never adopted by Congress, signed into law by the president, or accepted by the courts. Rather, it is derived from the theory of collective choice on which formal policy analysis rests. According to this theory, to quote again Stokey and Zeckhauser, "the purpose of public decisions is to promote the welfare of society." In this view, the preferences of individuals should determine social policy insofar as those preferences are connected to the expected welfare or well-being of those individuals. The work of policy analysis consists of identifying those preferences and aggregating them, on a willingness-to-pay basis, to determine which policies maximize social welfare overall and are therefore scientifically correct.

What is crucial about formal policy analysis is that it sets forth the principal goal of public policy, namely, welfare maximization, in advance of any political or legal deliberation. It is plain, then, that the views, beliefs, or opinions citizens hold about the goals we seek as a community can have no bearing on formal policy analysis. After all, these views are either consistent with the principle that social welfare is the goal of public policy or they are just wrong. Policy analysis seeks to satisfy only the preferences individuals entertain about their own welfare and is not interested in their views about policy as such. Perhaps citizens have such opinions; perhaps they may argue for or against policies on moral, cultural, or social grounds unconnected with their own welfare or well-being. Policy analysis must resist all such arguments as irrational, since the goal of public policy is to promote social welfare. The point of satisfying the preferences of the individual, after all, lies in the connection he or she makes between the satisfaction of those preferences and his or her own well-being. If the individual believes no such connection exists—if he or she pursues or opposes a policy for moral, cultural, or other principled reasons that have no connection with his or her expected welfare—how could such values enter the social welfare calculus on which public policy should be based? The individual may deny a personal welfare interest in the policy he or she pursues for moral reasons. Social, moral, or political values of this sort, even if they dominate political discourse, have no business influencing public policy. This is because the science of policy analysis has determined that social welfare is the goal of public policy.

A clear example of a social value would be the separation of church and state, that is, the principle that Congress shall make no law to establish a religion. Cost-benefit analysis—or the comparison of relative willingness to pay for different outcomes—is not even remotely relevant to the principle of church-state separation. A long historical, political, and legal process determines freedom of conscience as a social value. Perhaps freedom of religion is not cost-beneficial; it is possible that a society with an established faith may spend less on religion than a society that tolerates diversity. Even if this were true, a cost-benefit critique would hardly alter our national commitment to tolerance.

Occasionally, public opinion surveys find that by large majorities, Americans would disapprove of one or another of the Bill of Rights—for example, the Fifth Amendment guarantee against self-incrimination. A determination of the amounts individuals are willing to pay, for example, to enforce religious uniformity or limit freedom of the press hardly seems relevant to the legitimacy of our legal rights, democratic values, and social commitments—freedom of conscience, equality before the law, habeas corpus, trial by jury, universal suffrage, and so on. Policy analysis concerns not these social values and commitments but interests of a different sort, that is, preferences of the kinds consumers typically reveal in the choices they make in markets, rather than the views or opinions that may motivate political deliberation, discourse, and action.

An important distinction must be drawn between preferences consumers seek to satisfy in their market behavior and the principled views they may pursue through political action. A person who smokes, for example, may have a strong consumer desire for a cigarette, and in that sense a policy analyst must conclude smoking enhances his or her welfare. The more he is willing to pay for a cigarette, the more smoking benefits him, according to this theory, which identifies willingness to pay with welfare. Yet that same individual might believe that smoking is terrible and that society should tax and otherwise discourage it. One may distinguish, in other words, between what the consumer wants for him- or herself (consumer preference) and what he or she believes is right or best from the point of view of the community or in general (citizen preference). Policy analysis would seem to focus entirely on our consumer desires while excluding our views or opinions as citizens. Otherwise, it would have to admit into its calculations principles, views, and arguments that oppose welfare maximization as the target of public policy and disagree with the idea that environmental and other initiatives should be based on a cost-benefit test.

Policy analysts may respond to this criticism by distinguishing between two kinds of social goals or values—distributional equity and allocative efficiency.[11] Policy analysis, on this account, primarily concerns economic or allocative *efficiency*, which is to say, the extent to which the benefits of a policy exceed the costs for society as a whole.[12] While seeking to make the social "pie" as big as possible, policy analysis may leave distributional or *equity* goals, that is, how the pie is divided, to the political process.[13] One might then concede that insofar as social values comprise equity concerns, they are not central to policy analysis. This is not necessarily a criticism of policy analysis; it only recognizes a division of labor between economic expertise and political judgment.[14]

The political process and the deliberative discourse essential to it, however, are not limited to equity issues. Rather, many policies—including those that affect the environment—must be considered in relation to values, principles, and moral commitments that have little if anything to do with either equity or with efficiency as economists understand those terms. The protection of ancient forests or endangered species, for example, rests on moral and spiritual considerations that may have nothing to do with maximizing human welfare or distributing goods equitably. Likewise, social policies concerning the death penalty or abortion arise from principles about privacy, the sacredness of life, and the appropriateness of retributive (rather than distributive) justice. The supposition that public policy must be justified in terms either of equity or efficiency, although commonplace among economists, is a strange view indeed.

TWO CONCEPTIONS OF COLLECTIVE CHOICE

In a recent book, James G. March, who teaches decision making and management at Stanford University, presents a basic distinction between two conceptions of rational collective choice. He distinguishes between economic (preference based) and ethical (principle based) decision making. When decision makers adopt the first or economic approach to collective choice—the model associated with formal policy analysis—they choose among alternatives by evaluating their consequences in relation to the prior preferences of individuals. This approach seeks to maximize the well-being of society as a whole by satisfying the preferences of its individual members, based on the assumption that individuals always prefer what they believe will benefit them.

When decision makers take a principled approach, March writes, they "pursue a logic of appropriateness, fulfilling identities or roles by recognizing situations and following rules that match appropriate behavior to the situations they encounter."[15] Individuals typically do not ask, What outcome will most benefit me as an individual? but, What do I believe is appropriate for society as a whole, given our shared principles, beliefs, and commitments? As we determine who we are as a community and, accordingly, the appropriate rules by which we are to regulate economic activity, the duties of deliberation take precedence over the algorithms of aggregation. "The reasoning process," March writes, "is one of establishing identities and matching rules to recognized situations."[16]

March notes that many academic economists and other policy analysts emphasize the first conception of social choice in which, ideally, the self-regarding preferences of individuals, determined independently, can be aggregated by a mathematical algorithm into a collective outcome. This algorithm is the social welfare function economist Kenneth Arrow and many others have brilliantly analyzed. March argues that in spite of the academic interest in such an algorithm, people typically make decisions, both individually and collectively, through the second or principle-based approach. In pursuing the logic of appropriateness, they ask themselves, implicitly or explicitly, such questions as, What kind of situation is this? What kind of person am I? What sort of an organization, community, and so on, are we? The crucial follow-up question has to do with determining *rules:* What principle should a person such as I, or a community or nation such as ours, act upon in a situation such as this?

It is easy to think of examples of policy questions which require decisions based on deliberation about moral principles rather than aggregation of personal wants. Consider, for example, such controversial questions as whether society should permit abortions or execute people for capital crimes. Does life begin at conception? Is abortion murder? Is the death penalty a form of justice or just another murder? Citizens have opinions about these matters. These opinions express principles they consider to be objectively right and therefore binding on society as a whole. In a democracy, the institutions of government are constantly seized by moral issues and perplexities of this sort. For example, when the Supreme Court found that abortion under typical circumstances falls within a woman's protected zone of privacy, it determined on moral and philosophical grounds the social values we respect. Those who disagree as a matter of principle must then try to initiate the process of amending the Constitution. Policy analysis—insofar as it pursues preference satisfaction, utility, and economic efficiency—appears to have little to contribute to the abortion question or to the discussion of any other principled social value or decision.

Each of the two conceptions of rational decision making that March mentions provides a framework for rational choice—one by emphasizing consequences for preferences, the other by appealing to rules appropriate to the identity of the decision maker in the given situation. The first approach asks the *economic* question: What will maximize the satisfaction of the preferences of the individual members of society over the long run? The second approach asks the *political* and *ethical* question: What do we stand for as a society? Which rules should we follow with respect to problems such as abortion, the death penalty, immigration, welfare reform, pollution, the extinction of species, or wilderness preservation, given our history, culture, and sense of shared identity as a nation?

The first conception of rational collective choice, policy analysis as typified by cost-benefit analysis, provides a fairly precise formula by which society can infer from the preferences of individuals a social or collective choice. The basic idea, of course, is to imagine the outcome individuals would themselves reach by trading in a perfectly competitive market. If markets fail to exist for certain public goods—unowned environmental resources are often cited as examples—then the government should allocate those resources as a market would have allocated them if they could be traded as private property. In that way, these resources will belong to those willing to pay the most for their use and, therefore, to those who will derive the most value from them. Society would then achieve the goal this theory prescribes, namely, to maximize the satisfaction of the preferences ranked by willingness to pay.

The second approach emphasizes the role of democratic processes and institutions, as constitutionally prescribed and constrained, in determining societal goals and purposes. This deontological view does not lay down the goals of society in advance of political deliberation and choice. It does not presuppose that the point of environmental or any other social policy is to maximize the satisfaction of preferences, taken as they come, bounded by indifference and ranked by willingness to pay. On the contrary, this approach assumes that people will possess not only conflicting preferences but also contradictory views or opinions about public policy. Some of us may agree with the goal presupposed by policy analysis: social policy should maximize welfare defined in terms of preference and willingness to pay. Many of us, however, may support quite different views about the principles to which policy should respond and the goals on which it should be based.

Pollution Control

Pollution control provides a clear example of the opposition between utilitarian and rule-based or deontological conceptions of collective choice. A utilitarian approach regards pollution primarily as an external or social cost of production and therefore may seek to internalize this cost in prices paid for goods and services that pollute. A principle-based perspective, in contrast, regards pollution as a form of coercion, invasion, or trespass to be regulated as a violation of the rights of person and property. From this perspective, pollution constitutes a tort or nuisance—like a punch in the nose. On this view, pollution control protects the rights of individuals against trespass, which is not the same thing as—and it may conflict with—satisfying consumer desires or preferences.

If society adopted a utilitarian approach, it would bring pollution up or down to optimal levels, that is, levels at which the benefits of controlling pollution further do not equal the costs.[17] The opposing principle-based framework, in contrast, minimizes pollution until the cost of further reductions become prohibitive. In other words, when it adopts the deontological approach, society regards pollution as a kind of crime. It may have to tolerate some pollution, as it must any form of crime, since the world is imperfect. (To prevent all theft, for example, society might have to invest too much in hiring police; this does not show that theft is just a cost of business, however, rather than a crime.) Society is morally correct to push polluters always to do more to control their effluents, since zero pollution is morally appropriate, even if it is an unreachable ideal.

A great normative and conceptual divide separates utilitarians who regard pollution as a diseconomy or social cost of production and deontologists (including libertarians) who see it as a kind of trespass or invasion of personal and property rights. To understand the difference, one might consider the case of *Boomer v. Atlantic Cement Company*, which played in the New York State courts as Congress worked on the Clean Air Act. There, plaintiff Boomer, a farmer, sought to enjoin Atlantic, a major manufacturer, from spewing dust and fumes on his land. New York State is a jurisdiction that usually grants injunctions in nuisance cases. In this instance, however, the trial court awarded Boomer compensatory damages instead, since Atlantic, an immense plant supporting the local economy, would have to cease operations to cease polluting. Thus, the court effectively gave the polluter the power of eminent domain—the power to coerce the plaintiff off his land at a price set not by the plaintiff but by the court.

What the court did was efficient from an economic point of view: it allocated resources according to market-based prices. This approach establishes economically "optimal" levels of pollution—levels at which those who benefit from polluting activities could still benefit even after compensating their victims for whatever damage they suffer. These "optimal" levels, however, can be understood only in terms of a hypothetical market where people will always sell property rights to the highest bidder—not in terms of an actual market where people like Boomer just want to be left alone. By denying Boomer injunctive relief, the court departed from the common law protection of property rights and instead gave the polluter effectively the right of eminent domain to coerce its neighbors off their land at a price set by appraisers and not by the neighbors themselves.

Many commentators believe that in enacting the Clean Air Act, Congress in part reacted against the outcome of *Boomer* to insist that the nation regard pollution not as an external cost of production but as an enjoinable nuisance or tort. The Clean Air Act, in setting air quality standard at no-risk levels, treated persons as ends-in-themselves rather than as means in the overall maximization of social wealth. In this legislation, Congress plainly sided with those who see pollution as a trespass to be enjoined. Congress rejected the idea that it is a cost of production to be internalized or reflected in the prices polluters must charge for the goods they produce.

Both common and public law in the United States adopt a deontological approach to pollution. Our environmental law firmly rejects the economic analysis of pollution, that is, the idea that it should be treated as a third-party or external cost of production. Instead, our law and the social values it makes explicit declare pollution to be a kind of assault, trespass, or tort that society will in principle not tolerate and therefore seeks to minimize to the extent technology allows. For this reason, as economists Maureen Cropper and Wallace Oates observe, "the cornerstones of environmental policy in the United States," such as the Clean Air and Clean Water Acts, "*explicitly* prohibited the weighing of benefits against costs in the setting of environmental standards."[18] On the one hand, our legal and moral tradition tells us to minimize pollution as a tort; on the other, social science tells us to optimize it as an externality. Public law stands on a thousand years of common law wisdom and experience—rather than on a recent academic theory about economic efficiency, social welfare, and rational choice.

Endangered Species Act

The Endangered Species Act requires all agencies of the federal government to "insure that actions authorized, funded, or carried out by them do not jeopardize the continued existence" of endangered species.[19] In interpreting this statute in the landmark case of *Hill v. TVA*, which had to do with the snail darter and the Tellico Dam, the Sixth Circuit Court of Appeals concluded that the law expresses a moral principle and, therefore, is not subject to a cost-benefit test. "The welfare of an endangered species," the Court said, "may weigh more heavily upon the public conscience, as expressed by the final will of Congress, than the write-off of those millions of dollars already expended for Tellico."[20] In affirming this lower court finding, the Supreme Court noted that the statute explicitly prohibited a cost-benefit test. "One would be hard pressed to find a statutory whose terms were any plainer than those . . . of the Endangered Species Act," Chief Justice Warren Burger wrote for the Court. "The language admits of no exception."[21]

More than 80 percent of Americans on a recent survey agreed with the statement "Because God created the natural world, it is wrong to abuse it." As the anthropologists who conducted the survey concluded, "It seems that divine creation is the closest concept American culture provides to express the sacredness of nature."[22] By huge majorities, Americans say they believe that animals such as wolves and whales possess a dignity that makes a legitimate claim to our respect and concern. As philosopher Ronald Dworkin points out, most of us attribute intrinsic value to other species. "We think we should admire and protect them because they are important in themselves, and not because we or others want or enjoy them."[23]

What is particularly interesting about the commitment Americans make to protecting species is that it flows from a moral principle rather than a conception of self-interest. The recently issued *Global Biodiversity Assessment* acknowledges that concern for the continued existence of threatened species "is almost entirely driven by ethical considerations precisely because it is disinterested value."[24] This kind of concern involves "a moral 'commitment' which is not in any way all self-interested."[25] The *Assessment* adds: "Commitment can be defined in terms of a person choosing an act that he believes will yield a lower level of personal welfare to him than an alternative that is also available to him." The individual does not want less welfare per se, but "adherence to one's moral commitments will be as important as personal welfare maximization and may conflict with it."[26]

In other words, people may want to protect species because it is the right thing to do not because of any benefit they expect to gain themselves. The welfare or well-being of the individual is not the principal concern; in fact, the individual is willing to sacrifice personal welfare (for example, by writing a check to the Nature Conservancy) in order to comply with a moral principle. Some economists believe that no one who is rational can ever act on any other principle than self interest, that is, to advance his or her own well-being. For example, the economist Alan Randall has written, "What the individual wants is [in his estimation] good for the individual."[27] From this point of view, it is either impossible or irrational for any individual to seek any good other than his or her own. If individuals are assumed to have no moral interests other than their own well-being, then the goal of society, indeed, might be simply to maximize the well-being of its members.

Of course, people act upon and care about all sorts of values and principles other than their own welfare. People assert and debate values and principles that reflect their views of what the nation should do, not necessarily what they believe will benefit them. Policy analysts take one position about environmental policy—resources should be allocated to maximize welfare—but other citizens assert views incompatible with that principle. They say we should protect nature because of its intrinsic qualities, because God made it, or as a heritage for future generations. These conflicting principled positions constitute the substance of political debate. It is simply not the case that policy analysts alone know the right principle while all others report only on their own welfare. Everyone has something principled to say about our the nature of our national purposes and common good.

INFORMAL POLICY ANALYSIS

So far, this chapter has followed Stokey, Zeckhauser, and many other economists in identifying policy analysis with cost-benefit analysis. For many practitioners, however, policy analysis is not the same as cost-benefit analysis. The essential difference is this: Cost-benefit analysis asserts that the appropriate goal for environmental and other social policies is welfare maximization. This approach to policy analysis assumes at the start that the fundamental purpose of the nation is to maximize the satisfaction of the given preferences of individuals, whatever they are, ranked by willingness to pay. It is doubtful that anyone outside the economics profession agrees with this assumption; indeed, even within the profession, it may represent a minority view. Accordingly, we might look beyond the standard works such as the Stokey-Zeckhauser *Primer* to understand the current state of policy analysis.

Many practitioners of policy analysis describe it as the art of finding the best means to achieve *given* ends, usually those determined independently by the political process. Giandomenico Majone characterizes this view as follows: "The analyst's job is only to determine the best means to given goals."[28] David Weimer and Aidan Vining define policy analysis as "client-oriented advice relative to public decisions and informed by social values."[29] After surveying policy analysts to find out what they thought they did, two scholars have characterize the profession as comprising "people who transform, data, information, and other analytic inputs into policy advice (or enlightening information) relative to a particular decision for a particular client."[30]

Although the term "policy analysis" covers a multitude of practices, they seem usually to be client-centered, where the client is not the individual consumer, but a group responsible for or seeking to influence public policy. A political authority, such as a regulatory agency, typically commissions policy analyses as a way either to solicit advice or to justify a particular decision. Sometimes, different clients have competing interests or goals. For example, the Corps of Engineers might want to justify one resolution of a wetland dispute, the Environmental Protection Agency another. Policy analysts are bound ethically to advance and defend their client's goals and interests rather than their own. "Analysts are often asked to evaluate or compare proposals specified by clients," Duncan MacRae, Jr. has written. "Selection of alternatives of this sort need not involve research expertise; it can be based on a rough preliminary judgment of the expected effects of alternatives, their political feasibility, and their relevance to a client's public arguments."[31]

If policy analysis takes goals or values to be given, where do they come from? For the most part, from the client, who has a policy goal or agenda. Health policy presents many examples. The health insurance industry, the American Association of Retired Persons, the American Medical Association, the hospital industry, as well as government agencies all hire policy analysts. These analysts are supposed to help their clients understand their stake in the outcome of the political process and to represent or formulate a special interest in ways most consistent with the goals or the good of society as a whole.

These policy analysts confront the task of determining, for example, how society can both provide health services to the aging and to the poor and yet keep within some budget constraint. Policy analysts who tackle this issue do not question the societal goal to provide health care or health insurance. They seek to recommend how society can provide the most health care at the least cost, for example, by keeping the program within a stated budget, such as the amount society now spends on Medicare and Medicaid. At the same time, analysts may try to formulate policy solutions in ways that serve their clients—by recommending outcomes that deliver benefits to their clients or shield them from costs.

Policy analysis as an informal craft or art, then, marshals information, evidence, and arguments in favor of a particular policy option (say, a single-payer plan) over others. The arguments can come from anywhere—from consideration of political and technical feasibility, a reckoning of costs in relation to care provided, a concern with public sympathies and values, and so on. Analysts who work for groups lobbying the government (i.e., special interests) try to show how the proposals these groups present are consistent with the public interest. (Motto: "What's good for my client is good for the country.") The argument has to be framed in terms of public or social principles and values, not in terms of special interests. Accordingly, social values matter very much to this informal kind of policy analysis.

Policy analysts who work for government agencies may try to present an agency's preferred options in the most favorable light, for example, by showing how they follow or serve larger social goals, values, or commitments. Analysts, in general, examine the relative merits of competing options to solving a particular policy problem. They may assess how well various alternatives fit with a client's general position and may even try to educate the client to change or modify that position. In all cases, however, they address the public interest as a whole. Public policy is argued and justified in terms of the public interest and not, at least ostensibly, in terms of private or special interests.

This characterization of policy analysis as a kind of sophisticated and empirically informed political discourse, according to one practitioner, "promises to make policy research more intellectual, value conscious, and debate centered."[32] The point of this discourse, like that of political debate in general, is to arrive at a position that is broadly acceptable to the client and the broader society. Policy analysis seeks to build a political consensus with respect to a particular issue on the basis of empirical information, historical examples, conceptual clarity, and appeals to shared values. Policy analysis as a form or argumentation, then, does not differ in its virtues or purposes from political deliberation.

It is fair to characterize policy analysis, then, as an objective inquiry into the best policy options among given alternatives in the context of a particular body of evidence, experience, and normative commitment. Objectivity in this kind of discourse, as in any other, consists in intersubjective agreement or consensus attained through adherence to certain virtues of inquiry, such as intellectual honesty, openness to criticism, attentiveness to evidence, conceptual clarity, and so on. Intersubjective agreement or consensus based on these virtues of inquiry seems to be all that we can mean by "objectivity" wherever it is found. An open-minded inquiry based on intellectual virtues, in other words, is the only path we know this side of religious revelation to establish the correctness of any belief. Policy analysts may play a leading role in this kind of political but still objective inquiry into our shared purposes and social values.

Policy analysis as kind of informal discourse engages in political argument or persuasion that feeds off of and influences social values. Many policy analysts celebrate this "activist" role. One commentator has said that "[a]nalysts are not neutral observers, but participants, whose theory and methods help them view the context more systematically. The purpose is to share insights among participants rather than definitively predict behavior or arrive at general truths."[33] One might say that policy analysts are professional citizens: they get paid to engage in public life. This is a much more interesting and more productive endeavor than the narrower practice of formal cost-benefit analysis.

POSTSCRIPT: TWO CONCEPTIONS OF DEMOCRACY

The distinction between formal and informal policy analysis—one rooted in the theory of welfare economics, the other open to broader political discourse—may be traced to two conceptions of democracy which, in the last several decades, have opposed each other. One is reductionist: it supposes that the values of society as a whole can be derived mathematically or mechanically from the preferences of its individual members. In this approach, the appropriate function of government is to aggregate these preferences—a task for which voting is a familiar if somewhat clumsy mechanism. The opposing position contends that a conception of the common will or public good arises from the deliberative process in which citizens in principle have an equal voice. What is central to this conception of democracy is not the act of voting so much as the deliberative process that leads up to it in which citizens construct and refine their judgment about the common will through a processes of intellectual exchange with each other.

In the 1950s and 1960s, political scientists and theorists generally adhered to the first conception of democracy—a pluralist or strategic model of political choice based on conceptions of the individual found in welfare economics.[34] According to this approach, everyone is an egoistic, rational, utility maximizer and possesses preference orderings which, if rational, conform to certain well-known formal conditions.[35] As Thomas Dietz has written, under this rational actor model, "people try to maximize the benefits they receive relative to the costs they bear. That is, all actors are using the same rule in deciding what action to take—self-interested utility maximization."[36]

At its simplest, the strategic conception models collective choice on the idea of a social welfare function of the kind famously discussed by Kenneth Arrow.[37] In this conception, "individuals are supposed to begin with their diverse ends, desires, goals, or projects, and then to promote them as effectively as possible."[38] Democracy becomes a special case of instrumental rationality.[39] Many theorists of this school recognized, of course, that a rational person will form his or her own choices in the light of those that others are likely to make, so that this approach to political theory can emphasize cooperation, not just competition. John Harsanyi, for example, has argued that social morality arises in this context as a result of rational, utility-maximizing behavior.[40] In strategic or pluralistic conceptions of democracy, deliberation, consultation, cooperation, learning, and morality all may figure prominently. These virtues matter, however, insofar as they help individuals to determine their own best interests and society to serve those interests as fully as resources and technology allow.

Since the 1980s, many political theorists have moved away from the strategic model toward an ideal of democracy as a deliberative and cooperative enterprise.[41] This emphasis on deliberative, discursive, and collegial processes of collective choice draws inspiration and support from many sources, including communications theories associated with the Frankfurt School of sociology.[42] A second source is found in the civic republican literature centering in American law schools.[43] A third tradition emphasizes civic engagement in participatory democracy[44] and civic virtue.[45] These positions agree in rejecting the view that political processes fundamentally aggregate prior preferences.

In the models of civic republicanism or participatory democracy that oppose strategic or pluralistic approaches, citizens engage in deliberation not so that each can determine or refine his or her own interests, but so that together they can discover a good that is not simply a function of their individual utilities. Theorists who claim James Madison as the American founder of this tradition cite his defense of a representational system as necessary to "refine and enlarge the public views by passing them through the medium of a chosen body of citizens, whose wisdom may discern the true interest of their country."[46] Invoking this tradition, Cass Sunstein writes that the goal of a constitutional democracy "is to ensure discussion and debate . . . in a process through which reflection will encourage the emergence of general truths."[47]

Current research in the theory of democracy suggests that in voting, citizens and their representatives may perform a cognitive rather than an arithmetic task. Instead of simply aggregating their individual interests, they vote on a common view of their collective interest. In other words, the policy chosen is the one that a majority believes expresses the will of the community as a whole. Those who vote against a resolution are still bound by it, because they recognize the fairness, legitimacy, and inclusiveness of the process by which it was chosen. (If a discrete or insular minority is excluded from the political process, they would not be bound morally to respect its results.) This accounts for the obligation citizens feel to obey even those statutes they oppose.

In this essay, we have discussed two conceptions of policy analysis. The first, which rests on the theory of welfare economics, may be described as a kind of thoroughgoing cost-benefit analysis. Texts in the field of policy analysis, such as Stokey and Zeckhauser's *Primer*, advocate this approach. This conception of policy analysis has the advantage of being scientific insofar as it proceeds by an essentially mathematical algorithm from data—the given preferences of individuals—to a policy outcome. This model of policy analysis adheres to the pluralist or strategic view of democracy as an arrangement by which self-interested utility maximizers compete and cooperate to satisfy their preestablished preferences.

The second form of policy analysis, one more likely to be practiced than theorized about, presents itself more as an art than as a science. It draws on the republican or Madisonian conception of democracy in which citizens through deliberation precipitate a conception of the public interest or common will not necessarily derived from their preexisting interests or preferences. From this perspective, democracy functions as an educative process in which people may persuade each other and freely change their minds. Policy analysis then serves an educative role, informing rather than replacing the processes of deliberation.

Which kind of policy analysis is most likely to succeed? This may not be a question policy analysts will themselves answer. The answer may follow, instead, from a larger choice between two contending conceptions of democracy. If we accept the older, more established strategic conception of democracy, we may see that formal policy analysis provides a scientific methodology for deriving policy choices from a single social value, that is, social welfare, conceived as the satisfaction of the preferences of individuals as ranked by willingness to pay. The function of elections, legislation, courts, and the rest would be secondary, since economic science could for the most part determine public policy. On the second conception of democracy, which sees policies as arising from deliberation rather than aggregation, the second or more informal kind of policy analysis, which describes itself as an art rather than as a science, seems more appropriate. It may inform political decision making without seeking to replace it.

ACKNOWLEDGMENT

The author acknowledges with gratitude the generous support for this research from the National Science Foundation, Grant No. SBR–9613495.

NOTES

1. It is not clear that social welfare is a social value. Happiness or well-being in a substantive sense may count as a social value, since one might argue that a good society is one in which people are happier or more content. As is often pointed out, however, the satisfaction of consumer preferences on a willingness-to-pay basis bears no relation at all with happiness or contentment; social science research is unambiguous on this point. In other words, wealth does not correlate with happiness after basic needs are met. For discussion, see Kahneman, Daniel and Carol Varey, "Notes on the Psychology of Utility," in *Interpersonal Comparisons of Well-Being*, ed. Jon Elster and John Roemer (New York: Cambridge University Press, 1991), 127–163. It is important to recognize that formal policy analysis does not concern happiness or well-being in any sense which ordinary language embraces and which might therefore count as a social value. Instead, it is a technical concept of economic theory defined in terms of maximized willingness to pay. As Richard Posner points out, the "most important thing to bear in mind about the concept of value [in the welfare economist's sense] is that it is based on what people

are willing to pay for something rather than the happiness they would derive from having it." Posner, Richard, *The Economics of Justice* (Cambridge: Harvard University Press, 1981), 60.

2. Alan Randall, "What Mainstream Economists Have to Say About the Value of Biodiversity," in *Biodiversity*, ed. E. O. Wilson (Washington, DC: National Academy Press, 1988), 217–223; quotation at 217.

3. Edith Stokey and Richard Zeckhauser, *A Primer for Policy Analysis* (New York: Norton, 1978), 257.

4. Ibid., 263.

5. Paul A. Samuelson, *Foundations of Economic Analysis* (Cambridge: Harvard University Press, 1953), 223; James Quirk and Rubin Saponsik, *Introduction to General Equilibrium Theory and Welfare Economics* (New York: McGraw Hill, 1968), 104.

6. Alan Randall, *Resource Economics: An Economic Approach to Natural Resource and Environmental Policy* (Columbus, OH: Grid Publishing, 1981), 156.

7. A. Myrick Freeman III, *The Measurement of Environmental and Resource Values: Theory and Methods* (Washington, DC: Resources for the Future), 7.

8. David Pearce, "Environmental and Economic Values," in *Towards an Ecologically Sustainable Society*, ed. Britt Aniasson and Uno Svedlin (Stockholm: Swedish Council for Research [FRN], 1990).

9. David Brookshire, Larry Eubanks, and Cindy Sorg, "Existence Values and Normative Economics: Implications for Valuing Water Resources," *Water Resources Research* 22, no. 11 (October 1986): 1509–1518; quotation at 1514.

10. Michael D. Bowes and John V. Krutilla, *Multiple-Use Management: The Economics of Public Forestlands* (Washington, DC: Resources for the Future, 1989), 32.

11. "Allocation programs include measures to affect relative prices and/or the allocation of resources in an economy, motivated by considerations of allocative efficiency. Distribution programs consist of efforts to alter the distribution of incomes in society, motivated by considerations of distributive equity." Edward M. Gramlich, *Benefit-Cost Analysis of Government Programs* (Englewood Cliffs, NJ: Prentice-Hall, 1981), 13.

12. For a sound argument to this effect, see Thomas C. Schelling, "Economic Reasoning and the Ethics of Policy," *Public Interest* 63(1981): 37.

13. Environmental economists Joseph Seneca and Michael Taussig define efficiency as the "maximum consumption of goods and services given the available amount of resources." They characterize equity as "a just distribution of total goods and services among all consumer units." Joseph Seneca and Michael Taussig, *Environmental Economics*, 2d ed. (Englewood Cliffs, NJ: Prentice-Hall, 1979), 6.

14. Since individuals hold preferences about distributional equity as well as preferences about their own consumption opportunities, however, it is hard to understand the principle on which distributional or equity preferences are ruled out of policy analysis and delegated to the political process. Why would the political process be best suited to consider equity preferences, while cost-benefit analysis deals with all other kinds of preferences? It would seem that individuals are as capable of including equity preferences as they are all other kinds of values into their preference orderings. Accordingly, equity preferences should be included, like any consumer preference, in the social welfare calculus. For a persuasive argument to this effect, see Burton Weisbrod, "Income Redistribution Effects and Cost-Benefit Analysis," in *Problems in Public Expenditure Analysis*, ed. Samuel B. Chase (Washington, DC: Brookings Institution, 1968), 177–222.

15. James G. March, *A Primer in Decision Making* (New York: The Free Press, 1994), 58.

16. Ibid.

17. For discussion, see Larry R. Ruff, "The Economic Common Sense of Pollution," in *Microeconomics: Selected Readings*, 2nd ed., ed. Edwin Mansfield (New York: Norton, 1995), 498–514.

18. Maureen L. Cropper and Wallace E. Oates. "Environmental Economics: A Survey," *Journal of Economic Literature* 30(1992): 675–740.

19. 16 U.S.C. Sec. 1936, 1976.

20. *Hill v. TVA*, 549 F.2d 1964, 1074 (6th Cir. 1976), *aff'd*, 437 U.S. 153 (1978).

21. *TVA v. Hill*, 437 U.S. 153, 173 (1978).

22. Willett Kempton, James Boster, and Jennifer Hartley, *Environmental Values in American Culture* (Cambridge: MIT Press, 1995), 92.

23. Ronald Dworkin, *Life's Dominion* (New York: Vintage, 1994), 71–72. The chapter "What is Sacred?" provides the best introduction I know to the concept of intrinsic value.

24. Charles Perrings, coordinator, "Economic Values of Biodiversity." in *Global Biodiversity Assessment*, ed. V. H. Heywood (Cambridge: Cambridge University Press, 1995), 823–914, quotation at 830.

25. Ibid., 836, citing Amartya Sen, "Rational Fools: A Critique of the Behavioral Foundations of Economic Theory," *Philosophy and Public Affairs* 6, no. 4 (1977): 327–344.

26. Ibid., 836.

27. Alan Randall and George Peterson, "The Valuation of Wildland Resource Benefits: An Overview," in *The Valuation of Wildland Resource Benefits*, ed. Alan Randall and George R. Peterson (Boulder, CO: Westview Press, 1984), 6.

28. Giandomenico Majone, *Evidence, Argument, and Persuasion in the Policy Process* (New Haven: Yale University Press, 1989), 21.

29. David Weimar and Aidan Vining, *Policy Analysis: Concepts and Practice* (Englewood Cliffs, NJ: Prentice-Hall, 1992), 4.

30. Dan Durning and Will Osuna, "Policy Analysts' Roles and Value Orientations: An Empirical Investigation Using Q Methodology," *Journal of Policy Analysis and Management* 13, no. 4 (1994): 629–657, quotation at 629.

31. Duncan MacRae, Jr., "Policy Advice and Political Science," in *Advances in Policy Studies Since 1950*, ed. William N. Dunn and Rita Mae Kelly (New Brunswick, NJ: Transaction, 1992), 125–156, quotation at 131.

32. T. D. Cook, "Postpositivist Cultural Multiplism," in *Social Science and Social Policy*, ed. R. Shotland and M. Mark (Beverly Hills, CA: Sage, 1985), 21–61, quotation at 46.

33. Louise G. White, "Policy Analysis as Discourse," *Journal of Policy Analysis and Management* 13, no. 3 (1994): 506–525, quotation at 510.

34. See, for example, D. Black, *The Theory of Elections and Committees* (Cambridge: Cambridge University Press, 1958); James M. Buchanan and Gordon Tullock, *The Calculus of Consent, Logical Foundations of Constitutional Democracy* (Ann Arbor: University of Michigan Press, 1962); Robert Dahl, *A Preface to Democratic Theory* (Chicago, IL: University of Chicago Press, 1956); A. Downs, *An Economic Theory of Democracy* (New York: Harper and Row, 1956).

35. For a mathematically clear presentation of these conditions, see Amartya Sen, *Collective Choice and Social Welfare* (San Francisco: Holden-Day, 1970).

36. Thomas Dietz, " 'What Should We Do?' Human Ecology and Collective Decision Making" *Human Ecology Review* 1, no. 2 (1994): 301–309, quotation at 303.

37. Kenneth Arrow, *Social Choice and Individual Values* (New York: John Wiley, 1951)

38. Estlund, "Who's Afraid of Deliberative Democracy," *Texas Law Review* 71(1993): 437–1477, quotation at 1437.

39. See Brian Barry and Russell Hardin, eds., *Rational Man and Irrational Society?* (Beverly Hills, CA: Sage Publications, 1982).

40. See John Harsanyi, "Morality and the Theory of Rational Behavior," in *Utilitarianism and Beyond*, ed. A. Sen and B. Williams (Cambridge, England: Cambridge University Press, 1982).

41. See Cass Sunstein, "Beyond the Republican Revival," *Yale Law Journal* 97 (1988): 1539–1576; and Jon Elster, "The Market and the Forum: Three Varieties of Political Theory," in *Foundations of Social Choice Theory*, ed. John Elster and Aanund Hylland (New York: Cambridge University Press, 1986), 111–112.

42. Jürgen Habermas, *Justification and Application: Remarks on Discourse Ethics*, trans. Ciaran Cronin (Cambridge, MA: MIT Press, 1993).

43. See, for example, Frank Michelman, "Conceptions of Democracy in American Constitutional Argument: The Case of Pornography Regulation," *Tennessee Law Review* 56 (1989) especially 293–294; see also Cass Sunstein, "Earl Warren is Dead," *The New Republic*, May 13, 1996, 35–39.

44. See David Mathews, *Politics for People: Finding a Responsible Public Voice* (Urbana: University of Illinois Press, 1994); and James Fishkin, *The Voice of the People: Public Opinion and Democracy* (New Haven: Yale University Press, 1995).

45. See George Will, *Restoration: Congress, Term Limits and the Recovery of Deliberative Democracy* (New York: Free Press, 1992).

46. James Madison, *The Federalist*, No. 10, p. 62 (New York: New American Library, 1961).

47. Cass Sunstein, *The Partial Constitution* (Cambridge, MA: Harvard University Press, 1993), 253.

8

The Ethics of Cost-Benefit Analysis: Incommensurable, Incompatible, and Incomparable Values

Douglas MacLean

Cost-benefit analysis is a frequently discussed subject, but it seems to appear on the public radar screen, and swords are drawn, whenever an agency or commission proposes a more ambitious use of cost-benefit analysis to aid regulatory decision making, especially in areas involving important values that many people believe cannot be well served by thinking about them in terms of economics. I propose to take up this subject again here, for two reasons. The first is that the level of interest in cost-benefit analysis is currently high. Support for more cost-benefit justifications of regulation was a prominent part of the Republican Party's ingenious Contract with America, which succeeded in bringing them to power in the U.S. Congress in 1994. Regulatory reform proposals are once more under consideration, and most of them include strong cost-benefit requirements. Some of these reforms could introduce deep changes in the way many agencies would be required to think about and justify their rules and policies. A second reason for addressing this subject again is that I now think philosophical discussions of the ethics of cost-benefit analysis have in the past often been misleading or incomplete in important respects, with the result that their implications have not been clearly understood.

DOES COST-BENEFIT ANALYSIS DISTORT VALUES?

There are several ethical issues that surround the use of cost-benefit analysis. Much has been written, for example, about what counts as a cost or a benefit, the importance of how costs and benefits are distributed, how uncertainties are to be dealt with, and the effects of discounting the value of costs and benefits as they occur further into the future, which tends to favor projects that return benefits quickly and defer costs to later. These issues raise important ethical concerns about justice, our obligations to future generations, and other matters, but I do not attempt to address them here. I want to focus on a single and, I believe, somewhat more basic issue.

The issue I want to discuss is whether cost-benefit analysis leads us to distort or misrepresent some important ethical concerns by forcing us to think of all values as commensurable or by comparing them all in terms of costs and benefits. The obvious areas in which this issue is salient are in thinking about policies aimed at reducing risks to life and health, protecting the environment, or preserving cultural or natural treasures. When we apply cost-benefit analysis to evaluate a policy or a proposal in these areas, we are forced to think about our values in terms of the costs of the actions or policies that serve them. This is precisely the point of requiring that proposals be justified by cost-benefit analyses, and this is the reason that these requirements are supported by advocates of regulatory reform. Cost-benefit requirements are supposed to force us to consider what we give up in other areas when we dedicate resources to environmental protection or promoting health and safety.

Some proponents of cost-benefit analysis have claimed that the value of these things simply *is* the cost of actions or policies that flow from such concerns, so that a willingness to pay for such actions is an accurate and complete expression of the values in question. Money happens to be the natural scale on which to measure and compare the costs of the actions that express our values and concerns, and these values are "reduced," in just this way, to monetary terms. The issues of public health and safety, and especially of environmental protection and the preservation of natural and cultural treasures, are constantly increasing in importance, and while few people would insist on eliminating risks or ignoring costs altogether, many people are bothered by the pressures of regulatory reform, under the discipline of cost-benefit analysis, to reduce our deliberation about these important values to a comparison of economic costs and benefits.

PHILOSOPHERS' OBJECTIONS IN THE PAST

This problem, as I have said, is not new, but as many times as it has been raised or expressed, the problem remains curiously difficult to articulate. Some philosophical objections to cost-benefit analysis that appeared in the early 1970s illlustrate this phenomenon. Philosophers at that time associated cost-benefit analysis with the kind of utilitarian moral theories that had dominated discussions in philosophy in England and the United States for nearly a century. Classical utilitarianism, as especially developed by Bentham, Mill, and Sidgwick, was part of a socially progressive movement intended to help guide the progress of industrialization and technological development as well as to unshackle education from religious dogma and prejudice in ways that would lead to the betterment of all mankind. This progress was to be understood simply in terms of a general increase of happiness and a diminishing of suffering. By the early 1970s, a major objection to utilitarianism was emerging, which would come to be associated most strongly with the writings of John Rawls in the United States and Bernard Williams in England. The objection was that utilitarianism ended up devaluing *persons*, both their separateness and their complexity as individuals, by focusing exclusively on *experiences* of happiness and suffering. Cost-benefit analysis was generally seen by philosophers at that time as a way of applying utilitarian norms to public policies, and cost-benefit methods reinforced this general criticism of utilitarianism, both because the methods employed to measure values were often crude, and because analyses were applied in ways that many people felt revealed a lack of moral conscience among public officials and bureaucrats.

The worst example of this was the use of cost-benefit and cost-effectiveness analyses in support of decisions to escalate U.S. military involvement in the Vietnam War. Some philosophers were appalled and they saw a coarseness of moral thinking in public life that they regarded as the product of utilitarianism. Isaiah Berlin, for example, wrote in 1972 about "the calm moral arithmetic of cost effectiveness which liberates decent men from qualms, because they no longer think of the entities to which they apply their scientific computations as actual human beings."[1] And Stuart Hampshire, another eminent philosopher, criticized Secretary of Defense McNamara and his advisors explicitly for employing a "cold, quantitative, calculative Benthamism" to rationalize their decisions about Vietnam.[2] Hampshire complained that "[t]he utilitarian habit of mind has brought with it a new abstract cruelty in politics, a dull, destructive political righteousness: mechanical, quantitative thinking, leaden loveless minds setting out their moral calculations in leaden prose."[3]

This criticism may seem to us today to be not much more than invective aimed at some individuals Hampshire and others found repellent for their conduct in a war that many people believed to be immoral. What remains interesting in Hampshire's reaction, however, is the way he saw the problem, not as an isolated aberration of moral scruples, but as a natural expression of utilitarian thinking. Thus, he explained, "The error of the optimistic utilitarian is that he carries the deritualization of transactions between men to a point at which men not only can, but ought to, use and exploit each other as they use and exploit any other natural objects, as far as this is compatible with human happiness."[4]

The philosophical point was made at that time, in words calmer and more measured, in an introductory ethics textbook written by Bernard Williams.[5] His aim there was to call attention to a general problem in utilitarian theory rather than to any corruption of political thought that utilitarianism had wrought. He begins his criticism with the following observation: "In cases of planning, conservation, welfare, and social decisions of all kinds, a set of values which are, at least notionally, quantified in terms of resources, are confronted by values which are not quantifiable in terms of resources: such as, the value of preserving a quaint part of a town, or of contriving dignity as well as comfort for patients in a geriatric unit."[6] Williams thus begins by claiming that some values cannot be reduced to economic terms. He continues: "Again and again defenders of such values are faced with the dilemma, of either refusing to quantify the value in question, in which case it disappears from the sum altogether, or else of trying to attach some quantity to it, in which case they misrepresent what they are about and also usually lose the argument, since the quantified value is not enough to tip the scale."[7] The problem of applying cost-benefit methods to such issues, it seems, is that by forcing us to quantify certain values, in order that they may be registered at all, we are led to misrepresent them, usually in ways that understate their importance.

Williams's criticism seems perhaps to be different from the complaints of Berlin and Hampshire. He talks about a general distortion or misrepresentation of important values, but Berlin and Hampshire seem particularly concerned with the way in which methods like cost-benefit analysis lead us to ignore the moral centrality of persons and the moral value of other objects that are important in their own right and not just for their role in producing experiences of happiness or suffering. But in the end, I think, these criticisms are basically the same, for each of these philosophers is concerned most generally with how we must distort or misrepresent our values in order to get them all on the same scale of measurement, so that they can be compared. Thus, Hampshire says of the mechanical, quantitative thinking he deplores that "[s]uch calculations are the everyday stuff of political decision, and they seem to require a common measure that enables qualitatively unrelated effects to be held in balance."[8] He doubts whether there is any satisfactory way of making these comparisons, for he says, "Yet it is not clear that the taking of lives can be marked and evaluated on a common scale on which increases of pleasure and diminutions of suffering are also measured. This is the suggested discontinuity which a utilitarian must deny."[9]

For Williams, too, the pressures that lead to misrepresenting some important values come from the need to make them commensurable. With what seems to me a prescience about how some of the subsequent discussions of cost-benefit analysis would go, Williams writes, "In such matters, it is not that utilitarians are committed to thinking that these other values do not matter; nor are they confined to thinking valuable those things which can presently be handled by cost-benefit analysis. They are perhaps not even bound to think that every social value should eventually be handleable by something like cost-benefit analysis: they might say that they were not committed to the view that the common currency of happiness is money. But they are committed to something which in practice has those implications: that there are no ultimately incommensurable values."[10]

HOW DOES THE PROBLEM OF COMMENSURABILITY APPEAR TO COMMON SENSE?

This issue about the ethics of cost-benefit analysis has two aspects. One is the way in which thinking about what is valuable in terms of willingness to pay leads us to distort and misrepresent some of our important values. The other is in the idea that there are no incommensurable values, belief in which apparently drives us to the distortions and misrepresentations of values. These two aspects are closely intertwined, but I mention only in passing how measuring the strength of values in terms of our willingness to pay the costs of actions that express them introduces distortions and misrepresentations. I think there are good reasons to reject the claim that the value of anything is equal to its cost. That view can only be supported by an extreme kind of behaviorism about morality in general, which has little plausibility. It matches neither the intuitions of common sense nor our reflective moral judgments.[11] The things we value could be identical to their monetary costs only if at least two conditions were satisfied. We would have to accept, first, that all valued things are exchangeable in the way that money is exchangeable, and second, that nothing but our own experiences (or money itself, perhaps) can be valued as an end. But we don't believe either of these things. We all know what it is like to treat some things as not for sale, to regard some valued objects as irreplaceable, to be bound by duties of obligation or respect, which condition our moral lives in ways that are independent of their costs, and so on. We may have difficulties explaining and justifying such values, but we must take their existence for granted, I think, in discussions of morality and decision making.

At the same time, it is important to notice that rejecting a crude or extreme behaviorism does not tell us whether or not there are incommensurable values, or how incommensurable values, if they exist, pose a problem for rational decisions aided by analytic methods for structuring our thought. Philosophical discussions of this issue in the past, including the works I have cited, have in my judgment too often begun with the idea that a theory like utilitarianism, or a utilitarian method like cost-benefit analysis, can allow no incommensurable values. Then the discussion goes on quickly to observe how our values get distorted when we force them all onto some particular scale of measurement, usually a monetary scale. I propose here to reverse the order of thought. Let us accept our values, more or less uncritically, as they appear to common sense, and then inquire into how the problem of incommensurability is supposed to arise.

The first thing to notice is that when philosophers talk about incommensurability, that is rarely what they mean. They are nearly always concerned, rather, with the deeper problem of incomparability. They are concerned, that is, that some of our values cannot rationally be ordered at all, even working with the ordinal methods that many economists and decision analysts are content to work with. In some instances, we may need commensurability in order to compare values when, for example, the alternatives are uncertain and we must weight them by probabilities, or when we need to know not only how a set of valued things is ordered but the distances between the objects in the order, so that we may combine packages of benefits and costs in different ways. But for many purposes, a mere ordering will be sufficient. Incomparability, in any case, poses the deeper and more general threat.

THE PROBLEM OF INCOMPARABILITY

Sometimes in our ordinary speech we talk of values as being incommensurable when we do not mean that they are incomparable at all. We might talk of health as being incommensurably more important than wealth, or of love as being incommensurably better than fame, or of liberty as being incommensurably more valuable than efficiency. We might even say, speaking very loosely, that such pairs of values cannot even be compared. Usually, when we speak this way, we are exaggerating. We mean to say that one of the members of the pair is so much more valuable than the other that they cannot be put on a common scale. If we want to be a bit more technical, we might say that such pairs of values are lexically ordered, which means that no amount of the lesser value can compensate for any loss of the former. A lexical ordering is an incommensurable ordering, to be sure, but it is an ordering all the same, a clear and emphatic one. And we probably do not sincerely believe that many, if any, values are ordered in this incommensurable way. We often seem willing, when real decisions are being made, to make some sacrifices in love for a career, to make small concessions to important liberties for significant gains in efficiency, and so on. We probably don't really believe that many such pairs of values are actually incommensurable. In any event, we surely do not believe that these particular values cannot be compared at all. These are among the easiest comparisons we can make.

If we are going to find values that are incommensurable in the deep sense of being incomparable as well, we should not be looking at pairs of values in which one seems immeasurably greater than the other. We should look instead at values of different kinds, where different standards of judgment are employed to rationalize and explain a value, or where we appeal to different forms of reasoning. It is here, if anywhere, that our attempts to compare different values may break down.

One suggestion along these lines, which is particularly apt for the kinds of values that concern us in applying cost-benefit analysis, can be found in the writings of Mark Sagoff.[12] He believes that "[i]ndividuals have a variety of often incompatible preference schedules they reveal in the contexts appropriate to each, for example, in markets, family situations, professional contexts, and political circumstances."[13] It is not clear what Sagoff means in calling our preferences in these different areas incompatible, but his point in referring to different preference schedules is, I think, to call attention to the different kinds of reasoning and evaluation that determine our preferences in each of these areas. His aim is to criticize economic reasoning such as cost-benefit analysis when it is applied in situations other than markets, because it brings the wrong reasoning to bear on ordering these other kinds of preferences. Thus, focusing on measuring preferences by examining our willingness to pay for different things, Sagoff writes, "Willingness to pay. What is wrong with that? The rub is this. Not all of us think of ourselves primarily as consumers. Many of us regard ourselves as citizens as well. As consumers, we act to acquire what we want for ourselves individually; each of us follows his or her conception of *the good life*. As citizens, however, we may deliberate over and then seek to achieve together a conception of *the good society*."[14]

Sagoff does not talk about our different values or preferences being incomparable. He claims instead that we cannot combine them using economic concepts like optimality or efficiency. "If individuals possess conflicting preference-maps," he asks, "how can we say what an efficient policy is?"[15] Now, if he means that we cannot simultaneously be maximizing two objective functions together, then he is talking about a kind of incompatibility, but it is not a problem beyond the reach of economic techniques. He also claims, however, that "[a]ttempts to find a 'combined' or inclusive preference ordering . . . are bound to fail. They will fail for logical, not merely practical, reasons. . . . To try to combine [our different incompatible] preference schedules into one is to search for a single comprehensive role the individual plays; . . . [N]o such social role exists, unless it is the role of a social moron."[16]

Although he does not talk about the incomparability of values, Sagoff's views would seem to commit him to the view that our important values are incomparable. He does seem to think that we distort our values by thinking about them using economic concepts like efficiency. He says that "our public officials discuss the meaning of magnificent environments using a vocabulary that is appropriate to measuring the degree to which consumers may exploit them."[17] I believe Sagoff is right about this, but the harm in thinking in these terms comes in an ordering of preferences that incorrectly reflects our values.

If we could arrange all our preferences on either our consumer preference map or our citizen preference map, for example, and the ordering remained the same, then of course there would be no problem of incomparability. Some values may be misrepresented by being placed in the ordering at all, but it does not seem a particularly harmful misrepresentation if, from every role and preference schedule, the ordering remains the same. So the problem must be that preferences are ordered differently according to different preference schedules, and there is no higher order of preferences to which we can appeal. That would constitute a kind of incomparability of the sort that should worry us. Now, I think there is an important point that Sagoff is making here, which I will return to discuss below. But Sagoff's picture of individuals having different and separate preference maps seems to me an implausible one. As citizens, we do think about the common good, but we are also consumers of government services and taxpayers. We are reasonably concerned with the cost of programs that promote the good we commonly share. We might wonder which programs deserve priority for our limited resources, and we might wonder how important some of the values served by these programs are to each of us, individually, all things considered. Likewise, it is unreasonable to insist that as private individuals and consumers our only concern is for our level of welfare and happiness. We also think, even as consumers, about what things matter to us and give meaning to our lives. We might wonder how, as individuals, we want to balance our commitment of time, attention, and other resources to public activities against our more private or personal aspirations. We can reflect on, criticize, and adjust these different preferences. It seems to me tendentious to refer to this process as taking up a single, comprehensive point of view that only a social moron could adopt. It is more reasonable to think of ourselves as merely reflecting on some different things tat matter to us and finding some larger perspective from which we try to balance our different kinds of concerns in a single life. We cannot be expected to live our lives from the most detached and comprehensive perspective possible for us, but neither is our sanity threatened by our adopting it when needed. Although I think Sagoff's view implies an incomparability of values, I don't find his way of explaining and justifying the incomparability to be adequate.

Consider again the idea that incomparability will involve values of different kinds, where we apply different standards to explain and justify them. The general problem with pursuing this idea is that too many values will be incomparable, and the idea of rational choice will break down almost entirely. Following this line of thought, it might turn out that beer and wine are incomparable in value. We know well enough that people take their preferences for wines and beers quite seriously and that we have well developed standards for assessing the quality of each. But these standards are quite different, and the criteria that apply to one do not in general apply to the other. No one would praise a wine for being thirst quenching or for how the head enhances the taste, and no one would think to evaluate a beer on the basis of its nose or its aging potential. So if comparability means being able to make comparisons using the standards appropriate to the objects being compared, then beer and wine may turn out to be incomparable. But if this is true, then we are in real trouble, for even though we do evaluate them in different ways, we must somehow manage to compare them every time we order a meal at a restaurant or decide what to have with dinner. People generally have little difficulty in doing this, and some people find it only slightly more difficult to form a general preference for one over the other and to offer justifications for that preference. It would thus seem that we need to explore and understand this more reflective realm of judgment in order to determine whether or not some values are incomparable.

INCOMPATIBILITY AND ROUGH EQUALITY

Let us take a different approach. The values that are most easily compared are those in which our choices involve no loss. If I must choose between $100 and $200, or between $100 and $100 plus an orange, the choice is easy, because the second alternative contains everything in the first alternative plus some additional good. The harder choices are those in which we must give up something we like or accept something we do not like. If I have to choose from among thirty-one flavors of ice cream, the choice is made difficult by what I have to forego. This is an example of the common and important phenomenon of *incompatibility* of different values. Some goods exclude others, and for a variety of reasons.

The choice of ice cream flavors is not an agonizing one, because I can enjoy another flavor tomorrow. But with more important decisions, some of our choices permanently close off other attractive options. My choosing to play soccer means I give up the chance to develop my talents in swimming; my choosing to study philosophy means I give up the chance to be a physician; my choosing to marry and have children means I give up other styles of life; and so on. Do we find incommensurable or incomparable values lurking where we must choose among incompatible goods? To answer this question adequately would require a lengthy discussion of some difficult and important issues. I can scarcely do more than mention them here.

The goods that are most difficult to forego are those we find most desirable but will never have, just as the worst losses we can suffer are losses of irreplaceable goods. We might think that these goods involve incommensurable values, because they can never be compensated. Nothing would replace the loss of a spouse or a child, no matter how one's life goes on.[18] These losses are similar in nature to, although they are far more tragic than, the losses that result from the incompatibility of different goods, whether the incompatibility results from our situations, our choices, or our abilities. But in neither case does the irreplaceability of a lost or foregone good imply the incomparability of different values. This is easiest to see when the good is foregone because we have chosen an incompatible good instead. If we have made the choice thoughtfully and deliberately, then we have compared the alternatives and ranked one at least somewhat higher than the other. I think such choices may show clearly that the values are incommensurable, in the sense that we cannot find some measure of them which we can then compare, nevertheless our choice may have followed from a rational process although not a mechanical or algorithmic one, and that should be sufficient to show that the incompatible goods are not incomparable.

A similar conclusion should apply to the loss of someone one loves. Nothing can replace the loss, because the individual cannot be replaced. But that is not to say that we cannot compare the value of a loving relationship to other values.[19] Once again, the values may be incommensurable, and their comparison may not be possible in a mechanical way, but we can sometimes arrive at rough and not unreasonable judgments about the relative importance of, say, love and work. Love will usually come out on top, but sometimes it is sacrificed, and not irrationally, for the sake of a career or a pursuit that is incompatible with it.

The life-determining choices we all face frequently involve incompatible goods, which is only part of the reason that they can be so difficult to make. Further difficulties involve the complexity of the issues involved, and the pervasive ramifications our important choices have in other areas of our lives. Life-determining choices shape our subsequent values and desires, and thus they help to determine the standards that will later be applied to evaluate the choice and to determine whether the choice was a good one or not. Now this fact alone may be sufficient to show us why it is unreasonable to try to measure the alternatives on a single scale in some quantifiable way, but I do not see how this fact alone can show us that the alternatives are not rationally comparable. Our uncertainty about how to proceed to make such comparisons does not justify concluding that they are incomparable. If, after careful and full deliberation, we find that we still cannot say with any confidence that one alternative is preferable to the other, then we have no more reason to say that the alternatives are incomparable than that they are roughly equal. Rough equality is a kind of comparison, even if it is sometimes not a very satisfying one.

In situations like those we have just been considering—life-determining choices with no alternative preferable—I think some people are reluctant to conclude that the alternatives are roughly equal, because they do not feel indifferent about them. But this is a mistake. How can we be indifferent about a choice between incompatible values, or in the face of losing or foregoing an irreplaceable good? If the choice at an ice cream counter can be made difficult by the fact that any flavor I choose means foregoing other flavors, then we should not expect to feel indifferent about the prospect of giving up goods that are far more valuable and important in situations of incompatible choice. Rough equality may mean that I have exhausted the possibility of making a choice on a rational basis, but this does not mean that, if at that point we apply an arbitrary mechanism for making the choice, we are either irrational or indifferent.

PLURALITY OF VALUES, QUALITY OF LIFE, AND GENUINE INCOMPARABILITY

One of the reasons why philosophers have criticized cost-benefit analysis is that it often relies on a willingness-to-pay technique for measuring different values, and this technique reduces all values to a single dimension. If philosophers also tend to associate cost-benefit analysis with utilitarianism, it is in part because of the utilitarian insistence on a monistic conception of value. For the classical utilitarian, at least, there is a single good, and that good is happiness. Anything else has value only as a means for producing happiness or reducing suffering.[20]

Many philosophers, however, believe in a plurality of different values. They believe, for example, that there are different and incommensurable conceptions of the good life. Rawls is one philosopher who accepts this kind of pluralism, and he has offered as an example of different and incommensurable conceptions of a good life a life of gentleness and oneness with nature as compared to a life of competition, risk, and the exploitation of natural resources.[21] These are surely different and worthy conceptions of a good life. And it is hard to imagine how they could be ranked and measured on any single scale. Should we accept that they are incomparable in the deeper sense that we have been examining? These alternative conceptions seem like the kinds of incompatible but comparable values we have been discussing.

But if we think hard enough about such examples, it seems that even the idea of comparing such goods in any reasonable way begins to break down. To see this more easily, it may be better to compare a life familiar to us, such as a life devoted to a family, friends, meaningful work, and some measure of material well-being, to a life that may seem entirely alien to us but not necessarily bad. Perhaps we should compare the conception of a good life familiar to many of us to a monastic and contemplative life, chosen by some members of a very different culture, which renounces most of the goods familiar to us and strives instead for higher consciousness of a kind described in terms well understood in the alien culture but quite hard for us to fathom. Such extreme cases may exhaust our imaginative capacities, and we will have encountered genuinely incomparable alternative conceptions of a valuable life for human beings. We have reached incomparability at last.

In reaching this point, however, we can appreciate some important features about the comparability of values. We should realize, in the first place, that genuine incomparability of the sort that interests philosophers is less easily come by than is usually assumed. We can also say something about what makes different values comparable and when comparability breaks down. When we make life-determining choices, for example, in which there are plural and incompatible goods that we must compare, we are making assessments about the quality of life. "Quality of life," in this sense, is a formal notion. It refers only to the broadest framework available to us from which we can form reasonable preferences for the different goods in question. It is certainly not something that refers to some stuff that can necessarily be increased or diminished by discrete amounts. Nor does it refer to some large-scale super-value or a moronic super-role in which all our different roles and pursuits are combined. It is, rather, what we get when we apply reflection and imagination to our most difficult decisions. For most purposes, it gives us at least enough to work from, so that we may begin to make the necessary evaluations, judgments, and comparisons that will eventually determine a best choice or at least narrow the range of acceptable choices somewhat. Incomparability exists when the alternatives exhaust our imaginative and reflective capacities. It isn't impossible for this to happen, but it is rarer than is usually assumed.

CONFLICTS BETWEEN VALUES AND DUTIES

I have argued so far for the existence of one kind of incomparability of values. We have looked only at how we compare different good things, noticing the plurality of values, the incompatibility of goods that may exist, and the irreplaceability of some good things. I suppose that similar reasoning will apply to the bad things we try to avoid or minimize in life. There are different kinds of evils to confront, to be sure, and our capacities to think rationally about them may be limited in similar ways.

There is one further and different kind of incomparability that it is important to mention. Following the strategy of accepting our common sense values more or less as they appear to us, it is important to point out that most conceptions of common sense morality include not only the pursuit of a good life, but also a set of duties, prohibitions, and required rituals that govern our relationships to each other and to parts of the natural world in areas that have always been central to morality. Rules and prohibitions govern the taking of life, care of the dead, sex and marriage, some aspects of property rights, and family relationships. They vary in strictness, ranging from absolute taboos to matters of etiquette and manners, and they vary between cultures, but they form a universal element of common sense morality.

This area of morality includes many controversial elements, and in the light of some progressive theories like utilitarianism they tend to be criticized or made to be justifiable according to the standards of the theory, but they are undeniably a part of the common sense morality of every culture we know about. If we were confident in the ultimate truth of utilitarianism or of the currently fashionable consequentialist variations of utilitarianism, then perhaps we need not concern ourselves with this area of morality. But there is not yet a philosophical consensus in favor of consequentialism, and the virtues that emerge from common sense morality still retain considerable appeal, to philosophers and nonphilosophers alike.

We know that the combination of this rule-governed area of morality with the part of morality that aims at the good life is a source of many familiar moral conflicts and dilemmas. The pursuit of happiness and the reduction of suffering, for example, can conflict with prohibitions on the taking of life or with the demands of honor. It can often be the case that we have no rational means for resolving these dilemmas except through casuistic reasoning, on a case by case basis. Such conflicts are evidence of a different sort of incomparability. In this case, we do not have different goods that we have no basis for comparing, but instead we have demands from different sources, which we cannot compare because we simply do not know how to bring these different sources of moral life together. We don't know what the formal analog of "quality of life" would be that would allow us to compare these conflicting claims in our thought.

Cost-benefit analysis does not attempt to include or measure these prohibitions, rituals, and virtues, but the objection that cost-benefit methods distort and misrepresent our values may gain support from a concern for this area of morality, for resort to cost-benefit methods may make it more difficult to be sensitive to the role of this area of morality in expressing respect, love, awe, and other moral feelings that are essential to our relations to each other and to nature. This is the criticism, at any rate, that Hampshire has in mind when he accuses utilitarianism of deritualizing the transactions between people to the point that people as well as natural objects are merely resources to exploit.

INCOMPARABILITY AND COST-BENEFIT ANALYSIS

We have now admitted two different kinds of incomparabilities of value, one that occurs rarely and the other less often remarked on but far more common. We should return now to ask how these incomparable values affect cost-benefit analysis. The answer will depend on whether we think that cost-benefit methods necessarily include something like a revealed preference theory of value, as reflected in the idea that our values may fully and faithfully be registered by our willingness to pay for different goods. If we include this kind of value theory as part of cost-benefit analysis, then we seem to commit ourselves to a kind of value monism that allows for full commensurability of values. But we have good reasons to reject this theory of value. I have already explained why insisting that the value of anything is fully captured by its cost or by our willingness-to-pay for it seriously misrepresents many of our important values. The question worth pursuing is whether some kind of method, like cost-benefit analysis but without the willingness-to-pay value theory, can avoid distorting our values by insisting that we make commensurable what are in fact incomparable values. This is how we must frame the discussion if we can ever hope to apply moral reasoning to improve our regulatory and policy decisions.

Does an improved kind of cost-benefit analysis necessarily distort and misrepresent our values because it forces us to compare values that are genuinely incomparable? We have yet to see an argument that it must. Consider first the conflict between rules and prohibitions, on the one hand, and pursuit of the best life, on the other. Cost-benefit analysis is concerned only with the latter. Nothing in the method or in the problems to which it is being applied requires us to deritualize our transactions with each other. Our interest in these methods is only in helping us to make decisions aimed at improving the quality of life. Although it is possible to apply cost-benefit analysis in a coarse manner aimed at replacing decisions based on other sources of moral concern with policies aimed at pursing the good, there is no reason why it must be used in this way. But if we proscribe the use of such methods from those areas of life that we want to remain governed by other norms, we will still be left with all the important policy areas having to do with risks to life and health and environmental protection.

Arguments can be found that decisions in these areas based on cost-benefit analysis allow for risks that we know will result in some number of deaths, and that this is equivalent to killing; or that decisions based on cost-benefit analysis justify some amount of development and exploitation of the environment, which implies that nature is viewed simply as an economic resource. But these are also tendentious ways of describing the tradeoffs that we must inevitably make. If the argument is that any way of trying to think reasonably about making tradeoffs in these areas is equivalent to killing people or treating nature merely as an economic resource, then we must reject the argument, for it is an argument against rationality per se. This kind of argument would prohibit us from deliberately reforming any regulation aimed at reducing risk to health, no matter how costly or inefficient it is, even in order to replace it with a policy that would save more lives more efficiently. The argument would regard such a decision as a choice to kill fewer people who are saved by the inefficient policy but who would not be saved by the more efficient one.

If we consider now the application of cost-benefit methods to order the different values that are relevant to our efforts to improve the quality of life (again, without insisting that the methods must be committed to an unacceptable value theory that reduces all values to a willingness-to-pay metric), we will see that they are not threatened by the incomparability of values. Deciding how to balance our efforts to save lives and improve health, protect the environment, preserve natural and cultural treasures, and pursue the satisfaction of other preferences as well remains a staggeringly difficult task. But all of these difficulties occur within a framework of familiar reflection and imagination. We are attempting, after all, to pursue a very ordinary and familiar conception of a good life and a good society. We are simultaneously consumers and citizens, and in both roles we balance concerns for meaning with an interest in happiness and worries about our limited resources to pursue these ends. Whatever ways we find adequate to reflect upon these problems will be sufficient for developing and applying some kind of analytic method, if it is reasonable and helpful to do so. So there is no worry about incomparable values after all, or at least none that has been brought to light.

CONTINGENT VALUATION

If I have held out hope for a kind of cost-benefit method that does not succumb to the objections of moral philosophers about the incommensurability of values, as I have intended to do, I want nevertheless to guard against drawing the conclusion that we need not be seriously concerned that cost-benefit methods distort and misrepresent our values. This remains an important problem, and I think it is a problem that is not solved by most of the methods of policy analysis with which I am familiar.

One method of cost-benefit analysis relies on economic behavior to provide a measure of costs and benefits. This is cost-benefit analysis combined with revealed preference theory. Some decades ago, this method was defended by economists who were committed to philosophical behaviorism and were thus suspicious that concepts like preference and value had any meaning apart from components in the explanations of the actual behavior of people. This kind of strong behavior has been well criticized and can be dismissed. Accepting this theory forces us to distort our values in serious and obvious ways.

Although the revealed preference theory of values is no longer taken to be the only conception of value that can provide the basic data for cost-benefit analyses, it remains popular, and some analysts still prefer to look only at actual economic behavior to uncover our preferences for the benefits and costs involved in regulatory decisions. There is little reason to think that methods based on this behavior alone will ever adequately measure and express our concerns for important goods like protecting the environment, preserving a cultural treasure, or reducing risks and saving lives.

In recent years (decades, actually), a different method for uncovering and measuring values has become prominent. This technique has come to be called the method of contingent valuation. It is an alternative technique for providing data to an analysis aimed at informing and guiding our decisions. According to this method, people are asked in surveys and in structured experimental settings to express their preferences directly for the different goods and bads that we are able to identify. At its most promising, this kind of technique is something like a mirror of the kind of reflective thinking we attempt when we are weighing something like a life-determining choice. It is potentially an improvement on our individual deliberations, in fact, because there are nearly endless possibilities for refining the structure of this kind of experimentally induced and controlled deliberation.

If we are ever to do very well in making rational comparisons and deliberations about our policy options, it seems to me, this is the kind of approach to discussing and evaluating values that will best enable us to do so. A method similar in its structure to contingent valuation is certainly better than the most popular alternative means of determining our preferences and values, which are either to leave the decisions to the market or to surrogate market behavior, or else to leave them to the whims, caprice, and pettiness of our representative legislators.

Unfortunately, contingent valuation methods usually aim merely at filling the gaps in the economic behavior that provides the data for revealed preference theories. Thus, the surveys usually aim to find out what people are willing to pay for goods for which there is no reliable economic information.

I have already said why I do not find it useful to talk about our having different preference maps that correspond to the different roles we have. But there is a different fact about how our preferences change which is important to understand. The conception of rational choice that underlies most of economics and decision theory insists that a person's preferences are invariant in two respects. First, a preference for different outcomes should be invariant to different descriptions of the prospects, and second, a preference for different outcomes should be invariant to different methods of eliciting the preference. A large body of psychological literature now shows that the preferences of most people are not invariant in either of these ways.[22] Different descriptions of identical prospects can lead to different preference orderings in most people, and different methods of eliciting preferences for the same alternatives can also lead to different preference orderings, these are called preference reversals.

The threat of preference reversals to our understanding of rational choice was perceived some years ago by two economists, David Grether and Charles Plott, who wrote, "The inconsistency is deeper than the mere lack of transitivity. . . . It suggests that no optimization principles of any sort lie behind even the simplest human choices."[23] One possible conclusion from this work is that people are simply deeply and systematically irrational, but this conclusion demands a great deal of confidence in the theory of rational choice that is confounded by empirical evidence.

There is another interpretation of the phenomenon, however, that is supported by our best understanding of what causes these preference reversals. This interpretation is that preferences are not things that exist independently of choice situations, which the decision maker brings to those situations, but rather that preferences tend to be constructed in the decision-making process and so are dependent on numerous contextual features of the process.[24] One finds especially in situations that involve a complex and unfamiliar decision-making task that people are unlikely to hold fixed and stable preferences and are more likely to construct them in the decision-making process. This is especially true in areas of public policy like those involving environmental protection.

The method of contingent valuation presupposes fixed preferences. It posits a hypothetical market and asks people to imagine what they would pay in this market for changes in environmental quality. Asking people what they are willing to pay in these studies is to employ one method of preference elicitation, which is to assign a value to different alternatives. Now what psychologists understand about the causes of preference reversals is that when preferences are constructed in this sort of elicitation procedure, people will give higher ratings to things that are normally associated with price cues and will give lower ratings to things like environmental quality that are not normally associated with price cues.

Suppose, however, that a different method of elicitation was used. Suppose, for example that people are asked to choose directly between some sort of alternative involving higher environmental quality and an alternative with lower environmental quality but a greater bundle of desired consumer goods. In the direct choice method of eliciting preferences in situations where preferences are likely to be constructed, people will assign greater weight to the alternative that is most compatible with what they consider to be good reasons for choice. If environmental quality seems more important than the comparable bundle of consumer goods, then the alternative with higher environmental quality will tend to be preferred more strongly in the choice method than it will in the ranking method used in most contingent valuation studies. This change in preference for environmental quality resulting from different elicitation methods has been tested and confirmed in several experiments.

But if contingent valuation methods that elicit a willingness to pay for some change leads preferences to be constructed in one way, thus misrepresenting our "true" values, then the same can be said for methods of direct choice, that lead to different preferences. The conclusion that is important, however, is not that one or another of these preferences better reflects our real and considered values, but that our preferences and values are partly constructed in these decision-making processes. This is what we would intuitively expect to be the case in the kinds of life-determining choices we considered earlier. The purpose of reflective deliberation is not to discover our preferences but to help us construct them.

The kind of analytic method for helping us make difficult policy choices that we should be aiming for is thus a method that uses something like the structure of contingent valuation methods to help us construct and compare our preferences and values. This is a method of rational deliberation. But because our preferences are partly constructed in the process and thus inextricably context-dependent, we should resist methods of evaluation that aim to reveal pre-existing preferences, as willingness-to-pay methods do. We should instead be trying to develop alternative methods that probe our values and lead us to deliberate about them in ways we find helpful. The most adequate methods will be less determinate than methods based on willingness to pay, which presuppose preferences that exist prior to the process of elicitation and perhaps can be made commensurable on a single scale as well, but they may be more reasonable and thus better candidates for a method of reflective deliberation.

NOTES

1. Isaiah Berlin, *Fathers and Children* (Oxford: Clarendon Press, 1972), 55.

2. Stuart Hampshire, *The New York Review of Books*, 8 October 1970, 4. Cited in James Griffin, "Are There Incommensurable Values?" *Philosophy & Public Affairs* 7 (1977): 29.

3. Stuart Hampshire, "Morality and Pessimism," The Leslie Stephen Lecture, 1972. Reprinted in *Morality and Conflict* (Cambridge, MA: Harvard University Press, 1983), ch. 4, at 85.

4. Ibid., 96–97.

5. Bernard Williams, *Morality: An Introduction to Ethics* (New York: Harper & Row, 1972).

6. Ibid., p. 96.

7. Ibid., p. 95.

8. Hampshire, "Morality and Pessimism," p. 85.

9. Ibid.

10. Williams, *Morality*, 96–97.

11. This view, and its connection to behaviorism, are discussed and criticized in Amartya Sen, "Behaviour and the Concept of Preference," *Economica* 40 (1973): 241–259.

12. See Mark Sagoff, *The Economy of the Earth* (New York: Cambridge University Press, 1988).

13. Ibid., p. 55.

14. Ibid., p. 27; Sagoff's emphasis.

15. Ibid., p. 54.

16. Ibid., p. 55.

17. Ibid., p. 68.

18. This candidate for incommensurability of values is defended by Martha Nussbaum, "Plato on Commensurability and Desire," in *Love's Knowledge* (New York: Oxford University Press, 1990).

19. This point is made by James Griffin in *Well Being* (New York: Oxford University Press, 1986), ch. 5. This is an appropriate point to acknowledge the influence Griffin's writings on this topic have had on my own thinking about them, in the book just cited, as well as in "Are There Incommensurable Values?" *Philosophy & Public Affairs* 7 (1977): 39–59; and "Incommensurability: What's the Problem?" unpublished (1994).

20. Like most things in philosophy, this claim about classical utilitarianism is debatable. It is not obvious, for example, that John Stuart Mill or Henry Sidgwick were monists in this sense.

21. See John Rawls, "Social Utility and the Primary Goods," in *Utilitarianism and Beyond*, ed. A. Sen and B. Williams (Cambridge: Cambridge University Press, 1982).

22. For summaries of this literature, see A. Tversky, P. Slovic, and D. Kahneman, "The Causes of Preference Reversals," *American Economic Review* 80 (1990): 204–217; and A. Tversky and R. Thaler, "Anomalies: Preference Reversals," *Journal of Economic Perspectives* 4 (1990): 201–211.

23. David Grether and Charles Plott, "Economic Theory of Choice and the Preference Reversal Phenomenon," *American Economic Review* 69 (1979): 623–638

24. See the articles cited above in note 18. See also Paul Slovic, "The Construction of Preferences," *The American Psychologist* (1994).

9

Intergenerational Interaction on Resource Allocation

Gene D. Cohen

While the media, with its proclivity to portraying confrontation, alludes to intergenerational conflict, the behavior of individuals, families, and society on the whole has been moving in the opposite direction—toward intergenerational collaboration. This burgeoning phenomenon, referred to by the author as intergenerationalism, a new positivism, has important social policy ramifications (Cohen, 1995). Understanding the nature of intergenerational relationships is particularly important when a society debates policies that will influence resource allocations from an age group perspective.

MORE ACCURATE PICTURES OF INTERGENERATIONAL INTERACTION IN THE UNITED STATES

Beyond jaded journalistic anecdotes of escalating intergenerational tensions, witness the increasingly commonplace appearance in television dramas and sitcoms of older protagonists and three or more generations of interacting family members. So, too, with the cinema, which, apart from entertainment and escapism, often reflects the wishes and cultural ideals of our society. Consider the recent popular box office hit *Roommates,* apparently based on a true story in Pittsburgh. The movie follows the life course—107 years—of the cantankerous older protagonist known as Rocky, wonderfully portrayed by Peter Falk (known as Columbo in an earlier role). At one level, the film insightfully and poignantly portrays the give and take, back and forth, supportive exchanges between different generations within families during critical life-course-influencing transitions. This dynamic unfolds when Rocky, as an older man, widower, baker, and grandfather, takes in his grandson, a little boy who has lost both his parents. Over the next thirty plus years in the drama, several major intergenerational exchanges unfold:

Rocky, as a grandfather in his seventies, takes in his young grandson, over time tactfully influencing the boy's growth of character and career choice to become a physician. With the grandson off to medical school, Rocky lives by himself in the building where he raised his family over the past fifty years. The building is condemned, and Rocky refuses to leave despite orders from the authorities to do so. The crisis intergenerational interaction on resource allocation resolves with the grandson taking in his grandfather (now nearing ninety) as his roommate. The grandson marries, has two children, is working very long hours as a surgical resident, and tragically loses his wife in an auto accident. Rocky, now a great grandfather (nearing 100) once again assumes a major parental surrogate role, living in and playing a key role in helping his grandson the doctor resolve prolonged major grief, and assisting in the raising of the two young children over the next several years. The family has emotionally reintegrated, the grandson and great grandchildren are doing well, and Rocky at 107 is on his death bed receiving tender comfort from his extended family.

Though not its goal, the movie reveals several major developments that social scientists have described in our aging society:

- the growth of four and five generation families

- the increased numbers of the "old-old" (those over eighty-five), and the more visible rise of centenarians (including those who are functioning fairly well)

- the dynamic two-way helping exchanges between older and younger generations in families

- the increasing role of older members (at older and older ages) in helping adult children, especially given the rise of single parent headed households

- the role of older persons as a national resource—kin and culture keepers—in both helping to hold families together (i.e., ensuring generic social security for the family) and contributing to society at large

- the significant direct and indirect resources that older members provide to their extended families

Beyond Hollywood, witness the increasingly apparent real-world, positive intergenerational interactions in American society: the growing interest in families of finding ways to help adult children with challenges of care giving for aged parents; the growing interest among school children to do community volunteer work, with placements at nursing homes and other senior residences high on the list; the increased number and percentage of grandparents who are helping out in the care of grandchildren when the parents are going through divorce, or when criminal proceedings have taken a parent out of the home, or when AIDS has taken the life of a parent, or when street drugs have made a parent dysfunctional; the expanding role of the best-educated ever cohort of older adults contributes to the fabric and culture of society through community volunteerism, philanthropy, or their own later life occupational and artistic contributions. This latter role of older adults as a national a resource, despite its increasing presence, gets relatively little play in the popular press, typically eclipsed by coverage of far less common examples of intergenerational tensions.

MYTHS THAT FEED MISPERCEPTIONS ABOUT INTERGENERATIONAL CONFLICT

An assortment of negative myths and misinformation about older adults and family interactions has fed notions of intergenerational conflict.

"Kids Don't Care"

Basically, this myth perpetuates the notion that, in the United States, adult children gradually abandon their aging parents, that when the kids grow up, they go their separate ways. But the facts, based on formal studies, show that over 85 percent of older persons live within less than an hour away from a child and that approximately 50 percent are either living in a child's household or within ten minutes from a child (Sussman, 1988). General estimates, derived from these studies, are that one-third of older Americans will at some point live with an adult child. Even in cases of disability requiring community services, filial involvement is significant; data documents that children provide assistance to about one-fourth of elderly disabled men and more than one-third of elderly women. Moreover, the role of technology, that is, phones and other forms of electronic communication, are having an extraordinary impact on allowing families to better reach out and both touch and help, ranging from providing support for emotional stresses to counsel and monitoring of proper and sustained management of major medical problems.

Help Between Adult Children and Their Aging Parents Is a One-Way Street

Studies show that the two-way intergenerational help portrayed in the movie *Roommates,* described above, is not just Hollywood hyperbole, but an increasingly commonplace occurrence as reflected by a substantial body of scientific evidence. Research looking at the prevalence of help in both directions has found that over a ten-year period the prevalence of older adults providing help to younger family members went up about 15 percent and was found in approximately 70 percent of families. On the other hand, the prevalence of younger family members providing help to older members remained about constant, though similarly high, in about 70 percent of families. (Bengtson et al., 1985; Gatz, Bengtson, and Blum, 1990)

A related one-way street issue is the way that care provided by family members is examined mainly in terms of burden; only rarely does research address the positives of care giving, looking at how families are brought closer together by illness and when disease and disability in one's parents influences the younger individual's feelings about getting the most out of personal and family life. Help from older relatives to younger ones was typically in the form of gifts (found in 69 percent of families), help with grandchildren (found in 36 percent of families), and help with housekeeping (found in 28 percent of families). Also, the number and percentage of grandchildren under age 18 being cared for by grandparents is significantly on the rise. (Bengtson et al., 1985; Gatz, Bengtson, and Blum, 1990).

Growing Generation Gap

Research suggests (Bengtson et al., 1985) that as successive cohorts entering later life become more similar in educational attainment, income security, health, and general social values, objective bases for conflict between age groups diminishes. Consider the dramatic changes in educational level in older adults just since 1970. In 1970 the median number of years of schooling in the United States for those age sixty-five and older was 8.6 years—less than a high school education. By 1989, less than two decades later, the median number of years of schooling was 12.1 years—greater than a high school education (U.S. Senate Special Committee on Aging, 1991). Much of the perceived gap between the generations, particularly depicted in the late 1960s and early 1970s and personified in the phrase "you can't trust anyone over 30," was a pre- versus post-Sputnik generation phenomenon, rather than a generic age group issue.

The Elderly Burden the Health Care System

In fact, hospital and physician costs (expenses that reflect aggressive or heroic, high-tech interventions) in the last year of life for those over age eighty are significantly *less* than last year of life costs for both those ages sixty-five to seventy-nine and for those under age sixty-five (Scitovsky, 1988; Temkin-Greener et al., 1992). What the research shows is that *functional status* rather than age influences the aggressiveness and expense of clinical interventions, and that such costs are greater in the younger groups.

There is no denying the high cost of health care in later life or that health care costs more for older adults than for younger ones. This is not the point. The point is about how health care dollars for older Americans are spent; this is where the distortions continue unabated, often abetted. It is one thing for a society to struggle with significant dollar outlays for assuring health care for its older members, but when the perception is that most of these outlays are going to futile interventions for large numbers of elderly individuals in their last year of life the whole debate becomes both distorted and soured. Continuing media distortions about misdirected last-year-of-life costs for the old reflect how the myth makers scapegoat the elderly. Decisions about dollar commitments to health care for older Americans should be debated in their own terms, not derailed by disingenuous outrage about money being irresponsibly poured down the drain in a mythological scenario of futile care.

What is interesting in addition to the myths that have been advanced about end-of-life health care costs for those at an advanced age is what perspectives are *left out* of discussions. For example, there is a tendency on the part of the press to paint health care expenses for older adults as being sucked into a black hole. In fact, these expenses typically pay for dignified care provided by a diversity of health care providers who are typically in younger age groups; left out of these discussions is a perspective on the enormous number of jobs that health care for elderly patients creates for younger adults, especially for less skilled lower socioeconomic group workers among nursing assistants and home health aids.

Programs for the Elderly Deplete the U.S. Budget

Here, we confront a classic case of incomplete questions being asked. Typically one hears that 30 percent of federal monies go to programs for the elderly. The issue is not so simple, because federal funds comprise only one segment of public monies. A more complete question would be how much of national as opposed to federal outlays are directed toward older adults. If one looks at state and local funding, the picture is quite different. For example, Arkansas spends about 1.1 percent of state funds on its two major budget items for the elderly (the division for aging services and state Medicaid payments to those age sixty-five and over); New York spends about 8.3 percent on similar budget items; Massachusetts about 4.8 percent; and Wisconsin, about 3.5 percent (information obtained through personal communications at the state levels). Overall, states and municipalities spend about ten times more on education for the young than they do on older adults (Gist, 1992). None of these statistics provides the full picture of national spending on different generations, but they do suggest that the picture is much closer to intergenerational equity than the myth carriers continue to paint.

INTERGENERATIONAL EQUITY IN THE DISTRIBUTION OF HEALTH CARE RESOURCES

During congressional testimony, a congressman asked me, "If one took an historical perspective, wouldn't one conclude that the increased distribution of health care dollars to the elderly as compared to the young was a serious inequity in our society?" I said that taking an historical perspective helped answer the question, in that the historical increase of dollars for health care for the elderly represented a shift in illness from earlier in the life cycle to the later years. If we wanted to reestablish equity of dollar distribution we would need to reestablish equity of illness distribution back down across the life cycle. In taking an historical perspective, we could see that the need for increased health care dollars in later life represented society's *success* in postponing illness ever later in the life cycle, and that the goal of research on aging was to advance this postponement even closer to the end. The congressman graciously conveyed a twinkle of agreement. Unfortunately, in the health care cost debate, misinformed dollar considerations have overridden most such glimmers of common sense.

The Most Famous Greedy Geezer—The Rest of the Story

One of the most overworked pejoratives hurled at elderly individuals is that of "greedy geezer," despite the enormous magnitude of volunteerism and philanthropy emanating from older adults (Cohen, 1994). Moreover, the greedy geezer epithet is cast as if it captures the direction of personality change in later life, despite gerontologic research to the contrary showing the stability of personality with aging. The disparagement then continues, with further excess baggage piled on by linking purported greed on the part of elderly persons to purported adverse impact on young people. Consider this constellation of stereotypes in the 1843 case history of "the most famous greedy geezer"—the rest of the story.

The case history focuses on a well-known figure from London in the 1840s. He was described as a melancholic, mean-spirited, misanthropic old man, making the lives of all around him miserable through his miserliness. These manifestations had evolved over a period of decades, culminating in his later years. By historical accounts, he then became the beneficiary of an enlightened home visit by a multidisciplinary team, more than 100 years before the outreach-oriented community health movement. This team then used psychodynamic, dream-oriented psychotherapy more than fifty years before Freud's classic work, *The Interpretation of Dreams.*

What Dickens really had in mind with his 1843 case study of Ebenezer Scrooge (aka "the most famous greedy geezer") were: (1) that Ebenezer's misanthropic and miserly behaviors were not manifestations of personality change with aging, but symptoms of an atypical and undiagnosed depression in later life; depression, not aging, was responsible for the personality change; (2) that chronic disorders can be treated, independent of age; (3) that depression in later life can be effectively treated with, among other modalities, psychotherapy, including the use of dream work; and (4) that when you focus on the problems of older persons, it need not be at the expense of other age groups; witness the benefits to the community of London, and other age groups, including Bob Cratchit and Tiny Tim.

MEDICARE IN AN INTERGENERATIONAL CONTEXT: HISTORY FORGOTTEN

In intergenerational resource discussions, the history of the genesis of Medicare has become increasingly forgotten. The impetus for Medicare was not only coverage for older adults, but *protection for the family,* who would have to foot the bill if their older members could not pay. Medicare was, is, and always has been a family-in-mind program, not a we/they, old versus young competitive resource distribution problem.

In real dollars, despite Medicare coverage, older persons pay more out-of-pocket for health interaction on resource allocation care today than they did prior to the enactment of Medicare. Even with Medicare, they are not having an easy time. Moreover, the economic situation of older adults as a whole does not leave many with much room to assume more personal financial responsibility. While social security has helped keep many older adults out of poverty, the sixty-five and older age group still has the greatest percentage of individuals below 150 percent of poverty (i.e., at near poverty level), according to 1990 data. The percentage is yet higher for those most at risk for health care problems—hence, in need of coverage—the eighty-five and older age group (see Table 9.1).

Given the near poverty level data above, it is apparent that inadequate Medicare coverage for older adults cannot be compensated very much by older adults themselves, especially by those at an advanced age. In the absence of adequate coverage, older patients will either go without necessary care or families who are highly committed to the care of older loved ones could experience the return of excess burden that was historically relieved by the introduction of Medicare a generation ago.

Table 9.1
Age Distribution Below 150% of Poverty, 1990

Age Group	Below 150% of Poverty
< 65	21.2%
> 65	27.2%
> 85	38.6%

Note: The 1990 poverty level was $6,268 for single persons age sixty-five and older; the threshold for a two-person household with no related children was $7,900. In 1990, 150% of poverty level for a single person age sixty-five was $9,402.

CONCLUSION

As a whole, the myths, misrepresentations, and overstatements about intergenerational conflict are a distraction from the literally thousands of grassroots, local, independent intergenerational programs that have sprung up and continue to burgeon around the country. They are also a distraction from what those who study large samples rather than isolated anecdotes view as positively evolving intergenerational relationships within families themselves. Why should this be surprising, since, as the adage puts it, the elderly are the one minority group that everyone aspires to join, given the alternatives? In other words, when young people contemplate their future, they come face to face with their elderly future selves. When they contemplate older adults in the present, they come face to face with their parents and grandparents, for whom they want to do the best. Both scenarios are inconsistent with a fundamental conflict between generations regarding resource allocation.

To frame the country's resource problems as an intergenerational conflict issue is at best a misinformed view based on myth and misinformation, at worst a cynical spin that uses older adults as scapegoats. President Kennedy once said that "the great enemy of truth is very often not the lies—deliberate, contrived and dishonest—but the myth—persistent, persuasive and unrealistic" (Andrews, 1989). It is time to retire the myths and to challenge social policy not to be sidetracked by exaggerated reports of intergenerational conflict, but to be challenged to harness the possibilities being presented by the rise of positive, productive, and creative intergenerational interactions.

REFERENCES

Andrews, R. 1989. *The Concise Columbia Dictionary of Quotations.* New York: Avon Books, 177.

Bengtson, V. L., Cutler, N. E., Mangen, D. J., et al. 1985. Generations, cohorts, and relations between age groups. In *Handbook of Aging and the Social Sciences*, ed. Binstock, R. H. and Shanus, E. New York: Van Nostrand Reinhold.

Cohen, G. D. 1995. Intergenerationalism: A new "ism" with positive mental health and social policy potential. *The American Journal of Geriatric Psychiatry*, 3, 1–5.

Cohen, G. D. 1994. Journalistic elder abuse: It's time to get rid of fictions, get down to facts. *The Gerontologist*, 34, 399–401.

Gatz, M., Bengtson, V. L., and Blum, M. J. 1990. Caregiving families. In *Handbook of the Psychology of Aging*, ed. Biffen, J. E., and Schaie, K. W. New York: Academic Press.

Gist, J. 1992. *Entitlements and the Federal Budget Deficit: Setting the Record Straight*. Washington, DC: AARP Public Policy Institute.

Scitovsky, A. A. 1988. Medical care in the last twelve months of life: The relation between age, functional status, and medical care expenditures. *Milbank Memorial Fund Quarterly Health and Society*, 66: 640–660.

Sussman, M. B. 1988. The family life of old people. In *Handbook of Aging and the Social Sciences*, ed. Binstock, R. H. and Shanus, E. New York: Van Nostrand Reinhold.

Taeuber, C. M. 1992. *Sixty-Five Plus in America*. Washington, DC: U.S. Department of Commerce, Economics and Statistics Administration, Bureau of the Census.

Temkin-Greener, H., Meiners, M. R., Petty, E. A., Szydlowski, J. S. 1992. The use and cost of health services prior to death: A comparison of the Medicare-only and the Medicare-Medicaid elderly population. *The Milbank Quarterly* 70: 679–701.

U.S. Senate Special Committee on Aging. 1991. *Aging America Trends and Projections*. Washington, DC: U.S. Department of Health and Human Services.

10

Social Welfare Policies and Values

Edward D. Berkowitz

This chapter argues the case for incoherence. It asserts that no set of values has universal appeal in the realm of social welfare and that instead people's preferences differ over time and space. Our social welfare policy reflects a continuing struggle between democracy and expertise, an ambivalence over whether to emphasize rehabilitation or maintenance. One could illustrate these tensions by restating them in the form of questions. Should the majority rule on such questions as welfare reform and national health insurance or should we put our trust in experts to interpret these problems for us? Should we use our social welfare system to pay money to those in need or should we provide them with the means to transcend their circumstances?

Questions over values abound in social welfare policy. It seems to me that tensions over values arise most often in the social policy debates in which the system confronts its failures. Working people are supposed to receive health insurance, yet many such people do not. In response the government has tried to increase access to health care, but the questions of just how much the government wishes to ration care and just how much the nation can afford to spend on health care remain unresolved. The result has been something close to political stalemate on the issue of national health insurance (if not on the technical details of health care finance). Heads of households are expected to work but we are not quite sure what to do about single-parent families with young children. Should welfare mothers (or fathers for that matter) receive financial support from the government, so that their children can grow into productive adults? Or do cash grants to welfare recipients encourage dependency and discourage work so that such grants, however well intentioned, are inevitably counterproductive? Civil rights laws are expected to eliminate racial prejudice yet such prejudice persists. Should we take these laws a step further and promote affirmative action or does affirmative action encourage the very sort of discrimination that civil rights laws are intended to remedy? I have no answers to these questions, only a set of historical observations.

AN INCIDENT IN CHICAGO

I learned about diversity and social welfare policy in Chicago. The incident occurred at the tail end of the Carter administration. As a member of the staff of a presidential commission, I organized a hearing on welfare policy that took place at a gritty auditorium on the edge of Chicago's Loop. On the day of the hearing, the usual social workers and grassroots activists trooped into the auditorium, armed with the press releases that they had been disseminating for over a decade. The statements called attention to the small amount of money that Illinois welfare recipients received and demanded that something be done to improve the situation. These demands, presented half-heartedly and with the near certainty that they would amount to nothing, lingered in the auditorium and contributed to the sense of grievance that filled the hall: just what gave these genteel commissioners the right to sit on the stage in silent judgment of the poor? At one point, a woman stood up and insisted on being recognized. She wanted to know if any of the commissioners, hastily flown in from important jobs in mainstream America, had ever been on welfare themselves. What gave them the right to reform an institution of which they had no knowledge or true experience?

As it turned out, one of the commissioners had once been on welfare, and it was she who came to my rescue. At one point in the proceedings, I noticed a woman in the front row who looked ill. A few minutes later, she slumped down in her chair and began to take on the characteristics of an epileptic fit. Moaning softly, she rolled her head around and showed general signs of distress. The image leaped to my mind of newspaper headlines proclaiming the death of a welfare recipient during a hearing of a presidential commission. Trained at sympathy, the social workers in the audience could think of nothing that would help the woman: she was, perhaps, too far past the stage of social casework, at the very margin where life met death. That is when the commissioner who had been on welfare turned to me and said, "I think I can help that woman."

This particular commissioner occupied a prominent position in a prominent trade union, and for that reason President Carter had appointed her to the commission. Fully occupied by her job at the union, she nonetheless continued to preach in a small congregation somewhere on the south side of Chicago. "I can help that woman," she insisted.

It had been my idea to call in the paramedics so that they could take the woman off in an ambulance and admit her to Michael Reese or some other local hospital. When the big burly paramedics arrived, however, the woman seemed to recover long enough to insist that she had no intention of going with them. The prospect of spending time in the hospital obviously scared her. With the paramedics off to the side, the trade unionist-preacher-commissioner stepped down from the stage and walked to the ailing woman's seat in the auditorium. She put her hands on the woman and began to pray. The prayers soothed the woman and arrested her convulsive motions. Because of this faith healing, the woman recovered.[1]

DIVERSITY OF VALUES

This anecdote underscores the fact that different people hold different values concerning social welfare policy. People differ in their tastes for medicine and other forms of social welfare services. Not surprisingly, then, the government programs that come to people's aid express widely different values. As two leading authorities in the field, put it, "purposes are never unitary." They note that all programs are compromises, and all contain contradictions.[2] Hence, the task of isolating a consistent set of values that underlie one program, let alone an entire set of programs, may be impossible.

Even if we could isolate a central value that explains our policies, we would need to recognize that values change over time and space. In the nineteenth century, as David Rothman has demonstrated, poor houses stood at the cutting edge of social policy innovation. In the twentieth century, poor houses were condemned as dangerous and old-fashioned. Segregation, an important policy strategy in the nineteenth century, gave way to a preoccupation with integration in this century.[3]

Location has an important influence on values because the nature of the welfare state has always differed greatly from one place to another. Even in today's society, with its forces for cultural homogenization, it remains the case that Washington, D.C. residents of Anacostia hold different values than those who live in Foggy Bottom. It strikes me as reasonable that the welfare state in one area of the country functions differently than the welfare state in another area of the country. In support of this claim, Lester Salamon has demonstrated that in 1982 total per capita government spending varied from $1,670 in New York City to $506 in Dallas.[4]

Nor do time and space exhaust the list of variables. Others would insist on class and gender as important determinants of values. Still others would point to race as a formative influence over U.S. social welfare policy.

THE PROBLEM OF DEMOCRACY

Beyond the question of identifying values lies the matter of how well our policies express those values. As a student of social welfare policy, I would identify the tension between democracy and expertise as a major unifying theme of our history. In this field one could easily formulate a critique of pure democracy. Indeed, pure democracy has never functioned well as a model for social welfare policy. If one accepts the notion that social welfare programs should come to the aid of those people who are least able to help themselves, then the majority may not be in an ideal position to dictate the terms of that policy. In the short run, the majority of people might want to transfer as little money as possible to the poor and to keep taxes as low as possible. In the long run, however, the effects of this policy might be to restrict economic growth and hinder the country's development. The majority may not be inclined to consider these sorts of long-term consequences. In such a situation, we may wish to cede some of the authority over social welfare policy to experts. If we do that, however, we run the risk of allowing these experts to distort our true preferences.

The problem of protecting the minority has another dimension that derives from the fact that social welfare benefits do not go exclusively to the poor. In the case of middle-class entitlements, the tendency has always been to expand them and not to consider long-term financing consequences. Congress has, for example, received constant pressure to expand benefits for the elderly and the natural inclination among popularly elected officials is to grant the request. Creating these sorts of entitlements, Congress faces two sorts of risks. First, the costs of these entitlements may be too high for future generations to pay. Second, the very popularity of the entitlements may put the minority of individuals not entitled to the benefits at great risk since often, the members of these minorities need the benefits more than those receiving them.

Democracy and Expertise in America's Social Welfare History: Civil War Pensions

The tension between democracy and expertise extends far back into our history as the case of Civil War pensions indicates. As sociologist Ann Shola Orloff has detailed, during the 1880s and 1890s the pension system changed from a measure to compensate combat injuries and war deaths to a "de facto system of old age and disability protection." In 1890, veterans' pensions already consumed 34 percent of the federal budget. Because of the loose way in which the benefits were administered and the rising percentage of Union Army veterans who availed themselves of them, expenditures for these old age and disability benefits did not peak until around 1912. After 1906, for example, the law was amended to allow any Union army veteran over sixty-two years of age to collect a pension. At that point, 90 percent of surviving Union veterans were on the pension rolls. The cost of old age pensions for Civil War veterans amounted in 1913 to more than $160 million per year.[5] Sociologist Theda Skocpol has termed the system of Civil War social benefits a "kind of precocious social spending state."[6]

The problem was that not everyone was deemed worthy to participate in this precocious social spending state. Confederate war veterans had to depend on the generosity of the treasuries of the former Confederate states if they expected to receive a pension. These states were among the poorest in the nation, and they lacked the federal government's easy access to the dependable revenues provided by import tariffs. In fact, residents of southern states paid a disproportionate amount of federal taxes and received smaller returns on those taxes than did residents of northern states. Southerners were clear losers under the pension system. So were immigrants who arrived in the north after the Civil War. The system simply excluded them, despite their relative poverty compared to the rest of the population.[7]

A clear political bias affected those who received pensions and those who did not. Northern Republicans collected more of the pensions than did Democratic southerners and urban residents. In the period after 1896, the Republicans constituted the majority party, and so the system responded to the will of the majority. Whether it best met the country's interests, however, remained an open question. Progressive Era commentators condemned the system without reservation. I. M. Rubinow, a social welfare expert of the Progressive Era, complained that "it is a matter of common knowledge not only that pensions are obtained upon fraudulent representations of past services . . . but what is economically more important, a large proportion of the amount goes to individuals who have no need whatsoever of financial assistance."[8]

PROGRESSIVE ERA REFORM

Efficiency and expertise, accompanied by a removal of social welfare activities from the partisan political system, constituted important themes of the Progressive Era between 1900 and 1920. During those years, important changes occurred in both the public and private sectors. States experimented with pensions for dependent children and elderly residents and passed laws that required employers to pay compensation to employees injured on the job. Private corporations operating in national product markets invested in safety devices in an effort to reduce industrial accidents. Each of these public laws or private practices marked a conscious effort to remove control over social welfare benefits from generalists and place it in the hands of experts. Social workers replaced politicians as dispensers of public assistance. Industrial commissioners, often trained as economists, usurped the role of judges in awarding benefits to injured workers. Personnel officers took the place of foremen in supervising company safety procedures.

Although each of these Progressive Era developments limited popular control over social welfare benefits, some, such as workers' compensation, enjoyed wide support. In part that was because such laws solved the twin problems of access and excess. On the one hand, progressive reformers complained of a lack of access to social welfare benefits. Court-administered industrial accident compensation systems often failed to grant any compensation or provided grants that bore little relationship to "the gravity of injury or need," according to Rubinow. On the other hand, Progressive Era reformers worried about an excess of benefits for injured workmen who sued their employers and happened to win large settlements from sympathetic juries. As Rubinow noted, "We are startled by the very large and undoubtedly sometimes even excessive amounts of damages awarded."[9]

Tenuously uniting employers concerned about excess and employees concerned about access, reformers between 1911 and 1919 succeeded in creating workers' compensation laws in forty-three states. Such laws were intended to provide steady but unspectacular compensation to the victims of industrial accidents; they were administered in many states by agencies that claimed both legislative and judicial powers to make rules and settle disputes. With the passage of compensation laws, workers injured in the course of employment no longer needed to win a legal suit before they could receive financial recompense. Instead, they received a financial payment based on their rate of pay and the severity of their disability and reimbursement for their medical care directly from the state workers' compensation agency. In the nineteenth century, settlement of the matter had hinged on the question of who was at fault for the accident. Workers' compensation laws, at least in theory, eliminated the concept of fault and replaced it with the notion of objective need. The states expected experts, rather than generalist judges or legislators, to enforce the standard of objectivity.

Workers' compensation demonstrated that the progressive ideal of replacing subjective popular control with objective expertise was unreachable. Whenever possible, progressive reformers tried to insolate the agencies administering workers' compensation from political pressure. Still, the new agencies, often called industrial commissions, faced constant challenges to their jurisdiction. Lawyers contested compensation cases and discovered means of removing the cases from the new agencies to the courts. During the first year of the workers' compensation law in Maryland, 7.2 percent of claims were contested. In 1933, 20.2 percent of the claims were contested. The number of hearings to hear contested cases increased from 273 to 1,776 per year. Employers and employees used the legislature to gain advantage in the laws, depending on the political circumstances of the moment; the legislatures regarded the new agencies not as removed from traditional politics but as objects of political patronage. In the end, politics—the democratic impulse—subsumed workers' compensation programs.[10]

SOCIAL SECURITY

This tension between democracy (or politics) and expertise remained an underlying theme of our social welfare policy in the New Deal. In the 1930s, reformers had a chance to enact a new national social welfare law. Their thinking was shaped by the Progressive Era critique of the poor laws and of veterans' pensions. The poor laws were demeaning and restrictive. The new law would strive to treat its beneficiaries with dignity and to include all industrial workers within its scope. The veterans' pensions were expensive and poorly administered. The new law would include provisions to keep future costs within manageable limits. Unlike veterans' pensions, the new law would be administered by social insurance experts, not politicians anxious to satisfy voters.

As enacted in 1935, Social Security, defined as old-age insurance, enjoyed no great popularity. It was far from the people's choice. The fiscal design of the program clashed with the needs of the economy. The plan was for payroll taxes to begin in 1937 and for the first regular benefits to be paid in 1942. Starting in January 1937, workers had one percent of the first $3,000 of their wages deducted from their paychecks. Employers contributed an equal amount. Hence, Social Security, as it was planned by the president's advisors, took more money out of the economy in the form of payroll taxes than it returned in the form of retirement pensions. In 1937, for example, the program collected $765 million and paid out $1 million in benefits. Two years later, it collected $360 million and paid out $14 million. During these years, then, it reduced the amount of money in people's pockets and further depressed the moribund economy.[11]

The financial arrangements created severe political liabilities. During the nation's most severe depression, it was impolitic for a social welfare program to collect more in revenues than it spent in benefits. The Republicans deftly played upon this vulnerability in the 1936 campaign. Alfred Landon, the Republican presidential nominee, criticized the program as "unjust, unworkable, stupidly drafted and wastefully financed."[12]

As early as 1939, program administrators, anxious as they were to insulate Social Security from political pressures, realized that they needed to make some adjustments. Hence, they agreed to raise benefits and reduce future taxes, always the popular choice in a broad-based program. In this manner, old-age insurance became old-age and survivors insurance in 1939.[13]

The 1939 changes illustrated the continuing tensions between politics and program management. When the program was an idea, an abstraction, as it was in 1935, the politicians could dismiss many of its potential problems. The Social Security program before Congress in 1935 had no effect on any worker or employer until after the next election, and it was not the center of congressional debate. Soon after the election, the abstraction of 1935 became the tax of 1937. Social Security acquired the potential to create problems for its sponsors, such as President Roosevelt. The feeling grew among both Republicans and Democrats that something needed to be done about Social Security. In this way, Social Security administrators faced the sorts of popular pressures that had marred Civil War veterans pensions.

Social Security administrators responded to the pressures with considerable political skill. They worked to mold the image of Social Security so that it, rather than welfare or some other social program, conformed to perceived public preferences. In so doing, they established themselves as technical experts whose job it was to convert popular sentiment into practical social policy. The administrators realized the uphill nature of their task. As late as 1940, veterans programs and state programs such as welfare and workers' compensation continued to dwarf Social Security. Workers compensation payments exceeded Social Security payments by a factor of six; veterans programs cost fifteen times as much as Social Security. As late as 1950, more than twice as many people were on the state welfare rolls receiving old-age assistance or pensions than were receiving retirement benefits from the federal government under Social Security. The average monthly welfare payment was $42 in 1949, compared with an average Social Security benefit of $25.[14]

In 1950, Congress substantially modified the Social Security program, and the program administrators won a great victory. The Social Security system began to grow. As a result of the 1950 amendments, eight million workers, most of whom were self-employed, were brought into the system, and average benefits were increased by about 80 percent. In February, 1951, for the first time, the number of old-age and survivors insurance beneficiaries exceeded the number of people receiving state old-age assistance. It was a moment of epochal importance in the history of U.S. social welfare policy. After 1950, social insurance, not the poor law, defined America's approach to old-age security. Social Security, through the adroit management of popular opinion and esoteric expertise, had triumphed over its rivals.

HEALTH CARE POLICY

After 1950, Social Security enjoyed something close to a monopoly in the formation of social policy. As an example, the matter of health insurance was not debated in broad, general terms, but rather it was cast as an expansion of the Social Security program. Responding to popular pressure as interpreted by the experts in the Social Security administration, Congress passed Medicare in 1965. In doing so, Congress took the country as close as it would ever come to national health insurance.

The development of Medicare indicated the gap between popular perception and policy practice. The public tended to think in broad and politically salient terms such as national health insurance. An inner circle of policymakers attended to the details of legislation that had crucial implications for the future of American health care. These experts understood the importance of institutions such as the fiscal intermediaries who handled hospitals bills under Medicare and the supplemental carriers who processed doctors' bills. They realized that the manner in which doctors and hospitals received payments for treating Medicare beneficiaries was every bit as important as the great ideological battles over national health insurance.

In recent years, even as the public has been distracted by more general questions, the federal government has grown into the nation's single largest payer of medical bills and, indeed, into one of the largest health care financiers in the world. The terms of the federal government's reimbursements to hospitals and doctors are now crucial to the nation's health policy. As the power of the federal government has grown in this area, policymakers have instituted important new procedures. Diagnosis-related groups (DRGs) govern the terms of payments to hospitals. A resource-based relative value scale (RBRVS) helps to determine the level of the federal government's payments to doctors. Each of these things is a relatively esoteric, statistically based instrument developed by actuaries and others with quantitative skills in settings far removed from hospitals.

DRGs and the RBRVS entered the political scene almost surreptitiously. DRGs became law as part of a large piece of legislation that helped "save" the Social Security system from bankruptcy in 1983. Policymakers in the Reagan administration and in Congress tacked DRGs onto this legislation because they knew that Congress could not afford to oppose it. As one key participant remarked, "This was a train that was leaving the station. We needed to get that legislation to hop on to it."[15] The public never engaged in a lengthy debate over DRGs. Instead there was what an expert dryly called "a fairly short process of Congressional consideration."[16] The RBRVS had a somewhat similar history. It became law in part because of the need to save money in the Medicare program, in part because of the budget reconciliation process, and in part because of the policy predilections of key health policy makers in Washington. As with DRGs, no lengthy public debate occurred over this important change in physician reimbursement.

As these developments indicated, health policy had ceased to be an ideological battleground in which people on opposite ends of the political spectrum conducted a war of ideas. Instead it was a matter of technical adjustments performed by experts with profound consequences. Partisan politics was an inadequate means of accounting for the developments in the field. Instead one needed to know about key lobbying groups and about extragovernmental bodies such as the Prospective Payment Commission and the Physician Payment Review Commission.

THE PERSISTENCE OF POPULAR POLITICS

It would be a mistake to think that we are now governed by experts. If health care financing represented a muted triumph of expertise, other areas of social welfare policy exhibited a far more open style of policymaking. Contrary to the desires of many policy experts, Congress proceeded to make severe cuts in welfare programs such as Aid to Families with Dependent Children (AFDC) and Medicaid. In these programs, the age-old dynamic of striving to cut benefits in order to cut benefits held sway. As Newt Gingrich and his Republican minions conducted what historian Michael Katz has called the war against welfare, they undoubtedly reflected the popular will. A majority of the public wanted to see welfare benefits cut; the majority believed that mothers should not be paid money to have illegitimate children. Still, a sizeable minority pointed out most welfare recipients were children, who could hardly be held accountable for their poverty and who required maintenance from the state. As the debate over welfare reform raged, the tension between expertise and democracy once again asserted itself.

THE TENSION BETWEEN MAINTENANCE AND PARTICIPATION

Of course, the experts do not always agree among themselves. People do not agree on the answers to these questions in part because the experts do not agree among themselves. The tension between maintenance or retirement, paying someone to withdraw from the labor force, and rehabilitation or participation, encouraging someone to join the labor force, emerges as another central theme of social welfare policy. Disability policy and welfare policy provide good illustrations of how experts have differed on this matter.

During the 1950s, the logic of social security expansion, which favored equating the condition of disability with the state of retirement, collided with an emerging faith in vocational rehabilitation, which emphasized encouraging people with disabilities to join the labor force. The leaders of the Social Security program, such as Arthur Altmeyer and Wilbur Cohen, pressed for the creation of Social Security Disability Insurance. This program would allow workers with severe disabilities the right to retire from the labor force and receive Social Security benefits, in the same manner as regular workers retired from the labor force. The leaders of the vocational rehabilitation program such as Mary Switzer and Dr. Howard Rusk argued for the expansion of vocational rehabilitation. That would allow motivated people with disabilities to obtain employment counseling and other services from state-run but largely federally funded rehabilitation offices.

In a Republican era, Mary Switzer, the head of the vocational rehabilitation program, played upon Republican sympathies. She and her colleagues obtained a respectful hearing from Oveta Culp Hobby, Eisenhower's first secretary of Health, Education, and Welfare (HEW), and from Nelson Rockefeller, the first undersecretary of Health, Education, and Welfare.[17] These Republican administration politicians wanted to define a distinctively Republican social welfare program. In rehabilitation, they found an approach that assumed the existence of continuing prosperity, rather than the constant threat of depression, and that highlighted the capabilities of people with disabilities, rather than their inability to compete in the labor force.

In this manner, the rehabilitation approach meshed with a more general transformation of social welfare policy in the 1950s away from income maintenance and toward a new reliance on the services of professional caseworkers to facilitate labor force participation. If Social Security was an entitlement or basic right, rehabilitation was a discretionary service in which professionally trained social welfare workers acted as gatekeepers and case managers. A successful course of rehabilitation facilitated such goals as the integration of people with disabilities into the labor force and their independence from other government benefits; themes that meshed nicely with those of the emerging civil rights movement. As with civil rights, the benefits of rehabilitation could be expressed in the optimistic rhetoric that was common to policy discourse in the 1950s. Using the sexist language of the era, Secretary Hobby told President Eisenhower, for example, that no accountant could estimate the "physical rewards, the sense of independence, pride, and usefulness, and the relief from family strains, which accrue to one of the disabled when he returns to his old job or to a newly learned job suited to his limitations, and once more take his place as a man among men."[18]

Mary Switzer had no doubt of the superiority of rehabilitation to income maintenance. To emphasize income maintenance, she believed, was to create dependency when the proper focus should be on eliminating it. Rod Perkins, a Nelson Rockefeller advisor and assistant secretary of HEW for Eisenhower, noted that he opposed federal income benefits to the permanently and totally disabled because such benefits led a person "not to seek to rehabilitate himself and overcome his disability." Instead of expanding Social Security, Perkins recommended "large sums devoted to rehabilitation."[19]

When the leaders of Social Security pressed for passage of disability insurance in 1956, they found their way blocked by Mary Switzer and the supporters of rehabilitation. As Wilbur Cohen put it, Mary Switzer and E. B. Whitten of the National Rehabilitation Association were "very effective in raising questions in the minds of the Republicans" about the desirability of disability insurance.[20] When the Social Security Administration succeeded in gaining passage of disability insurance in 1956, Altmeyer wrote to Cohen that "we have licked the opponents and their dupes and accomplices (the Rusks and the Switzers) on the basic proposition. Now, let's press our advantage."[21]

The decade ended with the simultaneous adoption of both policies. In 1954 Mary Switzer used her Republican connections to obtain a major expansion of the vocational rehabilitation program. Two years later Congress passed Social Security Disability Insurance. The result was a strong government commitment to the notion that people with disabilities had the right to drop out of the labor force and a simultaneous commitment that people with disabilities should be encouraged to enter the labor force. In this way, the social welfare system maintained a constant tension between two conflicting values.

This tension remains visible in our disability policy. We still support a large rehabilitation program as well as a major civil rights law known as the Americans with Disabilities Act. These elements of our policy highlight the increasing capabilities of people with disabilities and the hope that such people will join the labor force. At the same time, many people are committed to the maintenance of both the Social Security Disability Insurance and Supplemental Security Income programs which, taken together, dwarf the vocational rehabilitation program in the level of their expenditures. When someone last did a serious study, the nation spent only two cents of its disability dollar on rehabilitation and fifty cents on direct monetary payments. We talk about rehabilitation a lot. People are forever coming up with schemes such as the recent notion of giving people on the disability rolls time-limited payments that would encourage rehabilitation, but we continue to put our money on income maintenance. It is not clear how much our values have influenced policy outcomes or even what the underlying values guiding our disability policy are.

One might argue that disability represents an obscure area of social policy, not the arena in which the nation has debated broad ideological questions. That distinction may fall to our welfare programs, which have been on the cutting edge of policy discussions at least since the late 1960s. Welfare is one of those endeavors that seems an affront to deeply held American values. Prosperity of the type that swept America in the period between 1946 and 1973 and again in the 1980s is supposed to have eliminated the need for welfare. Yet it manifestly did not. Instead the Aid to Families with Dependent Children caseload increased from 3 million people in an average month in 1960, to 4.3 million in 1965, to 8.5 million in 1970, and to 11.3 million in 1975. During the 1960s, the unemployment rate was halved, AFDC recipients increased by almost two-thirds, and AFDC money payments doubled. As early as 1962, many states, including New York and Pennsylvania, spent more for welfare than for highways. Here then is a prime area for the system to confront its failures and to debate the basic values involved.

A shift in values similar to the one in disability policy occurred in welfare policy during the 1950s. A personal debate between Wilbur Cohen and Arthur Altmeyer, two social welfare professionals who took an interest in welfare, defined the debate. Arthur Altmeyer regarded welfare in simple terms. In Altmeyer's opinion, people in poverty required financial assistance. As a corollary to this axiom, Altmeyer believed that poor people needed money, not advice. Welfare policy should therefore not center on rehabilitating the recipients. Altmeyer feared that intensive efforts to intervene in the lives of welfare recipients to make them more independent would be counterproductive. In the first place, such efforts would lead to undue interference in the lives of public assistance recipients. In the second place, such efforts would be used as excuses for not raising the monetary level of welfare benefits.[22] "I am afraid that in the name of rehabilitation, increased self-help, and provision of constructive social services we will depreciate the need for effective income maintenance programs and weaken such principles as unrestricted money payment and the right of needy persons to assistance," wrote Altmeyer in 1957.[23]

Since Altmeyer believed so strongly in unrestricted money payments, he deplored the practice of workfare, or requiring welfare recipients, including young mothers, to work in return for receiving state support. Speaking before a group of social workers in 1957, Altmeyer argued that a "mother had a right to assistance even if she refused to go to work," a view that apparently shocked the audience.[24] Altmeyer put the needs of children foremost in his mind, and therefore argued that "a mother making a good home for her children should have a free choice in deciding whether or not it is in their best interests that she stay at home or go to work."[25]

In these regards, Altmeyer followed the progressive precepts that he had practiced during the New Deal, untainted by newer considerations related to race or gender. Altmeyer did not feel that women could participate in the labor force on the same terms as men, in part because they had special obligations as mothers that limited the amount of work they should do. Altmeyer also realized that the debate over welfare in the 1950s was conditioned, as it had not been before, by the subject of race. To Altmeyer's mind, the conjuncture of race and welfare made it even more important to protect the rights of welfare recipients. State laws with specifications such as requiring a person to establish a year's residence before he or she could receive welfare were "aimed of course at the Negroes." So were guidelines such as removing a welfare mother who had an illegitimate child from the rolls. In North Carolina, for example, state authorities made the suspected father a resource and thus made the child ineligible. Similarly, a mother who was able to work was required to do so in North Carolina. "All of this depresses me no end," Altmeyer declared.[26]

For Wilbur Cohen, race and gender had not yet become the primary determinants of social policy. He looked at the problem almost completely differently than did Altmeyer. Money, far from being the "entire solution," sometimes only served "to perpetuate the problem." The solution lay in the ability of trained social welfare practitioners to resolve social problems. "I . . . certainly don't believe in cutting them off the rolls when we don't have a satisfactory substitute," Cohen said. He noted, however, that there were "lots of other elements we must emphasize other than assistance, such as training, research, casework services, medical care, rehabilitation, etc."[27]

Altmeyer simply assumed that most people were on welfare because they had no other choice; nearly everyone strived to be self-sufficient and turned to government help only as a last resort. Responding to this situation, the 1935 Social Security Act established a system of determining need that protected an individual's dignity. Cohen came to see the 1950s as a very different era. In the new era, as Cohen put it, "relatively few families are in need for reasons which can be described as being beyond their control." The typical welfare client was no longer elderly, and in some cases welfare served to maintain a family "which has little or nothing constructive to offer to children. . . . From an examination of the ADC caseload, it appears that a high proportion of the caseload has multiple problems of a psychological and social nature," wrote Cohen.[28]

It was only natural that more of the era's optimism would rub off on the forty-some-thing Cohen than it did on the sixty-something Altmeyer and make Cohen more sanguine than Altmeyer about casework and other forms of rehabilitation. Wilbur Cohen explained to Arthur Altmeyer how to blend social services and income maintenance: "We need to identify the 'Mrs. Lees' in the caseload, who need no service other than the grant, so that we can stay out of their lives except as called on; and, on the other hand, to identify those who need service, so that we can go to them with active vigorous services of a preventive and rehabilitative nature."[29]

Cohen enjoyed the chance to put some of his ideas into practice, first as an academic in the 1950s and then as a government official in the 1960s. In the 1950s he made a study of the general assistance caseload around Ann Arbor, Michigan. General assis-tance was a local program run by the individual counties without federal financial assistance. The program aided poor families with both parents present, or it helped single individuals who were not disabled and had no dependent children. In other words, the program came to the aid of those who fell through the cracks of the federal public assistance programs.

One case from this study concerned the H family. After six years on the general assistance rolls, county authorities referred the family to the Special Services Project, run by Cohen. The husband could neither read nor write and at age forty-seven faced the prospect of continuing unemployment. His forty-one-year-old wife had been married at age sixteen. Six of the eight children remained at home. All had severe problems in school. Two of the daughters had illegitimate children. The parents stayed together only out of apathy and did little to help their children. Indeed, the family "had lost its central bonds, becoming a collection of hopeless, miserable, distrustful people." The family members hid from their problems, denying them rather than facing them. The social workers judged that the "family was not fulfilling its basic responsibilities in child rearing" and set as a "treatment goal" to have the parents improve their care of the children. The treatment "method" involved weekly interviews with the parents, "helping them step-by-step to choose family goals and to accomplish them." Slowly, the family gave up their pattern of "drifting apologetically through life, hoping that no one would punish them too harshly and in return accepting impoverished living conditions as their due." Cured of apathy, they began to function better, and they left the welfare rolls.[30]

The case of the H family showed how social workers diagnosed and attempted to cure problems. Arthur Altmeyer gave little credence to this process because it permitted social workers to enter the lives of the poor in intrusive ways and detracted from the basic goal of income maintenance. In striking contrast, Wilbur Cohen became a convert to the cause of intervention, if only in these sorts of problem cases. He did not see the intervention as punitive, so much as he viewed it as a therapeutic and beneficial. Here then was another debate over income maintenance and rehabilitation that divided even such close friends and allies as Wilbur Cohen and Arthur Altmeyer.

THE TORTURED HISTORY OF WELFARE REFORM

Ever since the 1950s, we have tried to find the right blend of services and cash grants to end welfare as we know it. The debate has taken many twists and turns that need not be rehashed here. We might just look at the most recent legislative landmarks.

In 1988 President Ronald Reagan collaborated with congressional leaders such as Daniel P. Moynihan (D-New York) and with the National Association of Governors in sponsoring what became the Family Support Act of 1988. The law established comprehensive state education and training programs. It mandated transitional child care and medical assistance benefits and compulsory coverage of two-parent families for at least six months of each year. The law also contained a strong child support enforcement provision. Only seven years later, Congress tried another version of welfare reform that appeared to take the approach that the best form of rehabilitation was the end of permissive cash grants.

Through these changes, it was difficult to discern any consistent thread. Instead, the nation seemed to drift from confidence in rehabilitation, to a faith that a solution could be engineered through employment incentives, to a belief that only a harsh elimination of welfare altogether would solve the welfare problem.

CONCLUSION

I have to end as I began. Diversity, as much as consistency, characterizes our social welfare policies and values. As a way of bringing order to the chaos of social welfare, I suggest the importance of the two central themes that have animated this essay. Our social welfare policy may be interpreted as a continuing struggle between democracy and expertise and between rehabilitation and maintenance. Any resolution of these struggles must inevitably be temporary, for the only constant in our social welfare policy appears to be change over time.

NOTES

1. I draw many of the facts, if not the interpretation, for this chapter from my article on "Social Welfare" in *Encyclopedia of the United States in the Twentieth Century*, ed. Stanley Kutler (New York: Scribner and Sons, 1996), 272–292.

2. Theodore R. Marmor and Jerry Mashaw, *America's Misunderstood Welfare State: Persistent Myths, Enduring Realities* (New York: Basic Books, 1990), 222.

3. David Rothman, *The Discovery of the Asylum: Social Order and Disorder in the New Republic*, revised ed. (Boston: Little Brown, 1990); Rothman, *Conscience and Convenience: The Asylum and Its Alternatives in Progressive America* (New York: Harper and Collins, 1980).

4. Lester M. Salamon, *Partners in Public Service: Government-Non-Profit Relations in the Modern Welfare State* (Baltimore: Johns Hopkins University Press, 1995).

5. Ann Shola Orloff, *The Politics of Pensions: A Comparative Analysis of Britain, Canada, and the United States, 1880–1940* (Madison: University of Wisconsin Press, 1993), 134.

6. Theda Skocpol, *Social Policy in the United States: Future Possibilities in Historical Perspective* (Princeton: Princeton University Press, 1995), 38.

7. In addition to Orloff and Skocpol, cited above, see Jill Quadagno, *The Transformation of Old Age Security: Class and Politics in the American Welfare State* (Chicago: University of Chicago Press, 1988).

8. I. M. Rubinow, *Social Insurance: With Special Reference to American Conditions* (New York: Henry Holt and Company, 1916), 406.

9. Rubinow, *Social Insurance*, 93.

10. Edward Berkowitz, *Disabled Policy: America's Programs for the Handicapped* (New York: Cambridge University Press, 1987), 15–40.

11. See Edward Berkowitz, "Social Security and the Financing of the American State," in *Financing the American State*, ed. Elliott Brownlee (New York: Cambridge University Press, 1995).

12. See Edward Berkowitz, *America's Welfare State* (Baltimore: Johns Hopkins University Press, 1991), 41.

13. Ibid.

14. Mark H. Leff, "Historical Perspectives on Old Age Insurance: The State of the Art on the Art of the State," *Social Security After Fifty*, ed. Edward Berkowitz (Westport, CT: Greenwood Press, 1987), 42.

15. Berkowitz, *America's Welfare State*.

16. Interview with Paul Ginsberg, Washington D.C., August, 1995, conducted as part of a contract with the Health Care Financing Administration to explore the history of important policy developments in health care finance.

17. See Martha Lentz Walker, Beyond Bureaucracy: Mary Elizabeth Switzer and Rehabilitation (Lanham, MD: University Press of America, 1985).

18. Hobby to Eisenhower, October 15, 1953, in Volume 43, Nelson Rockefeller Papers, Rockefeller Archives, Pocantico, New York.

19. No author, Memorandum for the Welfare File, March 14, 1960, Box 9, President's Commission on National Goals.

20. Wilbur Cohen, "The Situation in Social Security," February 15, 1970, Box 70, Wilbur J. Cohen Papers, Wisconsin State Historical Society, Madison Wisconsin. The National Rehabilitation Association was the chief lobbying group for the state vocational rehabilitation programs.

21. Altmeyer to Cohen, October 8, 1956, Cohen Papers, Wisconsin State Historical Society. Howard Rusk was a prominent rehabilitation doctor.

22. Altmeyer to Cohen, February 15, 1957, Box 6, Cohen Papers.

23. Altmeyer to Harry Page, March 20, 1957, Box 6, Cohen Papers.

24. Altmeyer to Cohen, March 5, 1957, Box 6, Cohen Papers.

25. Altmeyer to Harry Page, March 20, 1957, Box 6, Cohen Papers.

26. One reason that welfare requirements became tighter in the 1950s was that more blacks were entering the rolls, in part because of new legal requirements that they receive equal treatment under the law. In addition, the increased mobility of blacks from the south to the north brought more blacks into contact with the relatively liberal welfare systems of the north. Altmeyer to Cohen, April 20, 1957, Box 6, Cohen Papers.

27. Cohen to Altmeyer, October 25, 1957, Cohen Papers, Box 6; Cohen to Jules Berman, Chief, Division of Program Standards and Development, Bureau of Public Assistance, SSA, December 30, 1957, Elizabeth Wickenden Papers, Correspondence Files, Box 1, Wisconsin State Historical Society.

28. Cohen to Altmeyer, no date, but probably around April 1958, Box 6, Cohen Papers.

29. Cohen to Altmeyer, circa April, 1958, Box 6, Cohen Papers.

30. Wilbur J. Cohen and Sydney E. Bernard, "The Prevention and Reduction of Dependency," pamphlet published by the Washtenaw County Department of Social Welfare, September 1961, in Cohen Papers, Bentley Library, Ann Arbor, Michigan. The case study is on page 28. Unless otherwise noted, all subsequent references to the Cohen paper refer to the collection in Madison, rather than the collection in Michigan.

11

Women, Gender, Values, and Public Policy

Cynthia Harrison

> No free communities ever existed without morals, and . . . morals are the work of women. Consequently, whatever affects the condition of women, their habits and their opinions, has great political importance.
> —Alexis de Tocqueville, *Democracy in America*

These words written in the 1830s by everyone's favorite political commentator, Alexis de Tocqueville, could understandably be mistaken for sentiments of contemporary observers ranging from Phyllis Schlafly to radical essentialist feminist and sometime fugitive from justice Jane Alpert.[1] Dating from the founding of the Republic and reaching even unto the 1994 election, women—that is, white women—have stood as the avatars of virtue and that ostensible virtue has pervaded the discussion of women's relationship to the political system. In the nineteenth century, men excluded women from formal political rights to protect their virtue; in the early twentieth century, women claimed political rights based upon their responsibility to employ their superior virtue in service of the public good. By the late twentieth century, belief in the efficacy of the virtue of women has surfaced again, but this time it has emerged less from the essentialist view that women are intrinsically more virtuous and more on the pragmatic assessment that, as political outsiders, women have had fewer opportunities to be corrupted. In 1996, with women holding about 10 percent of the seats in Congress and 20 percent in state legislatures, the political system continues to display considerable resistance to this infusion of virtue, but perhaps the critical mass of women has not yet been attained.

Regardless of their efficacy, women as political players have, from the beginning of the Republic, stood for the principle that values, as opposed to sheer economic rationality or pure contests of power, should govern political decision making. Women effectively brought this perspective to bear on public decision making long before they won a guarantee of suffrage. And when public policy has focused specifically on issues concerning women, children, and families, the debate over values has been unusually explicit.

However, Americans hold two core values that determine much of public policy in the United States: individual liberty and antipathy for government. We have other values as well, but none has the power of these two to structure policy responses to social problems, which accounts for the most attenuated social welfare system of all the Western democracies. Women, in seeking support for policy measures reflecting social concerns, found themselves occasionally in sync with, but more often at odds with, these two axioms of American political life.

This chapter undertakes two primary tasks: a brief historical examination of women as political actors in the interests of value-driven public policy measures; and an examination of the interplay between values, economic behavior, and public policy that underlay the emergence of a new wave of feminism in the late 1960s and, in consequence, a renewed contest over values. Finally, I raise for discussion some of the current controversies concerning issues of gender and public policy in which the debate over values is paramount.

WOMEN AS POLITICAL ACTORS: BRINGING VIRTUE TO POLICY

By the 1830s, morals might have become, in Tocqueville's words, the work of women, but such an ascription was relatively new. In the seventeenth century, women had occupied quite a different position with respect to morals: they were the weak link in the chain, or, as Edmund Morgan put it, "the weaker vessel in both body and mind."[2] Historian John Demos, also writing about New England, explained that "[s]ome basic taint of corruption was thought to be inherent in the feminine constitution—a belief rationalized, of course, by the story of Eve's initial treachery in the Garden of Eden"; the belief sustained the "popular assumption of woman's basic moral weakness."[3]

Given this view, the mundane responsibilities of men and women differed dramatically. The husband directed, the wife obeyed. His responsibility for moral and religious instruction extended both to her and to their children.[4] Indeed, a husband was not merely "to instruct his wife in religion but 'to make it easy to her.' "[5] So subordinated was the seventeenth-century woman that some ministers expressed concern that children would despise their mothers.[6]

Locke, Condorcet, and other enlightenment thinkers drew different analogies from biblical admonitions, striving to create a society that relied upon reason, responsibility, choice, and virtue, and the notion of women as irretrievably corrupt began to diminish (Rousseau to the contrary notwithstanding).[7] As women came to dominate the membership of church congregations, ministers found explanations for women's piety: women's trials, including childbirth, turned them toward God; their exclusion from "worldly business" gave them time to devote to pious work. By the early nineteenth century, general opinion held women possessed of a "religious temperament," fostered by the "sensibility, delicacy, imagination, and sympathy" natural to them. Ministers relented from their focus on Eve and found other more promising biblical models that would demonstrate women's goodness. In the first third of the eighteenth century, women's church-related benevolent associations proliferated, inaugurating women's public-spirited activism.[8] The world's work required an infusion of such righteousness.

Indeed, with the new Republic launched, American women gained access to a practical education to fit them to be stewards, in their husband's absence, of family affairs and to undertake the education of the Republic's future citizens.[9] Men needed freedom from family obligations to devote themselves to commercial concerns; thus, women would take over domestic responsibilities formerly belonging to their husbands. The times adjusted the ideology so that women were no longer "weaker vessels" but lieutenants overseeing domestic operations. The spreading demand for education of girls opened new opportunities for women as teachers. One minister advised them: "We look to you, ladies, to raise the standard of character in our own sex; we look to you, to guard and fortify those barriers, which still exist in society, against the encroachments of impudence and licentiousness."[10] By 1818, one observer could note that "[m]ost men are so entirely engrossed by business as to have but little opportunity of fully understanding the characters of their children."[11]

Equipped by both religion and education and a new ideology which placed responsibility for the success of the American experiment in Republican government in the hands of mothers, women seriously undertook their new mission to inject moral values into public life. In maternal associations, women founded support groups for Christian mothers. In moral reform associations, they undertook to improve the community by extirpating the sin of licentiousness, expressed in the lust of men and the prostitution of women. These women insisted on a single standard of purity and marital fidelity for both men and women.Their tools were education and exposure: they would ostracize men who employed prostitutes but redeem the prostitutes themselves, whom they viewed as victims.[12] Most women did not move from religious reform associations to more explicitly political ones, but once the ideology confirmed the possibility of women influencing the wider world to good effect, such organizations became more likely. Women's political activism emerged from esteem for home and family, which lent their causes moral authority and fostered the enhancement of the status of women as well.[13] But antislavery activism breached the boundaries of women's separate sphere and women abolitionists quickly found themselves defending their right to speak in public and to play a role in public affairs. By 1848, a new movement explicitly dedicated to securing women's rights emerged from a meeting at Seneca Falls, New York. The women there—Quaker sisters Lucretia Mott and Martha Wright, and Elizabeth Cady Stanton were among the organizers—viewed work on behalf of women's rights as a moral cause, but it was only one of many. And even women who did not support the revision in the social order that political rights for women would signify—that "all men and women are created equal"[14]—nevertheless themselves continued to work on behalf of abolition, purity, temperance, and protection of women and children in need. The Civil War then drew all reform activity into its vortex.

Afterward, women both inside and apart from the suffrage movement found central places within a national explosion of reform. Waves of immigrants, first from Germany and Ireland and then from southern Europe, served as workers for employers delighted to pay starvation wages. Overworked and destitute, immigrants lived in congested urban slums, which American-born reformers found threatening to the American way of life. Along with poverty-induced problems of crime, domestic violence, and child abuse, many immigrants brought with them a culture which included alcohol.

Alcoholism soon became identified as the overarching problem, and the Women's Christian Temperance Union, founded in 1874, undertook not only to modify alcoholism but to give more power to women, whom they identified as its primary victim. Frances Willard's motto, "Womanliness first—afterwards what you will,"[15] evoked the centrality of women's identity as moral force. Willard advocated the Home Protection Ballot, a right to limited suffrage to enable "the mothers and daughters of America" to play a role in the decision whether "the door of the rum shop is opened or shut beside their homes." Members of the Union set up numerous independent institutions (nurseries, schools, missions, shelters) in addition to working for legislation banning alcohol, mirroring, in Frances Willard's words, women's work in the home as "maids of all work."[16]

The public policy aspect of this "maternalism" flowered in the settlement house. By 1900, nearly a hundred settlement houses provided the opportunity to educated women to do good works, living among the urban poor. Like Hull House in Chicago, the best known of these ventures, the settlements became social service agencies for women and children in the cities, offering nursery schools, home nursing assistance, employment bureaus, and training in English. In the process, the settlement houses began to expose the wretched conditions of life under which the urban poor labored and began an acquaintance with city and state politics in order to ameliorate them. Settlement houses became centers of political activity, advocates for factory laws, sanitation laws, juvenile courts, mother's pensions, public kindergartens, compulsory education, and the abolition of child labor. Most supported suffrage, in the words of one old suffrage song, "giving the ballot to the mothers."[17] By the time suffrage was won in 1920, voteless women had succeeded by sheer dint of moral force (and political organizing of male allies) to win some laws in most states regulating conditions of work for women and children, reforming prisons and courts, ameliorating the subordination of married women and, on the federal level, protecting the purity of food, establishing a children's bureau (headed by Julia Lathrop, the first woman presidential appointee and former resident of Hull House), and creating a women's bureau in the U.S. Department of Labor.[18]

After suffrage, Congress, apprehensive about the appearance of a woman's bloc vote emphasizing a reform agenda, hastily passed legislation to demonstrate members' interest in the reformers' agenda, which included measures directed at the general welfare and provisions aimed specifically at women as interested parties: a meat-packing consumer protection law in 1921 as well as a law providing some small funding for infant and maternal health; a citizenship bill, permitting American women who married foreigners to retain American citizenship; another bill eliminating pay discrimination between men and women in the federal civil service; and, in 1924, a bill establishing a federal prison exclusively for women. In addition, in 1923 congressmen in both the House and the Senate introduced the newly proposed Equal Rights Amendment to the Constitution, designed to mandate legal equality between men and women; the following year, Congress sent the Child Labor Amendment to the states for ratification. Presidents Wilson and Harding named women to the District of Columbia courts, the U.S. Civil Service Commission, the U.S. Employees Compensation Commission, and to a variety of other posts, as well as to their customary positions at the Women's Bureau and the Children's Bureau, in the interest of bringing a woman's moral sensibility to public life.[19]

Ironically, suffrage signaled the end of women as a uniquely moral force in politics. Formal political access removed women's moral edge and, when no bloc vote emerged in the 1920s, male politicians breathed a sigh of relief and went back to business as usual. Although women continued to be active in community institutions and charities, the women's movement splintered, and no new central organizing principle appeared promptly to unify it again. To the contrary, political party leaders warned women against creating a special political vehicle to represent them and the revitalized right wing further intimidated centrist women's groups by accusing others, especially women's peace organizations, of Bolshevik sympathies.[20] Once the economy collapsed, recovery monopolized the political discussion. New Deal legislation provided an opportunity to offer federal protection to widows and orphans and to extend worker protections, but economic exigencies eclipsed other policy rationales. The Depression had made appeals to conscience superfluous; the war that followed would have a similar result. Women had not only ceased to occupy a unique role as moral advocates;as political actors, they had dropped off the screen almost entirely.[21] Women would again offer a concerted value-based challenge to policy makers, but not until later in the century. Then they would be arguing from a position dramatically different from that which their early twentieth-century forebears had defended.

THE INTERACTION OF VALUES AND PUBLIC POLICY: WOMEN'S ECONOMIC BEHAVIOR, FEDERAL POLICY, AND THE EMERGENCE OF FEMINISM

After World War II, values became once again a matter of intense discussion among policy makers, although women began the era as targets of policy, not agenda setters. Restoring the American social order meant reestablishing gender-specific norms for behavior. Once the nuclear dust cloud settled, the nation turned to constructing the American Way of Life as a bulwark against international communism. The postnuclear family presumed mothers and fathers with different, though equally valued, roles. Fathers were primarily breadwinners, expected, however, to share responsibility for the moral development of their children, especially sons; mothers were the frontline practitioners of day-to-day child rearing, helping and supporting their husbands in the role of income producer. Moms could do other things—club work, supplementary wage-earning—but they were expected to subordinate those activities to the primary demands of their offspring. Blurred gender roles marked Soviet-style state-controlled Communism; Americans modeled the ideal Judeo-Christian family to the world.

But within twenty years—the Cold War still at its height—commitment to the traditional American family was under attack on several fronts. Students adopted the stance of 1950s cultural rebels, who had sneered at the notion of sexual abstention until marriage and monogamy afterward. Young people charged their elders with hypocrisy, living lives designed for conspicuous consumption rather than emotional fulfillment. Policy makers took uneasy notice of the rise in fatherless families among the poor and the impact of broken homes, the result of liberalized divorce laws. And before the 1960s had ended, an insurgent feminism rejected the fundamental premise of social organization, division of family labor according to sex. Thus began a vigorous explicit debate on the most basic questions of which values public policy should encourage: traditional family values or a radical individual egalitarianism that presumed no essential givens about men or women. But the relationship between shifting values and the challenge to public policy was not one of simple cause and effect. Instead, public policy makers played significant roles in creating the shift in values that subsequently generated a cultural crisis concerning gender roles.

Though Rosie the Riveter remains the best remembered icon of World War II, she represents an anomaly. The gains women made in nontraditional employment were eye-catching but short-lived and of little consequence. Discriminatory hiring and dismissal policies and a veterans' preference bill that put upper-level government jobs out of the reach of women for decades to come helped reimpose gender roles with a vengeance. Veterans' educational benefits, which went primarily to male students, widened the gap in educational attainment between men and women. The war had forced couples to defer marriage and children and so both men and women sought the pleasures of domesticity once the war ended; the record numbers of new babies left mothers with little time for political activism. Moreover, continuing conflict among women's organizations' leaders made a widespread mobilization of women in the service of women's rights or a politics of morality all the more unlikely.

Nevertheless, the postwar period witnessed a change in behavior among women that generated a striking interplay between shifting values and public policy, that is, married women went to work outside the home for wages. Although waged work for single women became common after the introduction of factory work in the nineteenth century, by 1900, few married women worked outside the home and those who did were primarily immigrant women and African-American wives. The prevailing ethos decreed that the good middle-class white mother should remain at home with her children. Nevertheless, the proportion of employed wives had risen steadily during the twentieth century, from 6 percent in 1900 to 15 percent in 1940. Wartime opportunities and the expansion of white-collar and service jobs in the 1950s provided further encouragement. The baby boom that peaked in 1956 produced acute needs for teachers. Affluence generated more jobs in retail sales. As health insurance became a commonplace benefit of employment, care became more accessible and the demand for nurses grew. When banks and insurance companies computerized their operations, women became keypunch operators. The call for women workers broke down long-standing barriers against hiring married women and also gave black women new access to clerical and retail jobs. By 1960, almost a third of American wives worked for wages at least part time and the proportion grew every year. Even more telling, the labor force participation rate for wives with preschool children climbed 8 percentage points in a little more than a decade, from 14 percent in 1951 to 22.5 percent in 1963, despite an ostensible social norm against married mothers working.

If women had adopted a new role, they offered an old explanation: They were working on behalf of their families' welfare. For middle-class families of the 1950s, indeed, home production offered little in the way of efficiency—store-bought bread and manufactured clothes cost little more than the homemade variety—and full-time homemaking provided nothing in the way of cash to pay for braces, summer camp, and college. Few wives claimed that work for pay provided economic independence for themselves; instead, it made possible advantages for their children. During the 1950s, wives at work stayed in traditional women's jobs and posed no explicit challenge to the superordination of men either in the workplace or at home as breadwinner.

In deference to their traditional roles, working women did not resist the overt and unapologetic discrimination they encountered on the job. Salaries for women's work ran at about 59 percent of men's earnings. Significant differences appeared even when men and women did the same job. Newspapers categorized want-ads by sex (and race). Companies made no bones about barring women from managerial positions or low-level jobs on managerial tracks. School systems favored men for principals' jobs; library systems, overwhelmingly staffed by women, opted when possible for male directors. The federal government itself permitted managers (almost all male) to specify the sex of candidates for civil service openings, with men routinely chosen for the higher-paid posts. Employers justified their practices by pointing to women's family responsibilities; women, they claimed, cared first and chiefly for their families. They could not be assigned to responsible positions because they could not be counted on to work evenings or weekends and they would absent themselves from work when their children were sick.

Potential for change in understanding women's roles emerged from the international situation. Some policy makers worried about the underutilization of womanpower, in view of the conflict between the United States and the Soviet Union for global influence. In 1957, the Russians had launched two space satellites, demonstrating (many believed) a substantial superiority in scientific and technical acumen. The Russians made obvious use of women workers in all fields. Americans could perhaps be guilty of short-sightedness if they continued to neglect a potential pool of scientists and engineers simply because of gender.

Women workers did not themselves quickly adopt this line. During the 1960 presidential election, the "women's issues" that did come up—child care, women presidential appointees, a White House consumer adviser, presidential endorsement of the long-pending Equal Rights Amendment—drew little attention except from a small group of Washington-based women activists.

So the election of John F. Kennedy in November 1960 offered an opportunity to effect a change in policy based not yet on a shift in values but simply on an alteration of circumstance. Women activists connected to the labor movement found themselves in a key position thanks to Kennedy's offer of an administration post to Esther Peterson, then with the Industrial Union Department of the AFL-CIO. From this platform, she launched a salvo against employment discrimination, pointing to women's expanded role, their families need for their wages, and the nation's need for their work. The program she implemented, with the administration's blessing, had been developed by a cadre of labor union women some fifteen years before in the wake of World War II.

The President's Commission on the Status of Women (PCSW), the first such national commission, appointed by John F. Kennedy in December, 1961, at Peterson's request, fit with the Kennedy program to revitalize the economy and to exploit the talents of all Americans to ensure American dominance in the international arena. The commission disclaimed an overtly feminist agenda. It focused on social assistance; everyone agreed that children were and would remain women's special charge. Rather, the PCSW took as its mandate to help women meet their responsibilities at home as they made a maximum contribution to America's economic and intellectual life.[22]

Chaired by Eleanor Roosevelt, the most prominent woman in the country, the PCSW undertook a comprehensive examination of the status of women in America and made proposals for a wide variety of measures, both governmental and private, to assist women in their dual public and private roles. Recommendations included an executive order enunciating a federal policy against sex discrimination in employment, the extension of minimum wage and equal pay laws to all men and women not already covered, paid pregnancy leave and maternity leave, publicly supported child care services for all who needed them, educational opportunities for older women, the extension of unemployment insurance to household and agricultural workers, the equalization of jury service rules, the removal of all legal disabilities of married women, recognition of nonmonetary contributions of married women (thereby giving them the right to property in the marriage), a greater role for women in political life, and the continuation of federal efforts to monitor and stimulate action toward these ends. During the life of the commission, President Kennedy acted on its recommendation to eliminate selection by sex in the civil service. On November 1, 1963, he signed an executive order establishing two continuing federal committees on women.

On controversial issues, the PCSW temporized. It did not throw its weight behind the movement for a constitutional amendment to ensure legal equality for women, proposing instead the alternative of a carefully constructed appeal for a Supreme Court ruling. Its statement in support of equal treatment for employed women was mitigated by its inference that some discrimination against women made sense, that is, it spoke of the need to eradicate only "unjustified discrimination." It did not endorse wage work for mothers of small children, although it took a position consistent across class and racial lines: "It is regrettable when women with children are forced by economic necessity or by the regulations of welfare agencies to seek employment while their children are young."[23]

But if its recommendations represented merely the best of mainstream liberal thinking on women, they catalyzed a new movement. By its very existence, the commission conferred a new legitimacy on the subject of sex discrimination, a subject theretofore regarded by the media as laughable. More concretely, the commission inspired the creation on the state level of parallel agencies; virtually every one of the fifty states established a commission on women. The ongoing bodies, federal and state, not only accumulated a massive amount of data in support of the contention that discrimination thwarted women's legitimate aspirations, they educated a national network of women newly committed to women's issues.

If the PCSW had gathered the fuel and laid the fire for the women's movement, Congress provided the match with its enactment of the Civil Rights Act of 1964, which included a provision banning discrimination based on sex in employment. A peculiar coalition stood (or crouched) behind the measure: an alliance of racist Southerners and anti-labor Republicans who were long-time supporters of the Equal Rights Amendment (including House Rules Committee Chairman Howard Smith [D., VA]), incited and abetted by pro-ERA women members of Congress and amendment backers outside. Emanuel Celler (D., NY), who chaired the House Judiciary Committee, warned that the provision would sweep away fifty-year-old state labor laws enacted to protect vulnerable women, but the House of Representatives agreed to it nonetheless, and the Senate, lobbied hard by the pro-ERA National Federation of Business and Professional Women's Clubs, let it stay. Nevertheless, the Equal Employment Opportunity Commission (EEOC), set up to enforce the employment provision, refused to credit this particular congressional action and abjured the sex provision. The existence of federal and state commissions had created an aura of expectation; their recommendations had developed into a national agenda. The federal government continued to contribute its support. As a result, when the EEOC disclaimed the "sex" amendment, it provoked this national network into an organized, frontal assault. The women attending the third national meeting of state commissions on women, held in Washington, D.C. and sponsored by the U.S. Department of Labor, took a table at lunch and formed the National Organization for Women (NOW).[24]

NOW claimed feminism as its philosophy and brought about a resolution of the century-old conundrum for women's advocates. Until the formation of NOW, women activists, even those who called themselves feminists, sought simultaneously policy measures that would gain for women equal access to the whole panorama of public life *and* that would protect women's special relationship to children. Women's groups had repeatedly tripped over this internal contradiction, but NOW swept it away with a declaration in its statement of purpose: "We reject the current assumptions that a man must carry the sole burden of supporting himself, his wife and family . . . or that marriage, home and family are primarily woman's world and responsibility—hers, to dominate, his to support. We believe that a true partnership between the sexes demands a different concept of marriage, an equitable sharing of the responsibilities of home and children and of the economic burdens of their support."[25] A modern feminism, shriven of biological essentialism, had appeared.

NOW won the contest with the EEOC and Celler proved right. Title VII of the 1964 Civil Rights Act swept away the provisions in the law that assumed the greater frailty of women. The disposal of these laws cleared the field for the Equal Rights Amendment, which Congress sent to the states for ratification in 1972, almost fifty years after its initial proposal in Congress. Within a decade from the report of the President's Commission on the Status of Women, which spoke still of justified discrimination in employment, a consensus emerged among the nation's opinion leaders that sex discrimination was illegitimate and should in virtually all cases be illegal, and that distinctions based upon generally perceived differences between men and women could not serve as an acceptable foundation for public policy decisions. If poll results could be believed, the majority of citizens agreed.

This broad outline of a frenetic era leaves out much, but the central point remains apparent. A shift in federal policy emerged in recognition of new behaviors and new national needs, but it led, rather than followed, a wholesale shift in public values. The independent movement, fostered by the government's actions, quickly outdistanced its champions within the political establishment. With a new feminist paradigm holding sway, Congress readily responded with a spate of new legislation,[26] and the judicial system similarly revised legal doctrine in keeping with the new set of egalitarian values.[27] But the cycle was not complete. If modern feminism bespoke a new worldview, adherents of the old were not all at once persuaded. By the end of the 1970s, political debate converged on arguably the most fundamental challenge to traditional values in politics since the Civil War. For the rest of the century, a core conflict in values and public policy arose from the feminist challenge to fundamental conservative religious and political beliefs about the way the world should be organized.

Arguably, every women's political movement contested public policy decisions on the basis of values rather than participating in the traditional public discussions about rational economic decision making to achieve maximum efficiency. In the early nineteenth century, the movement to give women access to education on the grounds that they held responsibility to raise citizens of a republic introduced the idea that the domestic was political, an idea reinforced in campaigns against indecency and for temperance. (Few women, on the other hand, got involved in the debates about monopolies or tariffs.) Women's claim both for autonomy and for state protection from unchecked male privilege emerged from one shift in values—a new American commitment to independence and democracy—to a second transformation in public values that by the beginning of the twentieth century led to substantial revisions in gender roles. How the state invests power in families is nothing if not an exercise in values. The redefinition of family power from a private, domestic matter to a public, political matter required first a restructuring of values so that women's autonomy and safety could be successfully weighed against the preservation of a "natural" male authority. In the twentieth century, women activists went further to question all notions of specific roles assigned by sex and engaged the most profound discussion about public policy and values—family values—yet.

CONTEMPORARY CONFLICTS: MEN, WOMEN, AND SOCIAL RESPONSIBILITY

The feminist movement that emerged from the 1960s had as its premise a rejection of the foundational principle of traditional social organization: division of the world's work according to sex. At the same time, thanks to the civil rights movement, the centuries-old system of racial subordination was threatened (although hardly de-throned) by principles of racial equality now incorporated into both statutes and judicial decisions. Taken together, the values of racial and sexual equality spelled the end of the traditional world and its hierarchy of political and economic privilege. Those who saw these distinctions as divinely ordained (or simply in their interest) mobilized, delivering the presidency in 1980 to Ronald Reagan and, in 1994, the Congress to Newt Gingrich and Robert Dole.

Though some would argue that the animus against liberalism arises predominantly from anxiety about economic well-being, the vitriolic rhetoric about, for example, welfare mothers (one member of Congress referred to them metaphorically as alligators) suggests that something more is at stake. If the motive were strictly economic, presumably one would see men and women who were similarly placed with respect to race and class voting the same way. Instead, even white born-again Christians divide by sex in political judgments.[28] The most determined support for the Republican program comes from white married men—those who had lost most in the sex-race power constellation. And, although only a small proportion of federal tax dollars goes to support families in poverty, attacks on "welfare queens" resonate persistently while exposures of corporate scams, massive agricultural subsidies, and defense waste, fraud, and abuse attract minimal attention and never catch fire. Indeed, the central contest in public discourse today pits so-called family values (i.e., traditional male-headed family values) against feminist family values, which support a variety of family types, including the most vilified: the female-headed household. For many policy makers, the rise of the female-headed household has come to symbolize the decline of American society. First identified as a national problem by Daniel Patrick Moynihan in his 1965 White House memorandum on the Negro family, the woman raising her children alone now represents a willful defiance of national norms, more to be censured than pitied.

The question of waged work for mothers currently forms the focus of more than one policy debate, but the expectations differ depending on the economic status of the mother in question. Until the 1950s, a good mother stayed home with her children, regardless of class. If she lacked the financial support of a man, government programs sought to replace it. Women during that decade justified work for wages as part of their "natural" domestic roles, providing for their children's well-being—inadvertently both sustaining the values attached to motherhood and undermining its traditional definition. By the 1970s, feminists asserted that a mother had a right to work outside the home without aspersions cast upon her competence as a parent and that fathers held equal responsibility for child care. At the end of the twentieth century, we find policy makers defining work for wages to be the *essential* component of good mothering, but only for poor mothers— those receiving financial assistance from the state. Ironically, at the same time, the middle-class mother at home all day with her kids rates an admiring news story, especially if she interrupted a professional career. So we see policy makers applaud the ideal of full-time (if temporary) motherhood for the married, white, middle-class mother, while they decry it for the poor, single, presumptively black mother who requires public assistance to fulfill this role. But more is at stake than the fiscal burden on the public. The question turns not on money, but on values.

Honest policy makers acknowledged that the system of Aid to Families with Dependent Children (AFDC), established in an era when mothers of young children did not work outside the home, no longer fit a society in which all adults are expected to work for wages in the labor market for some substantial number of hours each week.[29] But conservative pundits took a different and successful tack: AFDC did not merely fail to solve today's poverty problem, it *caused* today's poverty problem.[30] This analysis permits them to call the abolition of AFDC reform.

Failure to create positive alternatives to AFDC (publically funded child care and preschools, national health insurance, guaranteed child support payments, expanded earned income tax credit [EITC], last-resort government jobs) saves money, but simple elimination of financial support also serves the interests of those who wish to reinstall the traditional sex-race hierarchy that feminism appeared momentarily to dislodge. Conservative policy analysts stated their goals frankly: more marriages and fewer divorces brought about by the diminution of alternative sources of economic security for women. The unspoken policy objective thus is to reassert male authority within the family by depriving women with small children of the option of refusing to enter or to leave an unsatisfactory marriage. Many would candidly state that people divorce too readily and that fewer options will result in more stable and therefore sounder families. A feminist analysis of the incidence of spousal abuse might well argue the contrary: husbands who know that their wives cannot escape are more rather than less likely to give in to a violent impulse, making for fewer sound families. But conservative theorists now argue that male violence emerges not from the difference in power between men and women, but from feminism's assertion that women should be economically independent of men.

Such a line of analysis can be seen in the writings of James Q. Wilson, David Popenoe, and David Blankenhorn,[31] who assert that the decline of our civilization can be attributed to the "natural" (read "biologically immutable") antisocial characteristics of the human male. But, according to David Blankenhorn, the untrammeled incivility of men can be laid at the feet of women, who have determined that fathers are not necessary to family well-being and who have therefore released men from their obligation to channel their aggression in socially wholesome ways, that is, competing with other men in the marketplace for the sake of material provision for their families. Unattached to families, divested of their roles as fathers, these men become marauders in the streets. To stop them, says Wilson, "[o]ur object ought to be to increase the number of urban young men who marry and remain married."[32] David Blankenhorn notes that men estranged from their role as fathers are, almost literally, going crazy:

> As their fatherhood decomposes, or is threatened, they lose self-control. Some pick up guns and start killing people. Typically, the people they kill are children, ex-spouses, and government officials who seem to stand between them and their former lives, especially social workers, judges, and child support-enforcement officers. As fatherhood fragments in our society, this species of violence is spreading.[33]

Blankenhorn thus implies that these men who murder ex-spouses and children, had they maintained safe haven within intact marriages, would be good citizens and family members. Therefore, the onus for their crimes falls on the person who separated them from the children, that is, the ex-spouse.

Blankenhorn's critique of feminism is explicit. He decries the notion that mothers and fathers can be parents in the same way. He insists rather on the need for a "gendered" understanding of fatherhood, one that relies upon an authoritarian masculinity that withholds love from children who fail to live up to fatherly standards.

The "new father" of the feminist utopia, who loves and cares for his children as a mother might, constitutes in Blankenhorn's assessment, fatherlessness. If mothers and fathers are not different, women can raise children alone. Blankenhorn attributes fatherlessness, the nation's most devastating problem, to this sentiment.

David Popenoe makes a specific argument about the responsibility of women to civilize men:

> The good society is heavily dependent on men being attached to a strong moral order centered on families, both to discipline their sexual behavior and to reduce their competitive aggression. Men need the moral and emotional instruction of women more than vice versa; and family life, especially having children, is a considerable civilizing force for men. (It is not uncommon to hear men say that they will give up certain deviant or socially irresponsible patterns of life only when they have children, for then they feel the need to set a good example.)[34]

This "woman's burden" to civilize men is misbegotten on two scores. First, it is driven by an exaggerated essentialism. The moral superiority of women was, we know, an invention of the nineteenth century. In the seventeenth century, social policy depended upon a directly contradictory precept: a woman needed a husband because a woman had a weak mind, a fragile psyche, a frail physique, and an atrophied moral capacity. Thus, ironically, those who once used to be the weaker vessel are now commissioned to turn society back to the straight and narrow path. Cotton Mather would be struck dumb.

But we need not hearken back to the seventeenth century to find the flaws in this idea—that women are not intrinsically saintly. Women trapped in poverty, like men trapped in poverty, demonstrate a variety of adaptations to their circumstances, some wholesome, some not. But it is surely fanciful to believe that an impoverished mother marrying a drug-dependent father with criminal propensities will create a happy, healthy family. We know from recent studies that the fathers of children of young teenage mothers are likely to be older than twenty. Can we suggest, as a matter of public policy, that marriage to a sixteen-year-old pregnant girl will change the character of the twenty-two-year-old who impregnated her? Dare we risk such a gamble? (Of course, the question presupposes he consents. David Popenoe notes that "[h]ow to get men to marry the mothers of their children in the first place is no less daunting a task than lowering the divorce rate."[35])

We can guess at reasons for the decline in the marriage rate, but in fact it remains a puzzle. We have some data on which to base policy decisions: cross-cultural evidence from other western democracies and data from global population programs. Also, we have experienced in this country a dramatic decline in the birth rate over the course of our history. We know that girls with a positive incentive to delay pregnancy don't get pregnant; girls with nothing to lose do. In this instance, then, a focus on economically rational incentives might serve both traditional values and feminist ones.

But the emphasis on values in the public debate over single motherhood supplants discussion about the economic realities of such families and what economic strategies might ameliorate them. If there is a lesson to be found in the history of the discussion about values and women's place, it is that family structure and women's behavior change more in response to economic imperatives than to exhortation and that worldviews tend to be mutable, possibly more contingent on economic circumstances than the reverse. If economic independence for women means that fewer women marry for financial security, a national discussion about the noneconomic function of marriage may be worthwhile. But if that discussion serves to divert the attention of policy makers from the immediate problem of economic security for impoverished children and desperate single mothers, we serve no one's interest. We may need now less talk about values and more about economics.

NOTES

1. Phyllis Schlafly, *The Power of the Christian Woman* (Cincinnati: Standard Publishing, 1981); Jane Alpert, "Mother Right: A New Feminist Theory," *Ms.*, August 1973, 52–88.

2. Edmund S. Morgan, *The Puritan Family: Religion and Domestic Relations in Seventeenth-Century New England* (New York: Harper & Row, 1966), 44.

3. John Demos, *A Little Commonwealth: Family Life in Plymouth Colony* (New York: Oxford University Press, 1970), 82–84.

4. Morgan, *Puritan Family*, 98.

5. Ibid., 44.

6. Laurel Thatcher Ulrich, "Vertuous Women Found: New England Ministerial Literature, 1668–1735," in *Puritan New England*, ed. Alden T. Vaughn and Francis J. Bremer (New York: St. Martin's Press, 1977), 227.

7. Linda K. Kerber, *Women of the Republic: Intellect and Ideology in Revolutionary America* (New York: Norton, 1986 [1980]), chapter 1.

8. Nancy Cott, *The Bonds of Womanhood: "Woman's Sphere" in New England, 1780–1835* (New Haven: Yale University Press, 1977), chapter 4, 127–129, 132, 146.

9. Ibid., 104.

10. Joseph Buckminster, 1810, quoted in Cott, *Bonds*, 148.

11. Sarah Pierce, October 29, 1818, quoted in Cott, *Bonds*, 120.

12. Cott, *Bonds*, 151–153.

13. Ibid., 205.

14. Elizabeth Cady Stanton, "Declaration of Sentiments," quoted in Miriam Schneir, *Feminism: The Essential Historical Writings* (New York: Random House, 1972), 77.

15. Sara Evans, *Born for Liberty: A History of Women in America* (New York: Free Press, 1989), 127.

16. Quoted in Evans, *Born for Liberty*, 127, 129.

17. *Give the Ballot to the Mothers*, words by Rebecca N. Hazard, recorded by Elizabeth Knight on Folkways Records, album no. FH 5281, *Songs of the Woman Suffrage Movement* (New York: Folkways, 1958).

18. Evans, *Born for Liberty*, chapter 7, esp. p. 160.

19. J. Stanley Lemons, *The Woman Citizen* (Charlottesville: University Press of Virginia, 1990 [1973]).

20. Nancy Cott, *The Grounding of Modern Feminism* (New Haven: Yale, 1987); Lemons, *The Woman Citizen*.

21. Jeannette Rankin, who alone voted against the entry of the United States into World War II, as she had during World War I, was an exception to this rule.

22. For a discussion of the events leading to the creation of the PCSW, see Cynthia Harrison, *On Account of Sex: The Politics of Women's Issues, 1945–1968.* (Berkeley: University of California Press, 1988). Its impact is described in Harrison and in Jo Freeman, *The Politics of Women's Liberation* (New York: David McKay, 1975).

23. President's Commission on the Status of Women, *American Women* (Washington, DC: U.S. Government Printing Office, 1963), 19.

24. See Betty Friedan, *It Changed My Life: Writings on the Women's Movement* (New York: Random House, 1976), 75–86, for her discussion of the relationship between the PCSW and the formation of the NOW.

25. NOW, "Statement of Purpose," in *Up From the Pedestal: Selected Writings in the History of American Feminism*, ed. Aileen S. Kraditor (Chicago: Quadrangle Books, 1968), 363–369.

26. See Cynthia Harrison, "Women's Issues and Rights," in *The Encyclopedia of the United States Congress* (Simon & Schuster, 1995), 2140–2147.

27. Leslie Goldstein, *The Constitutional Rights of Women: Cases in Law and Social Change* (Madison: University of Wisconsin Press, 1988).

28. "Pollsters View Gender Gap as Political Fixture: White Men Heed GOP Call; Women Lean to Democrats," *Washington Post*, August 15, 1995, 1, 11.

29. Historian Edward D. Berkowitz has pointed out elsewhere the problem with expecting a program designed to help mothers stay home to serve the function of moving them into the labor force.

30. The most prominent exponent of this position is, of course, Charles Murray, in *Losing Ground: American Social Policy, 1950–1980* (New York: Basic Books, 1994 [1984]). Critiques of his use of data abound. Daniel Patrick Moynihan offers perhaps the pithiest rejoinder when he notes that he identified the trends that Murray attributes to the Great Society programs in 1965 in order to encourage Lyndon Johnson to *create* the Great Society programs, in *Family and Nation* (San Diego: Harcourt, Brace, Jovanovich, 1986).

31. James Q. Wilson, "Culture, Incentives, and the Underclass," and David Popenoe, "The Family Condition of America: Cultural Change and Public Policy," in *Values and Public Policy*, ed. Henry J. Aaron, Thomas E. Mann, and Timothy Taylor (Washington, DC: The Brookings Institution, 1994); David Blankenhorn, *Fatherless America: Confronting Our Most Urgent Social Problem* (New York: Basic Books, 1995).

32. Wilson, "Culture," 74.

33. Blankenhorn, *Fatherless America*, 141.

34. Popenoe, "Family Condition," 98.

35. Ibid., 103.

12

Democratic Rhetoric and Genetic Engineering: Who Owns the Human Gene Pool?

Eric T. Juengst

October 1995 marked a considerable number of important anniversaries for the ethics of genetic engineering. It was thirty years since R. D. Hotchkiss introduced the label "genetic engineering" in a worried essay entitled, "Portents for a Genetic Engineering" (Hotchkiss, 1965). Twenty years before that, 1975, the federal Guidelines for Recombinant DNA Research were developed to regulate genetic engineering, after scientists went public with their worries in the early 1970s upon actually developing the tools to do what Hotchkiss anticipated (Krimsky, 1985). It was ten years since the submission in 1985 of the first formal protocol to conduct a clinical trial of gene therapy on a human being, and a few began five years after that, in September, 1990. (Thompson, 1994). Today, that first human gene therapy trial is considered a success, over one hundred others are underway, and squadrons of molecular geneticists and biotechnologists now blithely call themselves genetic engineers, oblivious to the ironic origins of the label.

One of the interesting features of the thirty-year history of genetic engineering is the extent to which it has been open to and influenced by concerns over social values and the public's voice. As the histories of Lysenkoism, racial hygiene, and social Darwinism illustrate, human biology has not had many positive experiences in its twentieth-century attempts to incorporate prevailing social values into its science policy agenda. Yet from the beginning, genetic engineering seems to have been recognized to involve social value commitments that seemed to require the approval of the democratic process. Hotchkiss sets the tone by concluding his prescient prediction of genetic interventions we are now capable of performing by prescribing that "[t]he best preparation will be an informed and forewarned public, and a thoughtful body scientific. The teachers and the science writers can perform their historic duties by helping our public to recognize and evaluate these possibilities and avoid their abuses. For these things surely are on the way" (Hotchkiss, 1965, p. 202). Thus, in calling for the guidelines whose twentieth birthday we celebrated in December, 1995, the scientists themselves were in the forefront of those who argued that "[t]he principle of Democratic oversight is basic to our society, and its application is essential for producing popular information and popular decisions. The social consequences of the recombinant DNA technology are too enormous and important to be left to specialists alone" (Nader, 1986, p. 159). As early as 1972, prospective gene therapists like W. French Anderson were suggesting that the decisions to proceed with human genetic engineering experiments should require consent from society as well as from the individuals involved (Anderson, 1971). Moreover, Anderson and his colleagues followed through fifteen years later by publishing the entire protocol for his first clinical trial in the Congressional Record for public scrutiny and comment, and subjecting his research to the most extensive public review process in the history of biomedical experimentation (Walters, 1986). Similarly, in 1990, Nobel laureate James Watson launched the U.S. Human Genome Project, with a public commitment to complement the molecular mapping of the human chromosomes with research designed to anticipate and address the social value issues of the project's work, on the startling rationale that

> science is not done in a vacuum and should not be pursued as if it could be. Good science affects and its social context, and the practical effects of good basic science are often the most wide-ranging of all. Science in turn is constantly affected by professional norms, social policies and the public perceptions that frame it. . . . Doing the Genome Project in the real world means thinking about these outcomes from the start, so that science and society can pull together to optimize the benefits of this new knowledge to human welfare and opportunity. (Watson and Juengst, 1992, p. xv–xvi)

Today, over $20 million has been diverted from scientific pockets into the hands of social policy analysts, humanities scholars, social scientists, and educators in the Genome Project's efforts to follow through on Watson's commitment.

I happen to think that these attempts to democratize and humanize our science policy regarding human genetic engineering are a good thing: we should celebrate, not regret, this season's anniversaries. On the other hand, it is still dangerously easy to go too far in this direction and end up with yet another episode in our country's history of socially abusive and ideologically distorted science policies. In this chapter, I illustrate how *not* to integrate social values into our science policies regarding genetic engineering by examining one increasingly popular approach to international genetic research policy that I will argue does risk launching us down this slope.

The flashpoint for most current international discussions of policies to govern genetic engineering is the question of whether or not to allow scientists to pursue germ-line gene therapy—genetic engineering interventions that would effect changes in people that would be passed along to their offspring as a natural part of their genetic inheritance. One approach to this question is to suggest that the human germ-line should be considered for policy purposes as a special asset in the "common heritage of humankind," susceptible to the same forms of international stewardship as the planet's sea-bed or great works of art. Paramount in that stewardship is the goal of preserving the value of our species' genetic heritage for future generations, just as we would preserve our other universal goods. This, in turn, leads to calls to protect our common genetic patrimony against the plunder and abuse of those who would divert it to their own private ends.[1]

I call the line of reasoning I have just sketched the common heritage (or CH) view in genomic science policy. When it is brought to bear on the prospect of human germ-line engineering, it usually leads to presumptive condemnations of the idea as an infringement of the integrity of the genome and an abridgement of the rights of future persons to inherit a germ-line free from any engineered alternations. The CH view has been spectacularly successful in public policy settings over the last decade, influencing positions advanced in Switzerland, Germany, Canada, the Council of Europe, the United Nations Educational, Scientific, and Cultural Organization (UNESCO), France, Austria, and at any number of international conferences.[2] Moreover, it seems to flow naturally from the claims of conscientious molecular geneticists that, in some way, their work really is the public's business. Unfortunately, as an approach to science policy, the CH view is conceptually flawed and socially dangerous.

WHY GERM-LINE GENE THERAPY SEEMS LIKE MINING THE SEA-BED

> If there is an obvious component of the common heritage of mankind, indeed, more obvious than the resources of the sea-bed itself, it is the human genetic system.
>
> —Agius, 1990, p. 140

It is not hard to see why the human germ-line and genes it carries are considered by so many to be special assets in the common heritage of humankind. The human germ-line is the lineage of living cells that weaves itself through each of us, developmentally linking the zygotes at our origins to the gametes we produce after puberty. Since the zygotes at our origins are created by the fusion of other people's gametes, and individual gametes of our own can, in exceedingly rare instances, fuse with cells from another person's germ-line to produce new zygotes, it is natural to think of the germ-line as a thread of living tissue that runs between parents and their children, each new generation to the last.

In fact, as long as one is willing to assume that our species grew from a single origin and has since been true to itself, the human germ-line might be interpreted as the golden thread of human biological life, the thread that connects all of us as one family, and through which we pass on that connection to our children, as a unique and universal human legacy.[3] Moreover, since all the genes that underlie our individual human capacities have (rationally) been transmitted to us through the fusion of our parents germ-lines into our own, the value of the legacy of human germinal connection is not merely our common identity as members of the human family. As the transmitter of genes, it is the germ-line connection that allows us to inherit from our parents and endow upon our children the range of functions, capacities, and abilities that have enabled our species to become so successful in dominating Earth's ecosphere. As appealing as this story is, however, for the social values that it seems to embody, it needs to be abandoned as a basis for science policy.

WHY GERM-LINE GENE THERAPY IS NOT LIKE MINING THE SEA-BED

There are two sets of objections to evaluating germ-line engineering proposals through the lens of the CH view. The first are scientific and conceptual: framing the issues in terms of a right to inherit a genetic pattern that has not been artificially changed requires assumptions about human biology that make the effort incompatible with standard scientific thought. The second set of objections are ethical and political: grounding our moral concern for posterity in the CH view risks being self-defeating by facilitating the very social abuses of genetic science that it seeks to prevent. The interests of posterity that are at stake in the genomic science policy decisions we make today are interests in social opportunities, not natural resources. Rather than fretting over biological risks of germ-line engineering we know nothing about, we should be fulfilling our obligations to the future by preventing the practice from exacerbating forms of genetic discrimination we already know all too well.

SCIENTIFIC AND CONCEPTUAL PROBLEMS WITH THE COMMON HERITAGE VIEW

The Human Germ-Line

Is the human germ-line really a resource for humanity, like the sea-bed, the atmosphere, or even great works of art? It may be helpful to begin with some simple terminological clarifications. The "germ-line" is a concept from embryology and histology and is used in those fields to label the lineage of dividing cells within an organism that link its zygote stage with its fully differentiated gametes. From the biologist's point of view, each organism's germ-line terminates in its gametes. The next zygote is not another cell within the parent organism's germ-line, because it is not the result of another episode of cell division within that developmental lineage. Instead, the zygote fuses the end-products of two germ-cell lineages and founds a third.

This means that, strictly speaking, while individual humans have germ-line cells and germ-cell lineages, the human species does not have a germ-line in the genealogical sense which the CH view requires. Moreover, it is important to biologists that the human species does *not* have a continuous germ-line, because that is precisely what distinguishes them as sexual eucayotes from asexual organisms that persist as continuous lineages of mitotically dividing cells. In effect, human beings gave up their germ-line relationships long ago, in favor of sexual ones.

Of course, proponents of the CH view are free to stipulatively define the phrase "the human germ-line" for their own purposes, or to use the biological germ-line concept in an explicitly metaphorical way. The notion of a "human germ-line" as a transgenerational network with its own ontological integrity fits well—suspiciously well, in my opinion—with our preanalytic cultural intuitions about human genealogies and family blood lines, and so is useful in setting the stage for the common heritage view. However, those who extend the concept this way should be aware that they are departing from the scientific understanding of the world when they do so. Biomedically speaking, there is no intergenerational human germ-line that could serve as an asset to the future, and efforts to ground social policy in such an idea may be greeted by the scientific community with the same scepticism they would give a policy that assumed that blood literally passes from parents to children in a familial blood line.[4]

The Human Genome

On the other hand, if our germ-lines do not literally link us to our families, the genes that are passed on during the merger of two germ-lines do. I have inherited (almost) exact copies of genes my parents carried and will pass on (almost) exact copies of the same genes to my children. Is it perhaps that inheritance to which the CH view refers? Given that what the CH view seems to value about our genetic patrimony is its ability to give us our human capabilities, this seems plausible. It is the gene-line, not the germ-line that is really at issue in germ-line gene therapy.[5] Perhaps it would be more correct, then, to say that it is the complement of human genes that each germ-cell lineage carries, the genome that it shares with all other human germ-lines, that is at stake in the CH view. UNESCO is now proposing in its draft declaration that "the human genome is the common heritage of humanity." (UNESCO, 1995, p. 97).

Does germ-line gene therapy endanger the rights of future generations to enjoy their rightful share of our common human genome, like undersea mining can deny them the fruits of the sea-bed? Again, the geographical metaphors that are used in discussions of "mapping the human genome" make it attractive—too attractive, in my view—to interpret the human genome like the sea-bed, as an explorable, exploitable, mutable place. But we shouldn't be misled by our metaphors into reifying the concept of the human genome inappropriately. Unfortunately, if it is to continue to mean the same thing for science and public policy, the human genome is not something that can play the role of the sea-bed in evaluating germ-line gene therapy.

From the geneticists point of view, the human genome is a heuristic abstraction like the anatomist's concept of the human skeleton. The human genome is defined as the full set of genetic loci that characterizes our species, together with the structural (noncoding) elements that connect them, just as the skeleton is defined as the full set of articulated human bones. In every individual, the gene occupying each genetic locus takes a particular molecular form, as one or another of the alleles or patterns the DNA can display in that locus: that is the source of the observable phenotypic diversity our genetic inheritance provides. The concept of the human genome, however, does not concern itself with all the substantive variations or different alleles that are possible at a given locus, any more than the concept of the human skeleton must account for the minute variations observable between the bones of different people. The human genome, unlike the sea-bed, is a formal scientific concept with no particular material referent in nature. That is why it does not matter to the Human Genome Project (unless we are quite mistaken about the nature of our species) whose chromosomes are studied by those conducting the genome mapping research.

Unfortunately, if the human genome is an abstraction and not a natural object, our worries about preserving its integrity for future generations become concerns about the future of an idea not a natural resource. Thus we might legitimately assert the right of future generations to inherit the *concept* of the human genome, uncensored and not misinterpreted, as part of their common scientific heritage.[6] But that would be to engage in a debate over the future of the stock of human ideas, not the range of human capacities. To that extent, it seems to be diverting us from our central concerns over the future effects of germ-line engineering.

Of course, we all have interests in preserving the integrity of our personal specimens of the human skeleton, and it's plausible to argue that we all have duties not to put the skeletons of members of future generations at risk (e.g., by using thalidomide recklessly). In the same way, advocates for individual members of future generations could defend their clients' right to inherit a complete complement of human genes, protected from major loci deletions (or additions). But they would not have to appeal to the CH view to do so; it would be more effective to simply argue that their clients had been directly harmed by the malpractice of the genetic engineers, just as people already argue in wrongful birth suits involving teratogens like thalidomide or accutane.

Moreover, interpreting the CH view this way, as defending every individual's right to an intact genome, will not take us very far in evaluating most proposals for germ-line engineering. As long as the intervention contemplated would only change alleles at a natural locus, rather than deleting existing loci or adding new kinds of genes, the concern to preserve the integrity of the human genome would be irrelevant to the problem. For practical purposes, the genetic engineer can go a long way toward both therapeutic and enhancement applications before it will become necessary to contemplate inducing knock-out mutations or adding new loci in humans.

The Gene Pool

The fact that human genes do come in multiple forms suggests still another refinement in the interpretation of the CH view. We could say, with Agius (1990) and others, that it is humanity's stock of alleles—the sum total of all our individual forms of each gene—that is really at issue in the CH view. After all, it is here rather than in our common genomic plan or private germ-lines, where the diversity that is often cited as the principal value of our genetic patrimony is displayed. Within our species' complete collection of Mendel's alleles, polymorphic DNA variations, mutations, and "pre-mutations," and functional configurations of genomic structure lie all the biological capacities that allow us to flourish as humans in so many different ways. Moreover, unlike the genome, this collection is real: it consists of specimens of DNA spread across the germ-cells of four billion organisms. Just like pieces of art in the worlds museums, these specimens of DNA can, in principle at least, be collected, preserved, restored, destroyed, stolen, sold, shared, transferred, and combined: in short, they do seem to be the sort of thing that, like the sea-bed, might be preserved and cultivated for the benefit of future generations.

The scientific term in English for the collection of human alleles and genetic variants is the "gene pool." The concept of the "gene pool" comes to us from population genetics and evolution theory. It was influenced surprisingly late, in 1950, by Theodosius Dobzhansky, who used it to help establish a Mendelian definition of "species" as "a reproductive community of sexual and cross-fertilizing individuals which share in a common gene pool"(Adams, 1979, p. 246). Dobzhansky seems to have coined the term by translating loosely from the Russian *genofond* or "gene fund," a term used in the 1920s by his mentors in Soviet population genetics. In fact, the gene pool is sometimes still referred to as "the aggregate genetic resources available to the population, its genetic reserves, on which it may draw in undergoing genetic change" (Adams, 1979, p. 242). This fits very neatly—too neatly, it seems to me—with our intuitive cultural notions that humans have, thanks to investments made on our behalf through the wisdom of evolution, accumulated a genetic endowment on which we might draw to meet new challenges, and over which we now have stewardship, to manage as a common inheritance.

Unfortunately, from a scientific perspective it is nonsense to extend the metaphor of financial management to the evolutionary process in that way. When evolutionary biologists use the investment metaphor to explain the dynamics of a gene pool, it is the unseen, stochastic hand of natural selection, not the species itself, which manages the species' gene fund. That is not simply because the biologists are usually ignoring self-conscious organisms like themselves that can intentionally try to intervene in the process. It is because the evolutionary process is, by definition, an unmanaged and unmanageable one. This can be seen in several ways.

First, the great rhetorical advance Dobzhansky made by substituting "gene pool" for "gene fund" is to underline the fluidity and flux of the evolutionary process. An endowment can be left untouched and inherited by new executors without necessarily increasing or decreasing its value. The frequency of different alleles in a gene pool are constantly fluctuating because everything that affects reproduction changes them, including the random genetic reconfiguration of the sexual reproductive process itself. As Dobzhansky says, "The gene pool is in constant motion; if a simile is desired a stormy sea is more appropriate than a beanbag [or bank account]" (Dobzhansky, 1970, p. 201). Contemporary geneticists go even further to suggest as metaphors phenomena that are more dynamic and have even less integrity than a pool, like rivers (Dawkins, 1995).

This dynamism means that it is no more possible to manage the human gene pool from the inside than it is for a pond to retain its integrity in the absence of a basin. Every human decision concerning reproduction tampers with the gene pool available to the next generation, and as a result there has been no natural gene pool to inherit since human beings started making reproductive decisions. From this perspective, humanity has committed an entire spectrum of artificial interventions in the gene pool, from the practices of celibacy and monogamy to contraception, adoption, and prenatal screening, to the care of people with genetic disease through their reproductive years. Unfortunately, left to its own resources, the CH view can give us no guidance for distinguishing within this spectrum between those practices which should count as illegitimate tampering and those that are consistent with the future's rights to their fair share of the gene pool.[7]

Second, despite the normative connotations of the financial metaphor, biology makes no value judgments about the kinds of evolutionary change that gene pools undergo as a result of natural selection. According to the architects of the CH view, one of the qualifications for being included within the sixty-six common heritage of humankind, is that the resources in question should be "such that they could be well managed only if they were managed on behalf of mankind as a whole." (Inglott, 1994, p. 195). However, from the evolutionary theorists' point of view, there are no wise or poor management decisions to make in attempting to manage the gene pool because whatever changes occur will count equally as bonafide evolution in the species. Unlike the sea-bed or the atmosphere, there is no way to deplete or improve or even preserve the human species' river of genes, because it has no settled natural state to use as a homeostatic benchmark.

Finally, recall that the gene pool is a concept that applies at the level of populations rather than individuals. Given their allegiance to traditional ways to transmitting genes to new generations, the proponents of the CH view cannot argue that, in securing their right to the transmission of the unique human genetic inheritance, free from any engineered alterations, individual members of future generations can demand access to the entire unabridged version of humanity's gene pool. At most, the CH view only supports the view that people should not be denied their rightful share of the gene pool's allele collection. But that introduces an evaluative distinction that quickly leads to harder questions. If it is not the species' entire collection of genotypes that individuals can claim as their heritage, how is their rightful subset to be determined? Surely not simply by reference to their own genealogies and the familial gene pools they can claim as their natural ancestry; that approach would quickly produce just the kind of genetic caste system that the CH view would seem to be designed to prevent!

The fact that the CH view cannot help its proponents draw lines between acceptable and unacceptable genetic interventions and around the rightful shares of the gene pool that it seeks to guarantee is a hint that the answer to these problems lies in another direction altogether. In the end, I suggest that it is not the genes one inherits that are important (or possible) to regulate in creating responsible genomic policies, but the social environment in which they are expressed.

ETHICAL AND POLITICAL CONSIDERATIONS

Perhaps I am too literal-minded about the scientific uses of the genetic concepts one finds decorating descriptions of the CH view. One could acknowledge the limits to the scientific senses of "germ-line," "genome" and "gene pool" in the debate over germ-line engineering, but argue that we should still hasten to the metaphors that attend them. Even if evolution has no goals for humanity, humanity can have goals for the evolutionary process, for both good and ill. So even if the effort is inconsistent with other policies and faces its share of practical and theoretical difficulties, might it not still be prudent to endorse the special use of the CH view in the case of human germ-line engineering to provide a political basis for resisting the abuse of this potentially powerful technology?

Unfortunately, there is another set of objections that suggests that even if we were to set aside the conceptual problems with the CH view it carries serious social risks of its own.

Historical Warnings

First, it is worth noting that the CH view is not a new idea. As a paradigm for thinking about the social policy implications of genetics, it predates the Human Genome Project and our debates over germ-line gene therapy by seventy-five years. Mark Adams, a historian of genetics, demonstrates this nicely in his study of the history of our "gene pool" concept and its roots in the "gene fund" concept of the Russian geneticist, Alexander Serebrovsky in the 1920s. Adams points out that, as central as it has become as a concept of population genetics, the "gene pool" has its origins in an effort to help reconcile the science of genetics with the best ideology of the Soviet Union in the 1920s. Central to the effort was a strikingly modern version of the CH view. Against those who argued that Mendelian genetics suffered an inherent social Darwinist bias in favor of the capitalist elite, Serebrovsky argued that

> [i]f we consider our population, the citizens of our Union, we can regard them from one point of view as a group of subjects with full rights who exercise their right to create their own happiness on earth, and from another point of view, we can look at their totality as our social treasure, just exactly as we look upon the total amount of wheat, milk cows, and horses which create the economic power of our country. Our country prospers not only because wheat grows and cows give milk, but also because it has people who produce work of a certain level of quality. This question is especially important when we move the "higher" levels of human creativity, to artistic, scholarly, and scientific activity, to administrative work and a whole series of other manifestations of human nature. And if these elements actually rest on a basis of heredity, then we have every right to look upon the totality of such genes which create in human society talented outstanding individuals, or to the contrary idiots, as national wealth, a gene fund, from which society draws its people. It is clear that, not only can we not close our eyes to our gene fund, but to the contrary, we must see if there are processes operating within the gene fund which are changing it, and if there are, to what extent it is for the better or worse. . . . In order for the reserves of various genes in a given locality to be properly managed, we must look upon this stock as a kind of natural resource, similar to reserves of oil, gold, or coal, for example. (quoted in Adams, 1979, p. 257)

Serebrovosky then went on to advocate a series of eugenic proposals to preserve and improve the glorious Soviet gene pool. The centerpiece to his scheme of Soviet eugenics was a plan to regulate human reproduction for the benefit of future generations. He argued that

[c]hildren are necessary to support and develop society, children must be healthy, able and active, and society has the right to ask questions about the quality of the output in this area of production. We propose that the solution to the question of the organization of selection in humans will be the widespread induction of conception by means of artificial insemination using recommended sperm, and not at all necessarily from a "beloved spouse."(Adams, 1979, p. 265)

Unfortunately, in the context of Germany's reviving power and militant eugenic policies, these proposals did not help Serebrovosky's career in Stalinist Russia, and Adams reports that the term "geno-type" disappeared for almost two decades before being revived, shorn of its explicitly eugenic associations as "the gene pool." Meanwhile, of course, much of the same kind of language was used by eugenicists all over the world to help exploit the power of the CH view to advance political policies of social exclusion. Although these eugenic efforts did not have the benefit of Serebrovksy's "the gene fund" (they used "the germ-plasm" instead), they were often much more successful. In the United States, immigration restrictions against people from the Mediterranean, prohibitions of interracial marriage, and the involuntary sterilization of 60,000 "feeble-minded" people were all justified in terms of protecting the integrity of the genetic stock on behalf of future generations. In some circles today, one can still find people decrying the long-term "dysgenic" effects of modern medicine in just the same way.

I am not implying that proponents of the CH view in the context of the germ-line debate have an underlying eugenic agenda or that the "gene pool" concept as it is used today is tainted in some way by its historical origins. Clearly, most proponents of the CH view today endorse it precisely in order to forestall the possibility of new eugenic programs. However, I do think that Serebrovsky's invocation of the CH view to advance his eugenic agenda does display the ways in which reifying the "gene pool" as a natural resource can open the door to unacceptable social policies as just easily as overeager attempts to privatize and improve upon our nature. Sebrovosky's invocation displays three ways in which the CH view can prepare the ground for unjust social policies and attitudes: it can encourage (1) genetic reductionism, (2) coercive reproductive policies, and (3) discriminatory social attitudes.

Genetic Reductionism

By putting the human gene pool in the same normative category as the human stock of ideas, the CH view places an inordinate amount of weight on the role of genes in human flourishing. It centers our expectations about each other's accomplishments and our suspicions about each other's faults on our genes. To do so is comfortably reminiscent—too reminiscent—of the role we used to give the soul in human affairs and the forces that were thought to affect it. But reducing the character and accomplishments of an individual to their genotype is a very narrow perspective on human nature that most biologists would reject; genes are very far away from most of the action that makes human beings interesting to live with. When this kind of reductionism is combined with an ethic of personal responsibility for health, it can also serve to saddle individuals in future generations with private genetic responsibilities for problems which could have been addressed today as public issues (e.g., environmental) by relocating the cause of the problem in their genes (Duster, 1990).

Coercion

Moreover, unlike protecting the sea-bed or the atmosphere, no interventions can be performed on the gene pool without interferring in the lives of individual human beings. If the global managers of the genome were to decide that the dynamics of the human gene pool required regulation, how would they go about it? Just as Serebrovsky's eugenic proposals foundered on their invasion of the marriage bed, any form of global management of the gene pool would require invasions into the sphere of reproductive privacy. When this view is combined with a genetic naturalism (Knoppers, 1991) that eschews interventions into the natural gene pool, one is left only with reproductive interventions, inappropriately transforming what should be strictly personal issues into problems for public policy (Duster, 1990).

Discrimination

Serebrovsky's egalitarian opponents were offended by the tendency of Western geneticists to base their eugenic theories on elitist views of human classes and races. Note, however, that even in sketching a Soviet eugenics, Serebrovsky makes normative distinctions between different human types, with those involved in scientific and administrative activities at the top of the list. Genetics is the science of human differences, and as long as proponents of the CH view admit that some items in the human species allele collection are more useful, pleasant, or desirable than others, the door will be open to classify the members of future generations according to the value of the share of the human patrimony they will have been allotted.

INSURING EQUALITY OF OPPORTUNITY WITHIN FUTURE GENERATIONS

If the notion of a common human genetic heritage is so murky and unhelpful, why is it that germ-line gene therapy strikes us so forcefully as a technology which bears on the interests of future generations and for which global management would be appropriate? To see the real issue that this technology raises, it is helpful to think about what the purposes of a germ-line genetic intervention could possibly be.

Phenotypic Prevention

The first possible purpose for a germ-line intervention would be a traditional medical purpose: to prevent the manifestation of a disease by treating it in an affected individual's pre-embryo phase or in the gametes of the patient's parents. This might be called phenotypic prevention, since it seeks to prevent the expression of a disease phenotype. Here, germ-line gene therapy enjoys the support of the medical model, and even the most conservative official statements have started to waffle toward making exceptions to allow it, even if they have to import additional moral principles to do so. In this situation, any effects of the intervention on subsequent generations can be rationalized as unintended and indirect side effects of the therapeutic intervention and placed in the same acceptable category as the many other ways in which people influence (or tamper with) their germ-line cells in the course of normal life (Lappe, 1991). Of course, if these germ-line interventions start achieving their preventive goals by enhancing some health maintenance system within the patient's body—just as somatic-cell gene therapies for hypercholesterolemia already are doing[8]—this class of interventions may begin to seem more problematic.

Genotypic Prevention

A second, and more controversial, possible purpose for germ-line gene therapy would be what one might call "genotypic prevention": the effort to use the practice to try to reduce the incidence of a particular genotype in the next generation of a population. This is the application in which the interests of future generations are clearly at stake. In order to achieve this goal, germ-line interventions would have to carried out on a mass scale as part of public health campaigns involving as much of the population as possible. This would involve a public commitment to the value judgment that the targeted genotypes are disvaluable enough to warrant efforts to exclude them from population entirely. Inevitably, the success of such programs would be evaluated in terms of their abilities to reduce the frequency of the targeted alleles in the population, and the resulting savings in cost and morbidity.

Clearly, one set of issues that any such use of germ-line therapy would face is that of balancing the public health against the liberty of those individuals asked to participate. Prospective parents are likely to resist efforts to police their germ-lines, and health professionals are likely to resist efforts to tie funds for services to their success in having their patients make decisions the state's way. But again, these are issues for the first generation faced with this prospect. What about the future?

As advocates for people with disabilities increasingly point out, there is another constituency that would be put at risk by the public health use of germ-line engineering: the community of people who will continue to carry the offensive genes during the life of the public health program, that is, the unengineered. The further into the future this use of genetics persists, the more their interests are damaged, in two different ways.

Social "Handicaps." First, if it is true that those who are freed from the pathogens they would have inherited by the public health campaign will actually enjoy a greater range of capacities than those who continue to carry their "genetic load," then those whose CH rights have been respected (by oversight on the part of the public health authorities or zealous conscientious objection to the program) will be at a distinct social disadvantage. From the perspective of their genetic heritage of course, they will continue to be in fine shape, having inherited just their rightful and natural share of the gene pool. However, their relative capacities, and thus their relative share of the range of human opportunities available to their population, have been decreased. They would be in the same position as people from the third world who lack antibiotics are today. The fact that their people have not traditionally had access to antibiotics does not mitigate their claims to gain their fair share of that social good and the opportunities it can provide for human flourishing. It is in this way that germ-line gene therapy risks the creation of a real genetic underclass where there was none before.

Social Stigmatization. Moreover, because of the genetic reductionism that the CH view encourages, those who are left behind in a public health program designed to defend the population against some genetic disease are at risk of having whatever real disadvantages they may face greatly exaggerated by overly deterministic readings of their genotypic handicap. Because a single genotype can almost never predict with certainty the burden of suffering someone will experience, and can certainly never sum up the overall worth of the person, any social discrimination on the basis of retrograde genotypes will be unjustified in the vast majority of cases. Advocates for pathogene carriers can point out that, by focusing public health measures on genotype as a cause of human suffering, the germ-line engineers risk stigmatizing gene carriers as vectors of suffering and irresponsible reproducers of the genetic underclass. In this context, germ-line gene therapy seems less like mining the sea-bed and more like introducing a culturally biased intelligence test into our school systems; it could function to exaggerate the advantages that some portions of the population already possess, and thereby widen the gap between the opportunities available to them and to the rest.

If I am correct that the most urgent long-term social policy issues to flow from the possible uses of germ-line gene therapy actually involve the interests of the unengineered, then it should be clear that something more than the CH view should be required for the creation of responsible public policy in this area.

Notice that from the beginning, no one has assumed that the entire "gene fund" is valuable to our species; Serebrovksy acknowledges that there are genes for idiots as well as geniuses in the Soviet national treasure. Some alleles do seem preferable to others at many loci. By what standard are these intuitive judgments made? Without offering the full argument for it here, let me propose what the subtext of this chapter has been suggesting all along: to the extent that it is the range of human capacities which is valuable in our common genetic heritage, the critical underlying principle that needs to be brought to the surface in contemplating germ-line gene therapy is the role of *opportunity* in human flourishing. We seek to restore normal capacities (and perhaps build new ones) to give ourselves more opportunities for the experiences that give our lives meaning: savoring relationships, creating art, meditating on nature, and so on. In other words, in prizing our genetic heritage and evaluating how to cultivate it, it is the opportunities for creativity that it makes possible, not the genes themselves, that we want to preserve. To do so means paying more attention to the social context of future generations than to their genetic resources.

CONCLUSION: ADDRESSING THE SOCIAL OPPORTUNITY INTERESTS OF FUTURE GENERATIONS

What are the most important social policy goals are in attempting to prepare for the future of genetic technologies with the interests of future generations in mind? Our emphasis in designing public policy about the genome should not be on preserving some typological nineteenth-century notion of the image of man. Instead, the emphasis should be on providing and protecting a range of opportunities for men and women to flourish. In the long run, that means that those who benefit from gene therapy, or even genetic enhancement, are not the ones we should be concerned about. Rather, the preeminent need will be to protect those among the future generations unfortunate enough to enjoy an untampered genetic inheritance from the social discrimination and the unfair disadvantages that they could face in living and working with their genetically engineered neighbors.

The outline of those policies are already clear in the policies that are emerging to secure the opportunities due people with disabilities. They take both negative and positive forms. First, we should eschew proposals to use germ-line gene therapy—or, for that matter, genetic screening techniques—as public health tools to reduce the incidence of genotypes associated with genetic disease and disability in the population, as if particular genotypes represented a form of expensive "pollution" that could and should be cleansed from the gene pool. This reduces the identities of people with disabilities to their genotypes and encourages others to discriminate against them. Second, we should continue to expand the social opportunities and protections available to people with genetic differences and disabilities by working to prohibit unwarranted discrimination on the basis of genotype alone. Finally, we should strive in our rhetoric about the interests of future generations to focus on the promises we would like to make to our children rather than fret about what we have (or have not) inherited from our parents. The human gene pool, unlike the sea, has no top, bottom, or shores; it cannot be used up. The reservoir of human mutual respect, good will and tolerance for difference, however, seems perennially in danger of running dry. That is the truly fragile heritage that we should seek to preserve in monitoring genetic research on behalf of the future.

NOTES

Ancestral versions of this paper were given at the International Conference on Genetic Engineering and Future Generations, at Villeta, Malta, September, 1995, and at the Sixth International Congress on Ethics in Medicine, New York, NY, October, 1995 as well as the George Washington University Symposium, "Democracy, Social Values, and Public Policy." The paper benefited from the comments received at each of those meetings, for which I remain grateful.

1. One of the clearer statements of this view is to be found in Agius (1990, p. 140):

The genetical relation among all generations is one of the most unitive factors among the community of the human species. Human genes are common to all generations. The collective human gene pool knows no national or temporal boundary, but is the biological heritage of the entire human species. They are a common heritage because they are handed down from one generation to another. In a relational context, the rules of inheritance assume a much broader perspective thatn those usually recognized on the indiviudal level. In fact, ownership rights are form the viewpoint of mankind as whole. . . . No generation has therefore an exclusive right of using germ-line therapy to alter the genetic constitution of the human species.

2. See Mauron and Thevoz (1991) and de Wachter (1993) for reviews of these statements, as well as UNESCO (1995) and Foundation for International Studies (1994).

3. For example, no cross-species contributions from neanderthals or the nephileme.

4. There are, of course, millions of particular lineages of germ-line cells in individual human beings. Strictly speaking, then, to express concern about the effects of pre-embryo transformation or gametocyte therapy "on the germline" means worrying about the risks of the intervention to the health of the individual transformed, that is, the risks of iatrogenic mutagenesis, or over expression, or epigenetic complications that are familiar to those working with somatic cell gene therapy. These are real concerns, but not concerns that flow from the communal nature of the germ-line, or risks that are likely to have a widespread impact on future generations requiring international management. Existing science policy governing biomedical research practices already insures that germ-line gene therapy will never emerge as a legitimate clinical tool unless those basic concerns can be satisfied first.

5. As long as one is willing to disregard any possible cytoplasmic modes of inheritance!

6. Perhaps we could even defend that right against those who would pass on the garbled notion of the human genome as a natural resource.

7. Of course, most advocates of the CH view do go on to make such distinctions; but they have to do so by importing other moral principles into their analysis. Thus, as an exception to its ban on "tampering" with the genome, the Council of Europe allows all practices which can be otherwise justified "in accordance with certain principles which are recognized with being fully compatible with respect for human rights" (Council of Europe, 1982). Similarly, Agius appeals to principles derived from his Whiteheadian ethical theory to explain how he can support some uses of germ-line genetic engineering, despite his commitment to the CH view (Agius, 1990).

8. By increasing the patient's number of low density lipoprotein receptors beyond their normal level. See Wilson, 1992.

REFERENCES

Adams, Mark. "From Gene Fund to Gene Pool: On the Evolution of Evolutionary Language. " *Studies in History of Biology* 3 (1979): 241–285.

Agius, Emmanuel. "Germ-line Cells—Our Responsibilities for Future Generations." In *Our Responsibilities Towards Future Generations*, ed. S. Busuttil, E. Agius, P. S. Inglott, and T. Macelli. Villeta, Malta: Foundation for International Studies, 1990, 133–143.

Anderson, W. French. "Human Gene Therapy," In *The New Genetics and the Future of Man*, ed. M. Hamilton. Grand Rapids, MI: Eerdmans, 1972, 110–125.

Council of Europe, Parliamentary Assembly. *Recommendation 934 on Genetic Engineering.* Strausborg: Council of Europe, 1982.

Dawkins, Richard. *River Out of Eden: A Darwinian View of Life.* New York: Basic Books, 1995.

de Wachter, Maurice. "Ethical Aspects of Germ-line Gene Therapy." *Bioethics* (1993): 166–178.

Dobzhansky, Theodosius. *Genetics of the Evolutionary Process.* New York: Columbia University Press, 1970.

Duster, Troy. *Backbook to Genetics.* New York: Rutledge, 1990.

Foundation for International Studies. "World Declaration on Our Responsibilities Towards Future Generations." In *What Future for Future Generations?* ed. E. Agius and S. Busuttil. Villetta, Malta: Foundation for International Studies, 1994, 305–311.

Hotchkiss, Rollin D. "Portents for a Genetic Engineering." *Journal of Heredity* 56 (1965): 197–202.

Inglott, Peter. "The Common Heritage of Mankind and Future Generations." In *What Future for Future Generations?* ed. E. Agius and S. Busuttil. Villetta, Malta: Foundation for International Studies, 1994, 193–199.

Knoppers, Bertha. *Human Dignity and Genetic Heritage.* Montreal: Law Reform Commission of Canada, 1991.

Krimsky, Sheldon. *Genetic Alchemy: The Social History of the Recombinant DNA Controversy.* Boston: MIT Press, 1985.

Lappe, Marc. "Ethical Issues in Manipulating the Human Germ-Line." *Journal of Medicine and Philosophy* 16 (1991): 621–641.

Mauron, Alex, and Thevoz, Jean-Marie. "Germ-line Engineering: A Few European Voices." *Journal of Medicine and Philosophy* 16 (1991): 649–666.

Nader, C. "Technology and Democratic Control: The Case of Recombinant DNA." In *The Genes in Wars: Reflections on the Recombinant DNA Controversy* ed. R. Zilinskas and B. Zimmerman. New York: Macmillan, 1986, 139–167.

Thompson, Larry. *Correcting the Code: Inventing the Genetic Cure for the Human Body.* New York: Simon and Schuster, 1994.

UNESCO International Bioethics Committee. "Revised Ouline of a (UNESCO) Declaration on the Protection of the Human Genome." *Eubios Journal of Asian and International Bioethics* 5 (July 1995): 97–99.

Walters, LeRoy. "The Ethics of Human Gene Therapy." *Nature* 320 (1986): 225–227.

Watson, James, and Juengst, Eric. "Doing Science in the Real World: The Role of Ethics, Law and the Social Sciences in the Human Genome Project." In *Gene Mapping: Using Law and Ethics as Guides.* ed. G. Annas and S. Elias. New York: Oxford University Press, 1992, pp. xv–xix.

Wilson, James, Grossman, M., and Roper, S. "Ex Vivo gene therapy for fainilial hyper-cholesterolemia." *Human Gene Therapy* 3 (1992): 179–222.

13

Democracy, Social Values, and Public Policy: Concluding Commentary

Kenneth F. Schaffner

The chapters in this book represent an extraordinarily broad range of disciplinary perspectives including ethical, economic, feminist, historical, political, religious, and social, as well as more general philosophical orientations. I write from the last perspective and my intent is both to summarize and to provide an organizational framework for the contributions. In addition, I touch on a few dimensions I found missing from this multidisciplinary collection, and also offer a few suggestions about further testing of the views presented and where these themes may be encountered in critical future situations. My comments fall under two broad categories: those pertaining to theories of value and those relating to other dimensions in the area of democracy and public policy.

THEORIES OF VALUE

Reduction

Robert Paul Churchill has raised the problem of reduction in connection with the themes of this book, by which I take him to refer to an attempt to find a single common basis for value claims. This has been a perennial problem in philosophy, where "happiness" has been the answer for philosophers as diverse as Aristotle and John Stuart Mill. Deontologists such as Kant sought a unitary basis in the categorical imperative. A search for a single basis for value claims also has its analogues in more contemporary forms of utilitarianism and economics, where it reappears as "preference satisfaction," a concept to which I return later.

Jennifer Trusted distinguished between absolute moral values and more transient social values, but found in her core moral values at least several diverse elements such as respecting persons, keeping trust, justice, and benevolence. Her valuational schema resonates with a recent consensus in the area of bioethics, where the multiple values of autonomy, well-being, and equity or justice are seen as powerful middle-level principles to be deployed in complex ways to clarify and adjudicate ethical conundra that arise every day in the hospitals and in biomedical research advances (Belmont Report, 1979; Beauchamp and Childress, 1994). Though some bioethicists attempt to find a unitary basis for ethical decision making, most are quite content with a plurality of values that better reflects the richness of experience and the complexity of the problems addressed.

Pluralism

This multiplicity of core values took on even greater diversity as issues of class, race, gender, generation, and religion were addressed. Cynthia Harrison's rich descriptions and analyses from the feminist perspective indicate the powerful role that conservative social forces have played in marginalizing half of the population and identified the factors that lead to the liberation of women. James Peacock and J. Bryan Hehir provided examinations of the role of religious values in secular and nonsecular societies, of their force, and then considered the difficulties of harmoniously integrating such secular and nonsecular perspectives. Gene Cohen pointed out the many myths that exist concerning intergenerational interactions and strove to provide more accurate analyses of the differences in perspectives and values in the young and the old within a framework for the accommodation of the prima facie differences. The tension between seeking a unitary reduction in value theory amid the patent diversity and pluralism of values and value perspectives was reechoed in two somewhat more formal problems discussed by the participants: commensurability and the role of preferences.

Commensurability

Both Douglas MacLean and Timothy Brennan raised the problem of commensurability in their contributions. To oversimplify the problem is this: If there is more than one basic value and the plurality of values cannot be reduced to one, how do we assess the comparative strength of different and possibly competing values? More concretely, using an example from bioethics that frequently arises in a variety of contexts, can we ethically permit an individual on the basis of *autonomy* to make a choice where there is a broad consensus that the choice will do that person clear harm? Here "harm" can mean events such as loss of a limb or even death. MacLean argued that any type of cost-benefit analysis, a frequently used tool in policy analysis, must commit to a thesis of commensurability, at least in the weak sense of a common scale of measurement for distinct values. MacLean pointed out that there is no mechanical method by which we can accomplish this. Brennan distinguished between philosophers' approach to value commensurability and economists' approach. In recent years many philosophers have tended to deny value commensurability (Williams, 1985; Stocker, 1990; Nussbaum, 1990). Economists, on the other hand, seem to believe they can paper over any philosophical disagreements with a nominal means of preference or monetary assessment. Brennan is skeptical of this tack, suggesting that the lack of attention to deeper philosophical analyses may lead to serious economic mistakes and/or lack of empirical and normative content in economics.

Preference Satisfaction

As already suggested, economists (and their contemporary utilitarian philosophical cousins) have argued that commensurability (and reduction) can be achieved at least for some important policy contexts by appealing to a notion of individual preference orderings. This is a prima facie attractive move, one that even Rawls subscribed to in order to ensure that quite diverse visions of the good life could be accommodated in a just state. (Rawls uses this approach as a "thin theory of the good" but only after a commitment has been made to his two major principles of justice [see Rawls, 1982].) In his analysis, Mark Sagoff raised two difficulties for such preference satisfaction approaches. First, these preferences are a theoretical construct, and it is not clear that they really exist. Empirically, they seem to be another just-so story. Second, the relation between preference satisfaction and happiness is not one of cause and consequence. Taken together with MacLean's and Brennan's arguments that deeper, more philosophical problems will need to be solved before preference satisfaction can be legitimated, these objections constitute a powerful indictment of a widely employed tool of policy analysis—an indictment that can only be quashed by much more in-depth philosophical and ethical analysis than has yet been provided in economics and philosophy.

OTHER SIGNIFICANT DIMENSIONS IN THE AREA OF DEMOCRACY AND PUBLIC POLICY

Economics and Rhetoric

There are three other themes that appear in this collection that have significant impacts on the intertwined issues of democracy, social values, and public policy that I think are worth highlighting. These are the roles of rhetoric, special-interest groups, and context. The importance of rhetoric in what seemed to be an economic policy debate was stressed by Klamer, who pointed out in the major case study he presented on NAFTA that Vice President Gore turned the debate around using well-designed rhetoric. Economics per se, Klamer points out, has little effect on public policy. The power of rhetoric in public policy, and of a kind of less "scientific" thinking than we encounter in mathematical economics, has been analyzed in a penetrating book by Deborah Stone (1988). Stone argues that "political reasoning is reasoning by metaphor and analogy" (p. 6). Further, she states, "Given a world of continua, there is an infinite choice about how to classify. . . . Policy is centrally about classification and differentiation. . . . Policy arguments are convincing to the extent that they give a satisfying account of treating cases alike or differently. Political reasoning, therefore, is primarily a reasoning of sameness and difference" (p. 308). Numbers, for Stone, are symbolic— more like poems and paintings—than objective things. Different individuals and groups will typically measure different things to make their case on a policy. This insight seems consistent with many of the views expressed here.

Special Interests

Klamer discussed at some length the role of special-interest groups and coalitions of these groups in the NAFTA debate. Democratic politics, certainly in the United States, is significantly affected by these groups. I would contend that we cannot understand the processes of change in this democratic society without paying close attention to the types of influence exercised by these interest groups, both on individual political figures as well as on the electorate. A story of the demise of the Clinton health care plan would be seriously incomplete if it did not address the roles of the National Federation of Independent Business (NFIB) and the Health Insurance Association of America (HIAA), and the latter's stunningly effective series of "Harry and Louise" commercials against the Clinton plan. Johnson's and Broder's recent lengthy monograph (1996) on the rise and demise of the Clinton health reform describes these two groups as playing "an especially critical role in the defeat of the Clinton plan" and adds that "both of them understood that this battle would require far more than a standard lobbying effort. Both were prepared to engage in living rooms across the country. The operations of both demonstrate vividly what the lobbies really did in this fight" (1996, p. 198).

The Importance of Context: Social, Historical, and Geographic

Policy thinkers frequently have tunnel vision; they are fixed on a problem and their horizons are limited. Several chapters addressed the importance of keeping in mind variations of values over time and space, an issue already addressed briefly on the problems of pluralism. James Peacock argued for the diversity over time and cultures and, following the lead of Max Weber, argued that policy theorists must pay attention to religious and cultural differences if they are to understand the nature of values. Cynthia Harrison led us through the major changes in the perception of women in American culture. Edward Berkowitz showed how values have changed regarding the Civil War pension problem and social security. Eric Juengst told us how different the Europeans are from Americans regarding genetic interventions, perhaps because of their geographic closeness to the site of the Holocaust.

MISSING DIMENSIONS IN THE AREA OF DEMOCRACY AND PUBLIC POLICY

Emotion

This collection covered many topics in its areas of focus on democracy, social values, and public policy, but there were two dimensions that were addressed only implicitly and in discussion that seem important for understanding this area. One of these dimensions is the role of emotion in public policy and democratic change. Most philosophical reasoning in ethics and political philosophy proceeds on the assumption that arguments are best when they are passionless. Klamer seemed to fall into this mode of analysis when he praised Gore's rational appeals and denigrated Perot's appeals to fear. But an older tradition, Aristotelianism, does not see ethics in this way and argues that right emotion is part of right action (Sherman, 1989). Thus courageous action is distinguished from recklessness by the *proper* experience of internal fear, not the absence of fear. Similarly, righteous anger *should* motivate individuals in the face of patent injustice. Recently, some philosophers have begun to appreciate this Aristotelian (as well as Humean) point, and Patricia Greenspan's (1988) and Alan Gibbard's (1990) books represent two excellent examples of that renewed appreciation. To some extent, Deborah Stone's (1988) work could be fitted into this perspective, though it is a political and not a philosophical analysis.

Power and Conflict Metaphors

The other missing dimension, a political one, was implicit in some of the more recent historical cases presented and has to do with the role of power in a democratic society: Who and which groups exercise it and to what extent it can be used to achieve a particular vision of the good for that individual/group. Harrison touched briefly on how the state invests power in families, but there was no in-depth investigation of this concept. In a democracy, power, in theory, lies with the electorate, but very sophisticated means have been developed by the special-interest groups to influence popular opinion and elected representatives. Rhetoric and emotion are two of the tools already noted. Interest groups seek to frame and turn a debate so that their vision becomes politically (and socially) operative, and the opposition's vision is marginalized or negated.

Strong disagreements about programs with large stakes for interest groups frequently lead to rhetoric more suited to military campaigns than to politics. There is the old saying of Von Clausewitz that "War is regarded as nothing but the continuation of politics by other means," but the political arena of fundamental public policy conflicts turns that quotation on its head: Fundamental policy debates are wars conducted by other means. A reading of Johnson and Broder (1996) reveals how many of the key players viewed themselves to be in battles and in a war. House Speaker Gingrich is reported to have characterized the defeat of the Democratic plan as "their Stalingrad, their Gettysburg, their Waterloo" (Johnson and Broder, 1996, xi). Clinton and his aides involved in planning his major speech on health reform had a "war room," a term the group debated about and carefully chose over others to best describe their efforts (see Johnson and Broder, 1996, 51). (It should be added, however, that Hillary Rodham Clinton determined that this was not a proper term and had the site renamed the "delivery room"; see Johnson and Broder, 1996, 52.) In this framework, the rhetoric becomes one of strategy, persuasion, as much disinformation as information, mantras, slogans, sound bites, pressure, legal bribes (campaign contributions), and foot soldiers (door-to-door workers). We had little debate about this dimension of public policy, and where public policy might fit into these types of conflict situations, though aspects of it were implicitly raised in Klamer's account of the NAFTA debate. Perhaps this dimension was lacking because we are all academics and not politicians, but it seems to be an important one for policy analysts to consider.

UNCOMPLETED TASKS AND FUTURE DIRECTIONS

In bringing my comments to a close, I want to focus on several directions that further inquiry might take. If there are any common themes discoverable in the rich set of issues described all-too-briefly here, I believe that the need to consider in-depth cases and to have a better understanding of ethical, economic, and political reasoning stands out. Several contributors addressed these themes. Cases themselves, such as NAFTA (Klamer), Social Security (Berkowitz), the origin of Medicare (Cohen), and the feminine revolution (Harrison) need a framework, perhaps several frameworks, in which they can be analyzed and generalizations extracted that may apply to other cases and to future policy debates.

The incompleteness of traditional economic analysis was stressed by so many of the contributors that it is evident, at least to this writer, that a major effort needs to be mounted to identify the outlines of a more robust approach to policy analysis. We can take a hint from Deborah Stone's comment quoted above that "political reasoning is reasoning by metaphor and analogy." I would propose that good policy reasoning, even that in economics, is also likely to be more analogical than deductive, more comparative and symbolic than quantitative, and heavily case based. Good policy reasoning will also be normative, and thus involve values, but of a pluralistic kind. Alternative analyses will permit policy analysis to sharpen the nature of the values that are in debate and may point the way toward compromise and consensus, or perhaps only toward a democratic process (voting by the electorate) in which essentially contrasting value visions will prevail. The importance of correct emotions would be recognized in such an approach, but the appeals made to confusing emotions must be acknowledged. The notion of strategic thinking in the sense of a campaign, or in extreme cases a war, needs to be kept in mind. Further, the significant role of historical and cultural contexts should be recognized.

In these brief remarks I attempt not to put more of a structure on this view of good policy reasoning that is developed elsewhere (Schaffner, 1997), but to point out that any account of good policy reasoning will have to be tested by application to historical cases, both recent and not-so-recent, and by prospective cases as well, to see how it does in the thick of argument and the social and political process. Current and near future areas that I believe are ripe for such applications include the social framework of health care delivery, criminal justice, welfare reform, and the social impact of the Human Genome Project on American society. Each of these broad areas has multiple subtopics that could serve as a fertile testing ground for various postmodern accounts of good policy reasoning.

REFERENCES

Beauchamp, T. *Childress Principles of Biomedical Ethics*. New York: Oxford University Press, 1994.

Belmont Report. DHEW Publication Nos. (OS) 78–0012–78–0014. Washington, DC: National Commission for the Protection of Human Subjects, 1978.

Gibbard, A. *Wise Choices, Apt Feelings*. Cambridge: Harvard University Press, 1990.

Greenspan, P. *Emotions and Reasons*. New York: Routledge, 1988.

Johnson, H., and D. Broder. *The System: The American Way of Politics at the Breaking Point.* Boston: Little, Brown, 1996.

Nussbaum, M. "The Discernment of Perception: An Aristotelian Conception of Private and Public Rationality." In *Love's Knowledge: Essays on Philosophy and Literature.* New York: Oxford University Press, 1990.

Rawls, J. "Social Unity and Primary Goods." In *Utilitarianism and Beyond.* ed. A. Sen and B. Williams. New York: Cambridge University Press, 1982.

Schaffner, K. *Practical Reasoning in Health Care.* 1997. In final preparation.

Sherman N. *The Fabric of Character: Aristotle's Theory of Virtue.* Oxford: Clarendon Press, 1989.

Stocker, M. *Plural and Conflicting Values.* Oxford: Clarendon Press, 1990.

Stone, D. *Policy, Paradox, and Political Reason.* HarperCollins, 1988.

Williams, B. *Ethics and the Limits of Philosophy.* Cambridge, MA: Harvard University Press, 1985.

For Further Reading

Aaron, Henry J., Thomas E. Mann, and Timothy Taylor, eds. *Values and Public Policy.* Washington, DC: The Brookings Institution, 1994.

Bok, Derek. *The State of the Nation.* Cambridge, MA: Harvard University Press, 1996.

Churchill, Robert Paul, ed., *The Ethics of Liberal Democracy: Morality and Democracy in Theory and Practice.* Oxford: Berg Publishers, 1994.

Dworkin, Ronald. *Life's Dominion.* New York: Vintage, 1994.

Elster, John. *The Cement of Society.* Cambridge: Cambridge University Press, 1989.

Etzioni, Amitai. *The New Golden Rule: Community and Morality in a Democratic Society.* New York: Basic Books, 1996.

Friedan, Betty. *Beyond Gender: The New Politics of Women and Family.* Washington DC: Woodrow Wilson Center Press, 1997.

Gillrog, John Martin, and Maurice Wade, eds. *The Moral Dimensions of Public Policy Choice: Beyond the Market Paradigm.* Pittsburgh: University of Pittsburgh Press, 1992.

Gutmann, Amy, and Dennis Thompson. *Democracy and Disagreement.* Cambridge, MA: Harvard University Press, 1996.

Ingram, Helen, and Steven Rathegeb Smith. eds. *Public Policy for Democracy.* Washington, DC: The Brookings Institution, 1993.

Lakoff, George. *Moral Politics: What Conservatives Know That Liberals Don't.* Chicago: The University of Chicago Press, 1996.

Larmore, Charles E. *Patterns of Moral Complexity.* New York: Cambridge University Press, 1987.

Moore Lappé, Francis. *Rediscovering American Values.* New York: Ballantine Books, 1989.

Mills, Claudia. *Values and Public Policy.* New York: Harcourt Brace Javanovich, 1992.

Rawls, John. *Political Liberalism.* New York: Columbia University Press, 1996.

Rokeach, Milton, ed. *Understanding Human Values: Individual and Societal.* New York: Free Press, 1979.

Trusted, Jennifer. *Moral Principles and Social Values.* London: Routledge & Kegan Paul, 1987.

Wilson, James Q. *The Moral Sense.* New York: Free Press, 1993.

Weimen, David, and Aidan Vining. *Policy Analysis*, 2nd ed. Englewood Cliffs, NJ: Prentice-Hall, 1992.

Wolfe, Alan. *Whose Keeper, Social Science and Moral Obligation.* Berkeley: University of California Press, 1989.

Index

About the Contributors

EDWARD D. BERKOWITZ is Professor of History and Public Policy at The George Washington University. He has written, coauthored, or edited ten books in the field of social welfare policy including, most recently, *Mr. Social Security: The Life of Wilbur J. Cohen.* He has served on the staff of a Carter-era presidential commission and as a policy analyst at the Department of Health and Human Services. His current project is a history of the Institutes of Medicine.

TIMOTHY BRENNAN is Professor of Policy Sciences and Economics at the University of Maryland, Baltimore County and Senior Fellow, Resources for the Future. He recently completed a term as senior regulatory staff economist with the President's Council of Economic Advisers. He coauthored the book *A Shock to the System* on policy issues pertaining to electricity competition. His other publications include articles on rights, freedom of speech, privacy, copyright, antitrust, and regulatory economics.

MILTON M. CARROW is Research Professor of Public Policy in the Graduate Program in Public Policy, The George Washington University and was previously a member of the faculty of New York University Law Center. He has served as President of the National Center for Administrative Law, a nonprofit research and training center established by the American Bar Association. His fields of interest are administrative law and public policy. His published works include *The Background of Administrative Law, The Licensing Power in New York City,* and *Law and Science in Collaboration,* with J. D. Nyhart.

ROBERT PAUL CHURCHILL is Director of the Peace Studies Program and Chair of the Department of Philosophy at The George Washington University. The author of numerous articles on public policy, especially national defense and security issues, he has also written a leading logic textbook and edited *The Ethics of Liberal Democracy* and *Crossing Cultural Boundaries*.

GENE D. COHEN directs the Center for Aging, Health, and Humanities at The George Washington University, where he is Professor of Health Care Sciences and Professor of Psychiatry. He is also founding director of the Washington, D.C. Center on Aging. Past positions have included President of the Gerontological Society of America, acting director of the National Institute on Aging, and the first chief of the Center on Aging of the National Institutes of Mental Health.

JOSEPH J. CORDES is Professor of Economics and Director of the Graduate Program in Public Policy at The George Washington University and served as Deputy Assistant Director for Tax Analysis at the Congressional Budget Office. Cordes has authored or coauthored over fifty articles dealing with tax policy, government regulation, and evaluation of government programs. His published research has appeared in journals such as *National Tax Journal, Journal of Policy Analysis and Management, Public Choice*, and the *Journal of Law and Economics*.

J. BRYAN HEHIR is Professor of the Practice of Religion and Society at the Harvard Divinity School and the Harvard Center for International Affairs. He also served for twenty years at the U.S. Catholic Conference of Bishops in Washington, D.C. Professor Hehir's teaching and research interest focus on the role of religion in international affairs and on American society, as well as on the role of ethics in international relations.

CYNTHIA HARRISON is Associate Professor of History and of Women's Studies at The George Washington University. She served for six years as the chief historian of the Federal Judicial History Office in Washington, D.C. She is past deputy director of Project '87, a joint education effort of the American Historical Association and the American Political Science Association for the bicentennial of the U.S. Constitution. She is the author of *On Account of Sex: the Politics of Women's Issues, 1945–1968* (1988) and numerous articles on women, politics, and policy.

ERIC T. JUENGST is Associate Professor of Biomedical Ethics at the Case Western Reserve University School of Medicine in Cleveland, Ohio. He has taught medical ethics and philosophy of science on the faculties of the medical schools of Penn State University and the University of California, San Francisco. His research interests and publications have focused on the conceptual and ethical issues raised by new advances in human genetics and biotechnology, and from 1990 to 1994, he was the first Chief of Ethical, Legal, and Social Implications Branch of the National Center for Human Genome Research at the U.S. National Institutes of Health.

ARJO KLAMER is Professor of Economics of Art and Culture at the Erasmus University, Rotterdam, and Research Professor at The George Washington University.

He is the author of *Conversations with Economists* (1984), *The Making of an Economist* (with Colander) and editor of *The Value of Culture* (1996).

DOUGLAS MACLEAN is Professor of Philosophy, University of Maryland. He has served on several panels of the National Academy of Sciences and has also been an advisor to the National Science Foundation's program on Ethics and Values and to the National Endowment for the Humanities program on Humanities, Science, and Technology. He has published many books and articles on moral and philosophical issues in risk analysis and the foundations of policy science, including *Energy and the Future* and *Values at Risk*.

JAMES L. PEACOCK is Kenan Professor of Anthropology, Professor of Comparative Literature, and Director of the University Center for International Studies at the University of North Carolina, Chapel Hill. He is past President of the American Anthropological Association and his fieldwork includes studies in Indonesia.

MARK SAGOFF is Senior Research Scholar at the Institute for Philosophy and Public Policy in the School of Public Affairs, University of Maryland. He is the author of *The Economy of Earth* (1988), was named Pew Scholar in Conservation and the Environment in 1991, and has served as president of the International Society for Environmental Ethics.

KENNETH F. SCHAFFNER, is University Professor of Medical Humanities at The George Washington University. Previously, he was University Professor of History and Philosophy of Science and Research Professor of Medicine at the University of Pittsburgh, where he also served as Codirector for the Center for Medical Ethics. His most recent book is *Discovery and Explanation in Biology and Medicine* (1993). He is an associate editor of *Philosophy, Psychiatry, and Psychology*, section coeditor for *Logic and Epistemology of Theoretical Medicine and Philosophy*, and also serves on the editorial boards of *The Journal of Medicine and Philosophy*, *Philosophy of Science*, and *Psychiatry: Interpersonal and Biological Processes*.

JENNIFER TRUSTED is a part-time Tutor in History and Philosophy of Science at the Open University and in the Continuing and Further Education Department of Exeter University. Publications include *The Logic of Scientific Inference* (1979); *An Introduction to the Philosophy of Knowledge* (1981); *Free Will and Responsibility* (1984); *Moral Principles and Social Values* (1987); *Inquiry and Understanding* (1987); *Physics and Metaphysics* (1991); *Beliefs and Biology* (1995); and papers in the *Journal of Applied Philosophy* and *Mind*.

ISBN 0-275-95985-6

9 780275 959852

90000>

EAN

HARDCOVER BAR CODE